READING TO WRITE: COMPOSITION IN CONTEXT

Peter Elias Sotiriou

Los Angeles City College

HEINLE
CENGAGE Learning

Australia • Brazil • Japan • Korea • Mexico • Singapore • Spain • United Kingdom • United States

Reading to Write: Composition in Context

Peter Elias Sotiriou

Publisher: Earl McPeek

Acquisitions Editor: Steve Dalphin

Market Strategist: John Meyers

Project Manager: Elaine Hellmund

For product information and technology assistance, contact us at **Cengage Learning Customer & Sales Support, 1-800-354-9706**

For permission to use material from this text or product, submit all requests online at **www.cengage.com/permissions** Further permissions questions can be emailed to **permissionrequest@cengage.com**

Library of Congress Control Number: 00-111352

ISBN-13: 978-0-15-506123-1

ISBN-10: 0-15-506123-2

Heinle
20 Davis Drive
Belmont, CA 94002
USA

Cengage Learning is a leading provider of customized learning solutions with office locations around the globe, including Singapore, the United Kingdom, Australia, Mexico, Brazil, and Japan. Locate your local office at **www.cengage.com/global**

Cengage Learning products are represented in Canada by Nelson Education, Ltd.

To learn more about Heinle, visit **www.cengage.com/heinle**

Purchase any of our products at your local college store or at our preferred online store **www.CengageBrain.com**

Printed in the United States of America
5 6 7 8 9   17 16 15 14 13

CONTENTS

PART III
A WRITER'S HANDBOOK   203

PREFACE

TO THE INSTRUCTOR:

Reading to Write is a unique composition textbook. It is both a reader and a rhetoric, based on the assumption that reading interesting and challenging selections is the most productive occasion for drafting, revising, and editing student writing. *Reading to Write* provides structured ways for the student to understand each reading selection, then uses this understanding to introduce issues related to reading and writing, grammar and usage, revising and editing. Instead of studying from three textbooks (a reader, a rhetoric, and a handbook), students using *Reading to Write* will find the bulk of their writing questions answered in one textbook.

Reading to Write contains twenty reading selections divided into five thought-provoking topics: literacy, breaking the law, the media, exercise and health, and issues in learning. Each topic has four selections, so the student will have a more complete understanding of the topic after completing all four reading selections.

Reading to Write is divided into three parts: Part I: College Reading and Writing, Part II: Reading Selections and Writing Topics, and Part III: A Writer's Handbook. Part I has four chapters devoted to ways to read in college, ways to write in college, and the ways writing is organized. Part II contains sixteen of the twenty reading selections with apparatus to read and write in each selection. Finally, Part III is a grammar, usage, and writing conventions handbook which addresses central problems students encounter and the basic skills needed for college compositions. As they complete each reading selection, students are directed to a specific part of the handbook, so they learn the grammar and usage material as they read the selections and write their essays.

Writing, reading, and grammar and usage activities are interconnected in each of the twenty reading selections. Students preread and prewrite about the selection, they outline and cluster the key information in each selection, they critically reread each selection, they are introduced to a specific reading and writing topic, they edit sample student paragraphs for errors in grammar and usage related to the selection, and they draft and revise their essay topic. Students are encouraged to write on a variety of topics, some based on a careful reading of the selection, others on their personal experiences that the selection calls to mind.

In the handbook, forty grammar and usage topics are introduced in a concise and clear fashion. At the end of the textbook a glossary provides definitions and examples of the grammar and usage terms treated in the handbook.

By the end of the textbook, students should have a firmer understanding of how to read and write in college. They should be able to read a selection critically and respond to it in a clear, organized fashion with relatively few surface errors. Students will thus be ready to more effectively respond to the myriad of writing requirements they will face in their college course work.

ACKNOWLEDGMENTS

The completion of *Reading to Write* was made much easier by the helpful and organized direction of my editor Stephen Dalphin and by his editorial assistant Amy McGaughey. Stephen listened carefully to my ideas for this textbook and gave me his enthusiastic support as I moved the manuscript through its various stages. Amy read through each page, cheerfully reminding me of a mistake I had made or a page I had omitted.

I would also like to thank the several reviewers of *Reading to Write* for their careful reading of the manuscript: Kathleen Beauchene of Community College of Rhode Island, R. Brent Bonah of Bunker Hill Community College, Norma Cruz-Gonzalez of San Antonio College, Cynthia B. Earle of New Hampshire College, Edwina K. Jordan of Illinois Central College, Laura Knight of Mercer County Community College, David Norin of Cloud County Community College, and Katherine Ploeger of California State University-Stanislaus.

Finally, as always, I want to thank my family—my wife Vasi and my sons Elia and Dimitri—who have lovingly given me the myriad hours I needed to move this textbook to its completion.

TO THE STUDENT

Reading to Write is a textbook that teaches you to write for college as you read. Instead of completing separate grammar, usage, reading, and writing assignments, *Reading to Write* incorporates all of these activities in your reading assignments.

How the Textbook is Organized

This textbook is divided into three parts. The first part introduces you to the ways college students read and write, the second presents various reading selections on topics of interest, and the third is a grammar, usage, and writing conventions handbook that explains the most common questions you have about editing your writing. Here are the titles and descriptions of the three parts of the textbook:

Part I: College Reading and Writing

In these four chapters, you will learn how to read college material, how to write essays at the college level, how college readings are organized, and how you can organize your writing. After each of these chapters, you will read a selection that treats a particular literacy question–the different reading problems people face and how they have learned to write. This first part will prepare you for all of the reading and writing assignments you will have in Part II.

Part II: Reading Selections and Writing Topics

This part contains sixteen reading selections on four engaging topics. Having already read four selections on Literacy in Part I, you will now read about: Breaking the Law (Selections 5–8), The Media–Television and Music (Selections 9–12), Exercise and Health (Selections 13–16), and Issues in Learning (Selections 17–20). Each of the four selections per topic will expand your understanding of the issue that is examined. The fourth selection is usually longer and a bit more challenging than the previous three. In each selection, you will be given opportunities to think about the topic before you read, read the selection critically, consider a particular reading and writing feature, complete grammar and usage exercises from sample student writing on the topic, and write about the issue, either by examining the selection more carefully or by responding to your own experiences that relate to the topic you have read.

With each writing topic, you will follow the necessary steps in the writing process: prewriting, drafting, and revising.

Part III: A Writer's Handbook

This part contains forty topics in grammar and usage that you likely need to review in order to revise and edit your writing more successfully. These are topics that students developing their writing skills have traditionally needed to study. The discussions are short and are followed by paragraphs of sample student writing that contain errors on the topic that has been introduced. Instead of doing isolated sentence exercises, you will be editing paragraphs on the topic that you have read, and you will more easily transfer this knowledge to editing your own drafts. After completing ten practices, you will be given a review practice that asks you to incorporate all of the grammar and usage issues that you have been introduced to up to that point.

How You Respond to Each Reading Selection

Each of the twenty reading selections follows a similar format–from prereading to drafting and revising. Here are the nine steps you follow as you read and write about each selection:

1.   *Before You Read:* Here you will answer a series of questions to see what you already know about the topic. These answers will better prepare you for reading the selection.

2.   *Previewing:* Before you carefully read the selection, you will quickly move through the beginning, middle, and end of it to get a sense for the main point the author is making.

3.   *Reading Critically:* Having previewed, you then will read the selection slowly and thoroughly, underlining important points, making comments in the margin, and placing question marks next to sections that you do not understand.

4.   *Outlining/Clustering:* Here you will be given the opportunity to summarize the key points made in the selection. You will be provided with a skeleton of an outline that you can complete as you read the selection or after you read. You may also place this information in a visual cluster, if visualizing material is an easier way for you to understand it.

5.   *A Second Reading:* This activity encourages you to reread the selection because you will find that a second reading of the material will greatly help your understanding. As you reread these selections, you will be asked to answer five thought-provoking questions that will encourage you to go beyond the literal meaning.

6.   *Reading/Writing Feature:* In this activity, you will learn about a feature of reading and writing that will help both your critical reading and college writing. You will relate this aspect of reading and writing to the selection that you have just read. You can then apply this reading and writing feature to the following reading selections and writing topics you complete.

7.   *Before You Write:* Here you will be asked to refer to the writer's handbook to learn about using grammar and **form in your writing.** You will be asked to complete editing practices that will involve your reading and correcting of sample student paragraphs on the selection that you just read. As with the reading/writing feature, you can then apply what you learned in these practices to the following writing assignments you complete.

8.   *Writing Topics:* Here you will choose a topic to write about in essay form. There will be two types of essay topics: "Writing about the Reading" and "Writing from Experience." The first type of question will ask you to refer to the selection closely as you write your essay, the second to apply what you have read to your personal experiences. You will likely have the chance to write both types of essay responses as you move through this textbook.

9.   *Responding to Student Writing:* This last activity will ask you to revise and edit your draft. You will be asked to answer a series of questions on your peer's draft, then to discuss your responses with her. Before you hand in your essay, you may want to use these same questions to do a final revision and editing of your work.

At the end of each set of readings you will be given follow-up questions to see if you can tie together what you have learned about each topic in a section titled "Follow-Up." You will be asked to review each selection and comment on which selection had the greatest impact on you.

After you finish *Reading to Write,* you will most likely have developed more effective ways to critically read college material and write in an organized, relatively error-free style. These are essential practices that you will continue to rely on as you complete your college course work. You will, I hope, discover that writing successfully at the college level is not that mysterious a process. In fact, you should come to realize that a systematic study of reading and writing will allow you to become a more productive college student.

PART I
College Reading and Writing

■══════■

In the following four chapters, you will learn the important reading and writing practices that you will need in college. Chapter 1 introduces significant reading activities; Chapter 2 focuses on writing; and Chapters 3 and 4 examine how reading and writing are organized. The knowledge gained in these four chapters will serve as a foundation for the rest of the work you will do in this textbook.

These four chapters are titled:

Chapter 1: Ways to Read
Chapter 2: Ways to Write
Chapter 3: Types of Reading and Writing
Chapter 4: More Types of Reading and Writing

After each of these chapters, you will read a selection that relates to one aspect of reading and writing. These selections are as follows:

Selection 1: "Literacy: A Family Affair" by Anita Merina
Selection 2: "The Eight Beatitudes of Writing" by Melannie Svoboda
Selection 3: "Finding Modern Ways to Teach Today's Youth" by Sharon Curcio
Selection 4: "Saved" by Malcom X and Alex Haley

As you read these selections, you will learn about the following reading and writing topics:

READING/WRITING FEATURES	GRAMMAR/USAGE	WRITING CONVENTIONS
Selection 1 Evidence	Sentence Fragments	Citing Author/ Title
Selection 2 Making Inferences	Sentence Fragments	Ways to Quote
Selection 3 Facts and Figures	Sentence Fragments	Introductions
Selection 4 Conclusions	Run-ons	Topic Sentence

READING/WRITING PREP

You may want to answer the following questions before beginning Part I. Answering these questions individually or in groups will prepare you for what you will learn.

1. What makes a successful college reader?
2. What makes a successful college writer?
3. What are some of the problems a poor reader has?
4. What are some of the problems a poor writer has?

CHAPTER 1

WAYS TO READ

You have undoubtedly come to this class and to college knowing how to read. As you advance from one level of education to another, your reading ways change. In college, the reading required to write paragraphs and essays is going to be more careful, more thorough. In this first chapter, you will learn how to be a more successful college reader. You will find that what you learn about being a more effective reader will improve your writing as well.

In college reading, the three connected steps to understanding the material are (1) prereading, (2) critical reading, and (3) rereading. As you critically read, you will find it helpful to paraphrase sentences, summarize large chunks of reading, and record your responses in a reading journal. These are all writing activities. You will see that writing is closely connected to all the reading involved in this textbook and in college. These activities are what I call in this textbook *writing about the reading.*

PREREADING

Many students begin reading a selection by starting with the first word and ending with the last. They may not have a very good idea about what they are reading or about the author who wrote the material. They simply assume that there is one straightforward way to read: you begin with the first paragraph and end with the last.

Many reading studies have shown that a more effective approach is to obtain an overall sense for what you are reading before you begin reading the first paragraph. These studies conclude that you are not wasting time to look over the material first. In fact, the research has shown that your understanding of the reading material will greatly improve if you have an overall framework in mind.

When you *preview* the material, you study the following parts of the selection:

1. *Author and title:* You look to see if the title can help you understand something about the reading. Selection 1 at the end of this introduction is "Literacy: A Family Affair" by Anita Merina. From this title, you realize that this selection will likely be examining how families teach their children to read and write. This article will likely show how families are important in helping children to learn to read. All of this information is called *background knowledge,* or what you already know about a topic. When you call to mind this background knowledge, you are able to put what you read into a more familiar setting, and your comprehension improves.

2. *Source and date of the reading:* Before you begin critically reading a selection, determining where the material comes from and when it was written is also helpful. If the selection is from a daily newspaper, you can conclude that the material is for the average reader. If the selection is from a college textbook, you can assume that the material will be more difficult to understand than a popular newspaper or magazine article. Furthermore, knowing when the selection was written will help you determine how recent the material is. For example, if an article on families and reading was written in 1950, you are correct to wonder if what it says is still applicable today, whereas an article on reading and the family written in 2001 will likely present the most recent research.

   "Literacy: A Family Affair" by Anita Merina was printed in 1995 and is published by the National Education Association (NEA). You can assume that what Merina is saying about reading and the family is recent and that it is probably focusing on the importance of reading in education because the NEA published it. Again you can make these assumptions before you begin reading, and they will help you as you begin to critically read the selection.

3. *First paragraph and last paragraph:* By reading the first and last paragraph of a selection, you gain a sense for what the selection is trying to do: what it is attempting to prove or show and how it ends or what conclusion it comes to. This knowledge will help you understand the entire selection more fully.

4. *Middle of the selection:* Move quickly through the rest of the selection, reading an occasional sentence or phrase. In this way, you learn the kinds of details that the selection presents and the ways in which it is organized.

Previewing should take just a few minutes. In the long run, previewing actually saves reading time because it allows you to make accurate predictions about what you are reading. When you can anticipate how a selection is organized and the kinds of details it presents, you tend to read the selection more quickly.

You may now want to complete the previewing activity for Selection 1 on page 11.

CRITICAL READING

Having previewed, you are now ready to read critically. At this point, you have some idea for what the selection plans to say and how it goes about saying it. Now you are ready to read *critically,* that is, being able to explain accurately what the selection is saying and providing the necessary evidence to support it.

A critical reader asks and answers the following questions as he or she studies the selection:

1. What is the selections saying, or what is it trying to prove?
2. What details are used to support what the selection is saying?
3. Are these details convincing?
4. If these details are not convincing, what is missing?

Critical reading is not passive reading. You should be reading with a pencil or highlighter in hand; underlining important words, phrases, or sentences; and making comments in the margins.

Some of the margin comments you should frequently write include the following:

1. A question mark (?) when you do not understand a part of the reading
2. Words like "interesting" when you come to a strong section of the reading or "not convincing" when a particular section seems weak to you
3. Any questions about the reading that you want to reconsider
4. Phrases that highlight the important parts of the selection

See Figure 1.1 for an example of how the first part of Selection 1 is successfully marked.

You may now want to complete the reading critically activity for Selection 1 on page 11.

FIGURE 1.1

"Literacy: A Family Affair" Anita Merina

1   Robert Mendez can read. This wasn't always the case. Robert says, "Until the age of 35, I was an adult who couldn't read. That meant I couldn't read to my children. I couldn't help them with their homework. I couldn't respond to teacher's notes from school. And when those times came around, I avoided them–avoided my own children. That's the pain–the personal hell–of being an illiterate adult. When you're illiterate, you're not able to read the names off a grocery list or your child's name on a report card. You can't get a better job because it means filling out a job application. Even when you're successful because you've used your ability to listen and to memorize to handle complex tasks like driving the freeways or to perform well at work, you're still a man who can't read."

[margin note: Keypoint]

[margin note: How you are handicapped by illiteracy]

2   Robert continues, "My fear of words developed when I was seven years old. It continued each time I was held back in class, each time I was called stupid by another child. At each time I faced printed words, the same fear and panic rose up again. I knew I didn't want that for my children, especially the younger ones who I could still help. So at 35, I battled back my demons, walked into a literacy center and asked for help."

[margin note: When Robert changes]

3   Across the country there are 90 million adults who can't read at a fifth grade level. Forty million of them can barely read and write at all. These are tragic numbers for America–devastating when you consider that children of functionally illiterate adults are twice as likely as other kids to be functionally illiterate themselves.

[margin note: Statistics on illiteracy]

PARAPHRASING

Sometimes you will be confused by the wording or structure of a particular sentence. You may want to underline this sentence and place a question mark in the margin to alert you to go back to make sense of it. At times, not understanding one sentence can prevent you from understanding the entire paragraph or several paragraphs. To paraphrase is to restate a difficult sentence in simpler terms that you understand.

Here are some steps to follow when paraphrasing a difficult sentence:

1. Read the sentence that comes before and after the one you need to paraphrase. When you know the placement or context of a difficult sentence, you have a better chance of understanding the difficult sentence.

2. Look up any words in the difficult sentence that are new to you.

3. Identify the core parts of the difficult sentence: subject, verb, and object or complement. These core parts will provide you with a key to the sentence's meaning.

4. See how any additional sentence parts like phrases or clauses change the basic meaning of the sentence.

5. Reread the sentence. Look away from the original sentence and write your version or paraphrase of it in the margin.

Study the following sentence from paragraph 3 of Selection 1 "Literacy: A Family Affair":

These are tragic numbers for America–devastating when you consider that children of functionally illiterate adults are twice as likely as other kids to be functionally illiterate themselves.

1. The sentence before introduces the statistic that there are "90 million adults who can't read at a fifth grade level." The sentence after quotes a person who refers to illiteracy as a "crisis."

2. A phrase that you may have difficulty with, "functionally illiterate," refers to people who can sound out some words but can't understand much of what they are reading each day, so they can't "function" effectively.

3. This sentence begins clearly with the subject "these," the verb "are," and the complement "tragic numbers." Merina is clear that the number of 90 million functionally illiterates in America is a very serious problem.

4. The ending of the sentence is a long clause that explains why these numbers are tragic: "when you consider . . ." Here you learn that the children of functionally illiterate parents have a much greater chance of being functionally illiterate themselves. This part of the sentence seems to be the most important point made in the sentence.

5. By following these necessary steps, you can paraphrase this sentence in the margin in the following way:

The number of illiterates is extremely serious especially because their children are two times as likely to be unable to get by with their reading skills.

Paraphrasing may seem tedious to you at first, but with practice it becomes a powerful tool for you to make sense of difficult sentences that you would normally skip over.

SUMMARIZING

Summarizing is a reading practice that is related to paraphrasing. To *summarize* is to restate accurately sentences, a paragraph, paragraphs, or an entire selection in fewer words than the original and in your own words. This is a very important college reading practice because by summarizing, you demonstrate an understanding of the important parts of the material that you have studied.

In summarizing an entire reading selection, you answer the following questions:

1. What is the purpose of the reading selection?
2. What details or evidence is used to achieve this purpose?
3. How does the selection end, or what conclusions does the writer come to?

You can write your summaries in informal paragraphs, in outlines, or in visual maps called *clusters*. A summary in outline form could take a format similar to the following:

I. _____ (purpose of the selection)

   A. _____

   B. _____ (key evidence explaining this purpose)

   C. _____
   (and so on)

II. _____ (conclusion made in the selection)

You can summarize reading material in visual form, commonly known as a *visual cluster* or *map*. A cluster summary could take a shape similar to that in Figure 1.2.

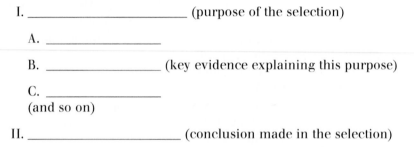
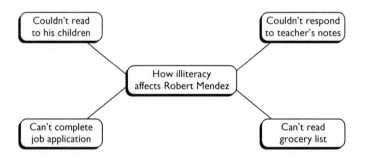

As a college student, you will be summarizing material in almost all of your courses; therefore, it is an important reading and writing practice for you to complete successfully. You will be summarizing each of the twenty reading selections in this textbook in the activity titled Outlining/Clustering, and in the Writing about the Reading exercise that follows each of the reading selections, you will be relying on these summaries for some of the information you choose to use.

You may now want to complete the outlining/clustering activity for Selection 1 on page 13.

A READING JOURNAL

Once you previewed the reading, read it critically, marked it, made margin comments, or summarized it, you may also want to write your understanding of the reading in a reading journal. A *reading journal* is an informal way to express many of your responses to the reading. Because this journal is informal, you do not need to concern yourself with spelling, grammar, and paragraphing. You just want to get many of your ideas down.

In your reading journal, include some or all of the following:

1. Questions you may have about the reading
2. What you liked about the selection
3. What you disliked about the selection
4. Comments on how this reading compares with other readings on this topic that you have read

The best way to keep a reading journal is to save a place in your notebook just for your reading journal entries. Date each entry and write out the selection title.

Here is an example of a reading journal entry on "Literacy: A Family Affair":

3/2 "Literacy: A Family Affair" Selection 1
This is an interesting reading. It's hard to believe that there are so many people who have a hard time reading. And in America!

There are some very powerful facts—like 90 million people are functionally illiterate and their kids are likely to follow in their path. This shows me that the problem will multiply in the future. So what can we do? Family literacy programs seem to be one way to deal with this problem.

I still have a few questions. Are there family literacy programs in our area? Are there illiterates in our neighborhood that I never knew had this problem?

Do you see how this student wrote down her most important reactions to the Merina selection? She talked about what she found most interesting, what frightened her, and the questions she still has. These are the questions that she will bring to the selection when she rereads it and further researches this topic.

***

REREADING

Critically reading a selection once may not provide all the answers you need to fully understand the material. If you choose to reread a selection, follow the same steps listed in critical reading: underline or highlight, make margin comments, paraphrase, and review your reading journal or summary.

You will find that college reading is different from most of the reading that you have done so far because it requires rereading for you to better understand the material. Rereading is not a mark of your reading failures but your understanding that college reading is often not fully understood the first time through.

The next chapter presents the steps involved in writing. You will see that the writing process is very similar to the reading steps you learned here.

Summary

1. Prereading is a necessary first step in understanding a selection. You look at the author, title, source, first paragraph, and last paragraph, and you read a few sentences and words in the middle of the selection.

2. Critical reading happens after your preview. You underline important points, make margin comments, and paraphrase difficult sentences.

3. A paraphrase is an accurate restatement of a sentence that is difficult to understand.

4. After critical reading, you may want to summarize what you have read or write a reading journal.

5. A summary is an accurate restatement of what you have read in your own words.

6. A reading journal is an informal writing whereby you make comments and ask questions about what you have read.

7. Rereading is a necessary final step to most of the reading encountered in college. You follow the same critical reading steps as you read the same selection again.

SELECTION 1: "LITERACY: A FAMILY AFFAIR" BY ANITA MERINA

This excerpt describes the current reading and writing problems in America. Anita Merina discusses the story of Robert, who had difficulty reading; the ways this problem hurt him; and how he finally solved it. She also describes several family literacy programs that have been successful in dealing with the problems of poor readers in America. This selection emphasizes the significance of reading in America in achieving goals and being a satisfied person.

BEFORE YOU READ

Before reading this selection, answer these questions in a writing journal or in class discussion:

1. Do you remember how you learned to read? Did you ever have difficulties in learning to read?
2. Do you know of an adult today who cannot read or write well? If so, describe this person.

PREVIEWING

Preview the following selection. Read the first and last paragraph. Then read a few sentences, words, and phrases in the middle paragraphs. Before you begin critically reading, write a few sentences on what it is like not to be able to read well.

Some of the problems a person faces who does not read well:

_____

_____

_____

_____

_____

_____

READING CRITICALLY

Now critically read the selection, and complete the following outline as you read or after you finish. You may want to make this outline into a visual cluster of the important information.

Anita Merina

Literacy: A Family Affair

1   Robert Mendez can read. This wasn't always the case. Robert says, "Until the age of 35, I was an adult who couldn't read. That meant I couldn't read to my children. I couldn't help them with their homework. I couldn't respond to teachers' notes from school. And when those times came around, I avoided them–avoided my own children. That's the pain– the personal hell–of being an illiterate adult. When you're illiterate, you're not able to read the names off a grocery list or your child's name on a report card. You can't get a better job because it means filling out a job application. Even when you're successful because you've used your ability to listen and to memorize to handle complex tasks like driving the freeways or to perform well at work, you're still a man who can't read."

2   Robert continues, "My fear of words developed when I was seven years old. It continued each time I was held back in class, each time I was called stupid by another child. At each time I faced printed words, that same fear and panic rose up again. I knew I didn't want that for my children, especially the younger ones who I could still help. So at 35, I battled back my demons, walked into a literacy center and asked for help."

3   Across the country there are 90 million adults who can't read at a fifth grade level. Forty million of them can barely read and write at all. These are tragic numbers for America–devastating when you consider that children of functionally illiterate adults are twice as likely as other kids to be functionally illiterate themselves.

4   "We're facing an **intergenerational** crisis of illiteracy," says Sharon Darling, president of the National Center for Family Literacy. "Undereducated adults and educationally at-risk children interlock," Darling says. "They're bound so tightly together that excellence in education is an empty dream for kids who go home each afternoon to families where literacy is neither practiced nor valued."

5   "Far too many at-risk children are at-risk because their parents are undereducated, even afraid of school or teachers," Darling continues. "That translates into one generation after another of parents not having the confidence to go into schools and take part in their child's education." Statistics show that a child whose parent dropped out of high school is six times more likely than average to drop out, too. "If you could get parents to come back and finish their educations," Darling says, "you could make them comfortable with school. Then they in turn, could teach their children by example to enjoy school and learn."

6   In a nutshell, that's what family literacy programs are all about. In the last 10 years, the number of family literacy programs across the country has jumped from 500 to more than 5,000. Whether you call the

program Even Start, Families for Learning, or Project Literacy, the goal of family literacy programs is the same–stopping the cycle of failure. Recent studies show they work. Not one of the 2,500 3- and 4-year old participants in a family literacy program evaluated in a 1993 study repeated a grade in elementary school. Without the program, Darling says, 25 percent of at-risk kids are likely to repeat at least one year prior to fourth grade. Moreover, once these children entered elementary school, they were reported to be highly motivated to learn and performed well.

7   Many educators deal with adult literacy every day–some more directly than others. . . . Robert Mendez is an educator too. In addition to his job as plant manager at Orchard Elementary School in Los Angeles, he's vice chair of the California Literacy Foundation, sits on the board of Laubach Literacy, and travels the country speaking to newly literate adults. Mendez has published articles and poetry in magazines, even spoken at a United Nations conference on literacy. But all of these accomplishments **pale** compared to the satisfaction Mendez gets from helping his son succeed.

8   "Every day I sit with my son Matthew and help him with his homework. I read with him, help with his reports, and take him to the library. Doing this brings me closer to him. This is what I tell adults who are sometimes frustrated with their progress and think about giving up. I tell them to hang in there, that it isn't important that you read quickly to your child–it's that you care enough to do it that's your success."

9   Robert adds, "Literacy is more than learning to read. It's getting rid of the luggage of guilt and shame. It's realizing you're opening doors to worlds you thought were closed to you. It's realizing that schools aren't places you dread walking into anymore. They're places where you've rediscovered the joy of learning. That's the **legacy** I want to pass on to my son."

SOURCE: *NEA Today*, April 1995, pp. 4–5.

OUTLINING/CLUSTERING

I. Some problems Robert faces in being unable to read well

    A. _____

    B. _____

    C. _____

    D. _____

---

intergenerational: between generations; **pale:** lessen in importance; **legacy:** anything handed down from an ancestor

II. Some startling facts about Americans who do not read well

    A. _____

    B. _____

    C. _____

III. Some important facts about family literacy programs

    A. _____

    B. _____

    C. _____

IV. What Robert learns about being able to read

    A. _____

    B. _____

A SECOND READING

Reread the Merina selection and answer the following questions as you read. Before answering these questions, you may want to write in your reading journal about any questions or comments you have about the selection.

1. Reread paragraph 5. Why do you think that a child of a high school dropout is "six times more likely than average to drop out, too"?
2. Reread paragraph 6. Why do you think that children who participated in family literacy programs did so much better in elementary school?
3. Paraphrase this sentence from paragraph 4: "We're facing an intergenerational crisis of illiteracy."
4. In paragraph 8, Robert describes how he works with his son. Why do you think these activities allow Robert to be closer to him?
5. Reread paragraph 9. Summarize the most satisfying reasons Robert finds for being literate.

READING/WRITING FEATURE: EVIDENCE

Every good writer of stories and essays relies on evidence to make what they are saying come alive. *Evidence* is simply the proof that the writer gives to support the point he or she is making. Anita Merina wants to show her readers how helpless people are who can't read and how successful they are when they learn to read. In this selection, Merina presents ample evidence to her reader to prove these points.

In stories, evidence usually comes in the form of *details,* specific recollections of an individual, an object, or an event. In essays and textbooks, you often read evidence that is a *fact or a figure,* like a name, date, or percentage. In either case, the quality of the evidence allows you, the reader, to be convinced or unconvinced of the point the writer is making.

Accurate and clear evidence is at the center of good reading and good writing. If you were to try to write about your reading education, for example, you should try to recall with clarity and honesty the specific moments in your reading experience. These are some of the questions that you should ask yourself before and as you write:

1. Who are the important people involved in my learning to read?
2. How did they help me? Can I recall specific moments about how they helped me?
3. Why were these moments important? What were some of the feelings I had as I was learning to read?
4. Has this evidence brought my reading experiences to life?

Look again at paragraph 6 from the Merina selection. This time read to see how the evidence Merina relies on shows the importance of family literacy programs:

> Recent studies show they work. Not one of the 2,500 3- and 4-year-old participants in a family literacy program evaluated in a 1993 study repeated a grade in elementary school. Without the program, Darling says that 25 percent of at-risk kids are likely to repeat at least one year prior to fourth grade.

Note that Merina tells her readers of the numbers and ages of the children in the study (2,500 three- and four-year-olds), when the study took place (1993), how many repeated a grade (none), and what would have happened if the children had not participated in family literacy (25 percent would have repeated a year before fourth grade). This evidence makes Merina's support of family literary programs believable.

This kind of evidence can be appreciated in quality reading and is what you should strive for in your own writing. You will learn more about evidence in Chapter 2.

BEFORE YOU WRITE

Before selecting a writing topic, you may want to study sentence fragments without subjects and complete Practice A1 (pages 206–207), study how to cite the author and the title of the reading selection, and complete Practice B1 on pages 254–255 of the handbook.

WRITING TOPICS

Choose a topic from the following choices.

Writing about the Reading

1. Write a summary of the selection "Literacy: A Family Affair." You may want to use the evidence you gathered in the outlining/clustering activity you completed. Write this summary in paragraphs.

Writing from Experience

2. Write a journal entry that begins to describe your recollections of how you learned to read. Try to provide as much evidence for your recollections as you can. Who were the people who helped you? How old were you? How did you feel about the ways you improved as a reader?

For this writing, do not concern yourself with sentence structure and paragraphing.

RESPONDING TO STUDENT WRITING

Use some or all of these questions to respond to your journal or to that of a classmate. Read carefully for meaning and make your comments specific.

If you are responding to the summary:

1. Are the points presented in the summary accurate?

2. What other key points from the Merina selection could be included in the summary?

If you are responding to the personal experience journal:

3. Is the evidence in the journal clear?

4. What other evidence could be included?

5. Provide a piece of evidence from the journal that is particularly revealing about how the person learned to read.

CHAPTER 2

WAYS TO WRITE

Writing is an activity that has many faces. Certainly you have done your share of writing even before coming to college. You have likely written letters to family and friends, perhaps written a diary to express your feelings, and certainly jotted down lists of things to buy at the supermarket or a quick note from a phone call. In school, you have likely taken notes in various courses and probably written exams and essays that required you to write more than a phrase or sentence. All of these writing activities, from the quick note to the essay of several paragraphs, share certain characteristics. They use the same language, follow the same rules of grammar and spelling, and attempt to convey a particular meaning to a person or group of people.

In college, you bring this knowledge of writing to your courses. Now you will likely be asked to write more and will probably be asked to think about and change what you have written. In this chapter, you will learn how to be a more effective college writer of paragraphs and essays. You will study four writing issues that apply to the writing that you do in this book and, I hope, to the writing required in all your college courses. These topics are as follows:

1. Prewriting
2. Drafting
3. Revising and Editing
4. How Paragraphs and Essays Are Structured

PREWRITING

Prewriting, also called *brainstorming*, asks you to think about what you plan to write, to jot down these thoughts in any order that they come, and to sort out these ideas into any patterns that you find. You can brainstorm by just sitting down alone and jotting down anything that comes to your mind in words, phrases, or sentences; or you can talk to fellow students, your teacher, or anyone who may have information on the topic you are considering. When you first begin prewriting, you may think that you are wasting your time. You may want your writing to come out perfect the first time, but as you continue to prewrite, you will find that your best writing comes from a series of stops and starts and from a lot of ideas that you never use in your final copy. Rather than being a waste of time, prewriting is *the* necessary step in getting started.

A way that college students have found to get their ideas down in prewriting is through a *free-writing journal.* As you learned in Chapter 1, the reading journal helps you figure out what you understand and don't understand about what you have read. Similarly, a free-writing journal helps you figure out what you know and don't know about the topic that you plan to write about. Free-writing journals, like reading journals, do not have to be written in sentences or paragraphs and can be half a page or several pages long.

Let's look at part of what Aldo wrote in his free-writing journal on the question that his composition teacher gave him: What are your recollections about learning how to write?

> Free-Writing Journal Entry #2
>
> I think I'm going to have problems with this question. I don't remember a lot about how I learned to write. Is she asking me how I learned to write the letters of the alphabet? my name? an essay at school? Those are the questions I'm going to ask her tomorrow.
>
> What I'd like to write about is my high school comp teacher, Mr. Shniad. He was really good, and I enjoyed writing for him. What did I write for him? Why did I like him? I don't remember too much. My friend Ron could help. He was in the same class. . . .

You see here that Aldo is really going over all the problems he has in answering the question. He doesn't know what his teacher really means by writing. All he knows for sure is that Mr. Shniad helped him learn how to write, and he enjoyed the class; but he doesn't remember all the details. These troubling questions–these stops and starts–are necessary for Aldo to finally figure out what he wants to say in this essay.

Before Aldo can go on, he needs answers to these questions. In the following class meetings, Aldo finds out from his teacher that he can write on any stage of his education as long as it focuses on this particular phase, so he decides to write on Mr. Shniad's composition class. He gets help from his friend Ron, who even saved many of the essays they wrote in this class. This gives Aldo a greater focus in writing this essay. He has narrowed his topic and now has material to write about.

Once you have a better idea for your topic and have thought about how you are going to explore it, you are ready to jot down this information in a *rough outline* or *visual cluster.* Both are ways to begin organizing what you have written in your free-writing journal. In both

FIGURE 2.1

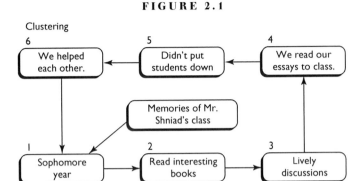

Clustering

systems, you are mapping where your writing will go. The outline or cluster does not have to be too specific; it merely serves to give your writing direction. Students often rely on the rough outline if they are more comfortable with words, whereas the more visually thinking students often put their ideas in a cluster.

Let's go back to Aldo to see how he outlined and then clustered his writing memories.

Outline on Mr. Shniad

I. Mr. Shniad helped me learn to write because his class was hard and enjoyable.
  A. It was my sophomore year in high school in a comp class.
  B. He had us read interesting books and talk about them.
  C. His discussions were lively, and the writing topics were interesting.
  D. He encouraged students to read their essays to the class.
  E. He didn't put the students down, and he found ways to make the writing better.
  F. He encouraged us to help each other.

This same outline can be put in a cluster that could look like the one in Figure 2.1.

Now Aldo can begin writing. He doesn't have to follow every detail of his outline or cluster. In fact, as he writes, he will find that the order of his ideas may change. He now has a road map. Like a road map, the outline/cluster gives the direction but does not provide the specific moments of the ride.

You may now want to select a writing topic from the two for Selection 2 on page 32 and complete the prewriting stage.

DRAFTING

Now Aldo can start writing his paper on Mr. Shniad's composition class. This second step in writing is called *drafting.* Drafting is writing down the ideas in sentences and paragraphs. It is a more formal kind of writing than journal writing. It is often wise to write your first draft quickly. Do not fret over spelling questions and punctuation rules at this time. Get your ideas down in sentences and paragraphs and see if you can stick to your outline or cluster. Also, don't worry if the paragraphs do not seem fully organized or as detailed as you would like them. In most cases in college, you will be able to write a second or third draft whereby you can answer these more specific questions.

Look at how Aldo begins the first draft of his essay on Mr. Shniad's composition class:

> I think my best teacher was Mr. Shniad. He helped me learn how to write. His class was fun and hard at the same time. We read a lot of intresting stuff and the students got a chance to talk about their writing. He always seemed to make our writing better by the nice comments he made on our essays.

Aldo will go back to make this first paragraph better but not until he's finished his entire first draft.

You may now want to complete the draft of the topic you chose for Selection 2 on page 32.

REVISING AND EDITING

Once your first draft is finished, you are not done with your writing. It's often wise to have your teacher and your fellow students read and comment on what you have read. Your teacher should give you important suggestions that you can use in a second and third draft, and your fellow students can also provide suggestions that you may want to include in your next draft or drafts. Changing what you have written is known as *revising.* You can revise your first draft on your own or with the help of others. Revising includes adding, taking out, or rearranging material, which can be a word, a sentence, a paragraph, or a series of paragraphs. Revising is a very important part of college writing because it allows you to think about what you have written and to make what you have written better, that is, clearer, more logical, more detailed, or more convincing.

Look at how Aldo revised his first paragraph:

I'm certain my best teacher was Mr. Shniad. He helped me to learn how to write clear essays. His class was fun and challenging at the same time. We read a lot of intresting material and the students got a chance to talk about their writing with him and other students in groups. He always seemed to make our writing clearer by the helpful comments he made on our essays.

Aldo made most of these changes after letting the first draft sit for a few days. It's always best to come to your writing again after a break because your mind is fresh. Aldo made some of these changes himself and received help on other changes from his teacher and from other students in his class. Do you see how the second draft of this paragraph is more focused, clearer? Aldo is speaking with more conviction now—he is certain that Mr. Shniad was his best teacher. There is more detail to his writing as well—Mr. Shniad taught him how to write clear essays, and students talked about their writing in groups. Also, Aldo is choosing more exact words—hard becomes *challenging,* stuff becomes *material,* better becomes *clearer,* and nice becomes *helpful.*

If Aldo has time, he will revise this paragraph a second time before he hands it in.

If you have revised your writing but you are pressed for time because you must hand it in, you are ready to edit your writing. You will find that revising can go on forever; however, in college and at work, deadlines must be met, and you will find that you must hand in writing that you are not completely satisfied with. That is a worry that all writers share: students, teachers, and professional writers alike.

Editing involves proofreading for surface errors: spelling, punctuation, and usage mistakes. Editing is best done at the very end of your writing because it is a mechanical activity, very different from the careful thinking you have spent in shaping the ideas that you have written. So it's wise to edit your work only after you have written your last draft.

Though editing is not the most creative part of writing, it is nonetheless important. Writing in college and at work that is filled with surface errors will not be taken as seriously as writing that is free of these errors. In this textbook, you will be given lots of opportunities to edit for grammar, usage, and convention errors in practice exercises, in your own writing, and in the writing of other students. You become better at editing by doing, so don't feel defeated if you do not learn all of these editing rules the first time that you have been introduced to them. It takes most students several editing experiences to learn how to identify a particular spelling, grammar, or punctuation error in their writing or in the writing of others.

Finally, let's look at how Aldo edited his first paragraph:

I'm certain my best teacher was Mr. Shniad. He helped me to learn how to write clear essays. His class was fun and challenging at the same time. We read a lot of int[e]resting material[,] and the students got a chance to talk about their writing with him and other students in groups. He always seemed to make our writing clearer by the helpful comments he made on our essays.

Aldo's classmate showed him how to spell *interesting,* and his teacher explained how to use commas with compound sentences. Aldo is now ready to hand this paragraph in for a final evaluation.

You will have many experiences in revising and editing your writing and that of your classmates in the activity titled Responding to Student Writing after each writing topic.

If you have finished your draft of the topic you chose for Selection 2, you may want to complete section on responding to student writing on page 33.

HOW PARAGRAPHS AND ESSAYS ARE STRUCTURED

Now that you have seen how most writers write as they prewrite, draft, revise, and edit, you are ready to consider how paragraphs and entire essays are organized.

The two key terms that explain the structure of paragraphs and essays are *general* and *specific.* A general statement makes a point but does not use facts and figures to make it. A specific statement makes a point by using details like facts or figures. Details can be examples, illustrations, steps, characteristics, causes, or effects. More is said about these kinds of specific statements in Chapter 3. A *paragraph* is a group of sentences that supports a general statement with specific statements, whereas an essay is a group of paragraphs that makes a general statement or statements and supports them with specific evidence. Essays can inform, persuade, narrate, or describe. They may even do several of these tasks in the same essay. More is said about the various types of essays in the chapters and selections that follow.

Let's take a final look at Aldo's first paragraph to see if we can identify its general and specific parts:

> I'm certain my best teacher was Mr. Shniad. He helped me learn how to write clear essays. His class was fun and challenging at the same time. We read a lot of interesting material, and the students got a chance to talk about their writing with him and with us in groups. He always seemed to make our writing clearer by the helpful comments he made on our essays.

Do you see how the first sentence is the most general of all? Aldo makes a statement that Mr. Shniad was his best teacher, though at this time he does not give us the reasons why. The most general sentence in a paragraph that states the controlling idea of the paragraph is often called the *topic sentence.* So this first sentence is Aldo's topic sentence. The second sentence is more specific, presenting characteristics of the class: fun and challenging. The next two sentences provide illustrations or examples of how the class was fun and challenging: the reading was interesting, the students talked about their writing, and Mr. Shniad made helpful comments on the students' writing. Aldo's first paragraph is successful because it smoothly moves from the general point to its specific points, where the specific statements make the general statement more convincing. This logical movement from general to specific describes all successful paragraphs and successful essays.

Essays, like paragraphs, successfully move from the general to the specific. Essays are more complicated than paragraphs because they move from general to specific and specific to general several times. Essays that describe a situation or narrate an event have a beginning, middle, and end; and essays that explain an idea or try to persuade you to accept a particular position have a beginning called an *introduction,* a middle called the *body,* and an end called a *conclusion.* Expository and persuasive essays have the shape illustrated in Figure 2.2.

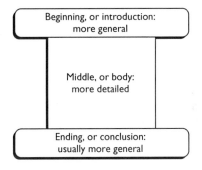

Beginning, or introduction: more general

Middle, or body: more detailed

Ending, or conclusion: usually more general

Aldo decided to use his first paragraph as his introduction because it generally included all the points he covered in his body. What Aldo introduced in his introduction—the interesting materials he read for Mr. Shniad, the conversations students had about their writing, and the helpful comments Mr. Shniad made—became separate paragraphs on each of these issues. This is what successful introductions should do. In one paragraph in the body, Aldo discussed specific titles of materials the students read; in two paragraphs, he recalls what students talked about in a particular writing topic on drug use; and in a final paragraph in the body, Aldo discussed specific comments Mr. Shniad had made on his final draft on drug use. The body of Aldo's essay thus followed logically from his introduction.

A conclusion usually either *summarizes* the important points the writer makes or *synthesizes* these points into a new idea. Aldo chose to write a conclusion of synthesis because he commented on how Mr. Shniad's writing course changed the direction of his writing from that point on. That is, Aldo came upon a new idea from the points his essay had made.

This final draft of Aldo's essay is explanatory; he wants to relate why he believes Mr. Shniad was his best teacher. Essays that explain are often called *expository* essays. Many of the essays that you write in college will be expository. Let's say Aldo intended to convince you that Mr. Shniad's way of teaching is the system that all teachers of composition should use. He would then be doing more than explaining because he would be wanting to persuade his reader, or *audience,* that Mr. Shniad's way is the best way to teach composition. Writers of *persuasive* essays want you, the audience, to change your mind on a particular issue.

Had Aldo told a story about one class meeting—who spoke, how Mr. Shniad responded, and what the students were asked to accomplish—he would be writing a *narration.* Narrations can be either fictional (untrue) or nonfictional (true), and they always tell a story. Had Aldo focused just on Mr. Shniad—how he spoke, dressed, moved his arms, and kept the class interested—then he would be writing a *description.* Description does not necessarily tell a story but tries to capture a person or object in words. As with narrations, descriptions can be either fictional or nonfictional.

You will encounter all of these forms of writing—exposition, persuasion, narration, description—in various writing assignments in this textbook. You may even use several of these writing forms in the same essay. Furthermore, you will also be reading these various kinds of writing in the selections in this textbook. The Malcolm X selection in Chapter 4 is an example of narration but has several elements of description in it. This selection can serve as a helpful model for your own attempts at description and narration.

In many ways, the writing topics you have studied in this chapter—prewriting, drafting, revising, and editing—are like the reading topics you studied in Chapter 1: prereading, critical reading, and rereading. In several parts of this textbook, you will see how reading and writing are interconnected activities.

Summary

1. Prewriting, or brainstorming, allows you to generate ideas about your writing.
2. Drafting allows you to begin to organize what you generated in prewriting into a paragraph or paragraphs.

3. Revising allows you to make each paragraph more organized, detailed, and convincing.

4. Editing is more mechanical because you are correcting surface errors; it should be done just before you hand in your writing.

5. Paragraphs move from general to specific. The most general statement is the topic sentence, and the specific statements are the details to support the topic sentence.

6. Essays generally have an introduction, which presents the important points the writer wants to make; a body, which contains paragraphs that present evidence for what is generally stated in the introduction; and a conclusion, which either summarizes or synthesizes the points the writer has made in the introduction and body. See how Figure 2.3 visually shows this relationship.

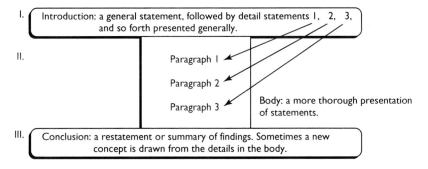

7. Essays can be narrative, descriptive, expository, persuasive, or a combination of these.

SELECTION 2: "THE EIGHT BEATITUDES OF WRITING" BY MELANNIE SVOBODA

In this article, Melannie Svoboda presents an organized discussion of the eight beatitudes—or declarations—concerning writing. You will read about her childhood memories concerning writing, the writing mentors who most influenced her, the obstacles she constantly faced as a writer, and the ways she has found to finish a particular writing project. This selection is an interesting blend of narration and exposition. Though Svoboda has many more years of writing experience than you probably have, her writing advice can, nonetheless, help your writing development. See this selection as an extension of the discussion about writing that you just finished in Chapter 2.

BEFORE YOU READ

Before reading this selection, answer these questions in a free-writing journal or in class discussion:

1. What are some of the biggest stumbling blocks you have in completing a writing assignment?
2. Who or what seems to have influenced your writing the most?

PREVIEWING

Preview the following selection. Read the first and last few paragraphs. Then read a few sentences, words, and phrases in the middle paragraphs, paying particular attention to the subheadings. Before you begin critically reading, write a short statement summarizing Svoboda's attitude toward writing.

Svoboda's attitude toward writing:

_____

_____

_____

_____

_____

READING CRITICALLY

Now critically read the selection and complete the following outline as you read or after you finish. You may want to make this outline into a visual cluster of the important information.

Melannie Svoboda

The Eight Beatitudes of Writing

1 My first article was published 20 years ago. As I mark this event, I am prompted to reflect on writing and the role it has played and continues to play in my life. I would like to share with you some of the lessons that writing has taught me. I call them the eight beatitudes, the eight blessings, of writing.

Craving a Better World

2 I do not know where the desire to write comes from, but I know it was inside me even as a child. When I was only in the third grade, I wrote my

first "book"–in a thick red tablet with yellow pages. Entitled *Sugar,* my book was about a little girl who wanted a pony with all her heart. When she asked her father if she could please have one, he said, "Yes, you may have a pony." In real life, I had wanted a pony with all my heart, but when I asked my father, he said no. I think my desire to write grew out of my desire to fashion a world more to my liking.

3   I continue to write, not so much to fashion a world more to my liking (I hope I have moved beyond that) but to make the real world better. That sounds **presumptuous,** I know, yet deep down I think most writers operate out of that hope. We must. Why else do we, with the little free time we have, choose to shut ourselves up and tether ourselves to a typewriter when we could be enjoying life's little, legitimate pleasures like watching television, reading novels, playing golf or knitting afghans? We write because, in one sense, we have to. C. S. Lewis described writing as a "lust." Writing flows from the innate desire to influence (no matter how slightly) people (no matter how few) for the better. Thus, the first beatitude of writing is this: Happy are they who crave to make a better world.

Willing Sacrifice

4 This brings me to the second beatitude. I distinctly remember how I wrote that first book in third grade. I started writing it in school on Friday. When I got home, I wrote some more. But when it was time to go to bed that night, I was still not finished. So eager was I to finish my story, I got up early Saturday to work on it. I can still see myself sitting at the kitchen table in my little white nightgown, writing in my tablet, with the house very still and the rays of the morning sun peeking in through the windows. That image has stayed with me all these years to remind me that writing is something to make sacrifices for readily. As I sat finishing my story that Saturday long ago, I was not feeling sorry for myself. I was not wishing I were somewhere else–for example, still in bed with my sister. No, I wrote eagerly, enthusiastically, feeling lucky to have been entrusted with this story to tell.

5   The writer Red Smith said: "There's nothing to writing. All you do is sit down at a typewriter and open a vein." Beatitude No. 2 says, Happy are they who willingly sacrifice for their story. Sometimes the sacrifice is a piece of cake, but at others, immensely difficult. Focus not on the notion of sacrificing to accomplish good, but on the privilege of even one small contribution toward that better world.

Refusing to Listen to Trolls

6 Beatitude No. 3 concerns **trolls.** Whenever I am writing something, the temptation to quit is always very near. An ugly little troll squats on my shoulder and whispers "sour nothings" in my ear. He says things like, "Your writing is no good!" And if I try to ignore him or tell him to go away, he says with greater persistence: "No one cares what you write!

Who do you think you are, anyway? Why don't you stop this foolishness already!"

7   To write a book is a serious undertaking, a major commitment. In the middle of writing my first book, I became discouraged and toyed with scrapping the project altogether—or at least putting it aside for a while. I shared these feelings with a friend of mine who, without hesitation, said firmly: "Melannie, that's the evil spirit talking! Don't listen to him! He knows your book is going to do a lot of good, so he's doing all that he can to stop you from writing it."

8   I was amazed by the conviction in his voice (not to mention the confidence he had in my writing). Since then, I have come to believe in the power of the evil spirit, especially the Demon of Despair. I have found that the strength of the temptation to quit a work is in direct proportion to its potential for good. The third beatitude of writing, then, is this: Happy are they who refuse to listen to trolls.

Trusting Urges

9 Writing has taught me a fourth beatitude—about trusting urges. Here is an example. Today I plan to work on Project A. I have been working on it for several days. In fact, I am in the middle of writing it and my deadline is fast approaching. But as I sit down in front of my word processor, I suddenly get the strong urge to start an entirely new project, Project B. The urge comes out of nowhere. It makes no sense at all. I try to reason with it, saying: "But I'm in the middle of Project A. I can't start a new project now!" But sometimes the urge, like a pesky little child, will not take no for an answer. "Write B! Write B!" it insists.

10   The writing process (like most things in life) has a mind of its own. We make plans about what we want to do, but sometimes we must lay aside those plans completely and follow other calls, give in to other voices. Rather than hitting the "recall" button on our word processor and bringing up Project A as we planned to do, we hit "new" instead and find ourselves staring at a blank screen. Writing has taught me the immeasurable value of flexibility. It has revealed to me the fourth beatitude: Happy are they who can trust their urges, lay aside their sensible plans and risk the altogether new. With writing, as with living, we do not always do what we set out to do. This article, incidentally, was a Project B, the outgrowth of a trusted urge.

Giving Away Our Hiding Place

11 I once lived with someone who had a curious skill: The more she talked, the less she revealed about herself. I would sit across from her at meals and marvel at her ability to use words without revealing anything significant about herself. Whenever we conversed, the image I had of her was of a bricklayer constructing, with every word, a wall that increasingly hid her from view.

12   This woman demonstrated to me that words are not always **revela-tory.** They are meant to be, of course, but we can manipulate them in such a way as to frustrate their essential purpose. We sometimes do this because (let's face it) words are downright dangerous, hazardous to your health. When we use words effectively, we give ourselves away. Like a little child playing hide-and-seek, our words are that loud sneeze or **titter** that lets the seeker know our hiding place.

13   Writing is such a perilous business. Living is a perilous business, too. When we write (as when we really live), we are putting ourselves on the line. In some cases, our necks go on the chopping block. We are proclaiming to the world in big bold letters: "Look! This Is What I Think! This Is How I Feel! What Do You Think of Me Now?" Is there anything more frightening than that? The fifth beatitude of writing is this: Happy are they who, in the risky business of life, dare to reveal their hiding place.

Being Grateful

14   Nothing fills me with more gratitude than my talent for writing, nor with more humility. As a writer, I feel I have been given a precious gift–not a gift I own, but a gift on loan. To work with words, to wrestle with them, to **woo** them, to **coax** them into some sort of meaningful sequence–what is more worthwhile, more potent, more fun? But writing is not simply something I do to words. It is also something words do to me.

15   Writing is a humbling experience. (I do not just refer to rejection slips.) Writing would be less humbling if at the start I knew what I thought and felt and, therefore, could not wait to get it all down on paper. No. More often than not, I write in order to discover what I think and feel (or what I do not think or feel.) Jayne Anne Phillips said it well: "Writers are basically seekers. That's what drives them." If I waited to publish until I have gotten something perfect, I would never publish anything at all. So I write not definitively, not once-and-for-all. I write **provisionally,** for the time being. Everything I write is implicitly stamped: "This is what I believe today. But ask me again tomorrow."

16   The sixth and seventh beatitudes go together. Happy are they who know that life is a pure gift–a gift never quite finished yet.

Connecting

17   The eighth beatitude of writing is about the joy of connecting. At the beginning, I described writing as an "I" hoping to share something with a "you." One of the greatest joys of writing comes when we realize we have connected with another person, when something we have written–perhaps only a sentence or a phrase–has deeply touched, moved or amused another human being.

18   C. S. Lewis said that friendship ordinarily happens when two people are engaged in a common activity. Eventually one of them makes a

revelatory remark, and the other one stops and says in wonder and amazement, "You too?" and quickly adds, "But I thought I was the only one!" That "you too?" experience is one of the most important we can have in life; it pulls us out of our preoccupation with ourselves, out of our paralyzing sense of isolation and joins us—if only for a moment—to another human being.

19   Writing links writer to reader, reader to writer, and reader to reader in a marvelous way. As a reader, I have felt bonded to an author by something he or she has written. As a writer I have received letters from readers as near as Akron and as far away as Nairobi, who tell me they have **resonated** deeply with something I have written. Call it what you want: connectedness, intimacy, linkage, union. The eighth beatitude of writing is this: Happy are they who have said, "You too?"

20   These are the eight beatitudes of writing. At least, this is what I think today. But ask me again tomorrow.

SOURCE: *America* 15 (November 11, 1995): p. 23.

OUTLINING/CLUSTERING

I. Svoboda's writing memories as a child

    A. _____

    B. _____

II. Five important insights concerning writing

    A. _____

    B. _____

    C. _____

    D. _____

    E. _____

III. How writing connects writer to reader

    A. _____

    B. _____

---

presumptuous: bold and overtly confident; **troll:** a dwarf in Scandinavian mythology; **revelatory:** in a disclosing manner; **titter:** a slight laugh **woo:** to entreat or urge; **coax:** to persuade by soothing words; **provisionally:** temporarily; **resonated:** increased in intensity

A SECOND READING

Reread the Svoboda selection and answer the following questions as you read. Before answering these questions, you may want to write in your reading journal about any questions or comments you have about the selection.

1. In paragraph 6, Svoboda refers to a troll. How does this image help you understand the third beatitude of writing?

2. Reread paragraphs 9 and 10–trusting urges. Summarize in a sentence or two what Svoboda is saying here about the writing process.

3. Paraphrase the following sentence in paragraph 10: "Writing has taught me the immeasurable value of flexibility."

4. Reread paragraph 18 on C. S. Lewis. What is the "you too?" experience?

5. Svoboda ends her article with this statement in paragraph 20: "At least, this is what I think today. But ask me again tomorrow." Why is this an appropriate way to end her discussion of the writing process as she understands it?

READING/WRITING FEATURE: MAKING INFERENCES

This selection is interesting to read and reread because you have to "read between the lines" to understand the many subtle insights that Melannie Svoboda has concerning writing. This kind of reading is rich in *inferences,* or insights that are not literally written down. A good reader often grasps these insights by studying the evidence or details in the selection and drawing the right conclusions from them. Writers who rely on their readers to make inferences are encouraging them to take their writing very seriously. A successful writer of fiction and nonfiction often writes narratives rich in inferences.

The questions you as a reader should ask when you make inferences are as follows:

1. What types of details does the writer use?

2. Do these details fit into any pattern?

3. Do any of these details not fit into this pattern?

Review paragraph 12. What adjectives does Svoboda use? What analogy is she using? What pattern do these adjectives and this analogy seem to fit into? Do you see how "dangerous" and "hazardous" are powerful adjectives used to describe how one writes? She is emphasizing how powerful words can be both in showing who we are and in sometimes hiding who we are. With her analogy of the child playing hide and seek and being found because she sneezed, we sense how playful, childlike, and vulnerable a good writer can be. All of these words, together, suggest the immense power and joy that Svoboda assigns to the written word. You could not appreciate the force that language has for Svoboda if you did not make certain, appropriate inferences from the language Svoboda chooses in the paragraph.

Now review paragraph 18. Can you infer why Svoboda uses C. S. Lewis to describe friendship as a "you too?" experience? The first appropriate inference you can make is that friendship has something to do with writing. This connection is exactly the one Svoboda makes in the following paragraph when she begins with "writing links writer to reader, reader to writer, and reader to reader in a marvelous way." The appropriate inference you can make is that for Svoboda, writing that grabs a reader establishes a friendship in which reader and writer share common experiences. Nowhere in these two paragraphs does Svoboda say this. It is up to you to "read between the lines" to make this connection.

So much of what we learn about what Melannie Svoboda considers good writing comes from inferences like these. Successful readers are willing to reread to make accurate inferences, and good writers of narrative, description, and exposition rely on their reader's ability to make these correct inferences.

BEFORE YOU WRITE

Before selecting an essay topic, you may want to study sentence fragments with adjective clauses and complete Practice A2 (pages 207–208) and study ways to quote and complete Practice B2 (pages 255–256) of the handbook.

WRITING TOPICS

Choose an essay topic from the following questions. Follow the steps in the writing process summarized on the inside front cover.

Writing about the Reading

1. Write an organized essay that accurately summarizes five of the eight beatitudes of writing that Melannie Svoboda presents in "The Eight Beatitudes of Writing." In your summary, rely on details from the selection and on the inferences you have made about each writing declaration. Finally, explain whether these five beatitudes relate to your writing experiences and whether you have other declarations of writing that Svoboda did not mention.

Writing from Experience

2. Melannie Svoboda discusses the many learning experiences that she had as a child and an adult that helped make her a professional

writer. Write an organized essay that describes a learning experience you had that was either beneficial or negative. This learning experience can be one you had in or out of school and need not be concerned with how you learned to write. Recall this experience carefully so that your recollections are rich in detail.

RESPONDING TO STUDENT WRITING

Use some or all of these questions to respond to your draft or to that of your classmate. Read carefully for meaning and make your comments specific.

1. Read the beginning of the draft. What does the writer say he or she plans to do? Is the beginning too long or too short?

2. Read through the middle of the essay. Are there enough details? Should other details be included?

3. Read the ending of the draft. How does it end? Are you satisfied with it? What would you like to see changed?

4. Do you find any paragraphs that seem to lose their focus? Choose one paragraph that can be improved. How would you improve its organization?

5. Edit for surface errors. Are there any obvious errors in spelling or in introducing the author or title of the selection? Edit for sentence fragments. Ask your instructor for help before you mark any sentence that you are not sure is a fragment.

CHAPTER 3

TYPES OF READING
AND WRITING

Now that you have studied ways to read and write, you are ready to learn how much of the writing that you will read and write is organized. Once you understand the ways writing is organized, your reading and writing will improve. Knowing the organization of a writing will enable you to predict what you will read next or what you need to write next.

Most of the writing and reading you will study in college centers around the following six organizational patterns or rhetorical structures. Each of these *organizational patterns* or *rhetorical structures* shapes a piece of writing in certain recognizable ways:

1. Thesis support
2. Cause and effect
3. Comparison and contrast
4. Sequence of events
5. Description and narration
6. Definition and classification

The basic features of the first three of these structures are discussed next, and in Chapter 4, you will be introduced to the last three.

THESIS SUPPORT

As a college writer, you will rely on the thesis-support pattern most often. In this pattern, the writer moves from general to specific statements, topics on essay structure that you learned in Chapter 2. In the thesis-support pattern, the argument of the writing, sometimes called the *thesis,* comes at the beginning. It is a general statement that presents a point for the reader to consider. The details that the writer uses either explain this point more fully or attempt to persuade the reader of the truth of the thesis. These details, or support, are specific statements: names, places, or things. These details are known as *examples*. When the example is carefully detailed, then it is known as an *illustration*. Both examples and illustrations are types of evidence.

Look at how the following description of a successful reader supports the thesis of the paragraph that a successful reader does not follow rigid rules:

> A successful reader is one who is open to what the reading has to say. She makes predictions about what will come next in the reading and can change these predictions as she reads. Further, the successful reader is flexible. She applies different reading ways to different readings. Most important, the successful reader sees reading as a discovery, not as a painful chore.

Do you see how this paragraph gives several examples for the various ways a successful reader reads? Do you also see that each example supports the thesis of the first sentence, that a successful reader is open? Did you also note that signal words, or *transitions*, alert you to these examples? These transitions are "further" and "most important."

You will use this thesis-support pattern often when writing essay responses in English and in many other college courses. In many of your essays, you will be required to develop a thesis supported by details. In many of your reading assignments, you will be asked to locate and paraphrase the thesis and show the support that the writer uses to explain this thesis.

Other words that are used to name a thesis are *argument, main idea,* or *point.* You may use these words in your writing as accurate synonyms for thesis, or you may recognize these synonyms in your reading.

Here is a list of other transitions that you can use to introduce support for your thesis:

for example	one example is
for instance	proof is found
specifically	the idea is supported by
in particular	

As well as being tools for your writing, these transitions can be relied on when you are looking for statements supporting a thesis in your reading. Study the following two sentences:

> To read successfully is to expect change and to be flexible. *For example,* reading specialists say that effective readers move comfortably from one organizational pattern to another as they read.

"For example" is a transition signaling a detail of support. Note that it is set off with a comma.

The support that you use to explain your thesis may not just be an example or an illustration. It may also come from some of the other organizational patterns that you will study in this chapter and the next: a cause, an effect, a part of a sequence, or a descriptive statement.

You may now want to read the first paragraph of Selection 3 on page 41. Can you summarize the thesis of this paragraph?

CAUSE AND EFFECT

Cause and effect is another powerful organizational pattern. Like the support for the thesis, causes are closely related to effects. The *cause* is defined as the source or the reason for change. For example, some reading researchers say that being read to as a child is one cause for being a lifelong reader. The *effect* is defined as the result or change. In the preceding example, lifelong reading can be seen as an effect of being read to as a child.

A cause or an effect may become the thesis of a piece of writing. For example, one could begin a study with the argument that being read to as a child is a cause for lifelong reading.

Also, causes and effects may serve as details that support an argument. Consider, for example, how this effect statement can serve as a detail to support the argument about being read to and lifelong reading:

The study showed that those subjects read to as children read at least one newspaper a day as adults.

Regular newspaper reading becomes an effect of being read to as a child.

The two kinds of causes are direct and contributory. *Direct causes* suggest necessary and single relationships. *Contributory causes* suggest multiple and probable relationships. You often come across direct causes in mathematics, chemistry, biology, and physics. For example, in chemistry, a loss of heat is a direct cause of cooling. It is always the case that less heat leads to cooler temperatures. In mathematics, multiplying a number by zero is always a cause for the product to be zero. Cause and effect can easily be separated in these two instances.

In studies like education, psychology, sociology, and anthropology, you will come across contributory causes. The earlier example about being read to and lifelong reading comes from an education study. Being read to as a child may be a contributory cause to reading a newspaper every day. Because a reader has so many experiences before becoming an adult, identifying one single cause for a particular behavior is impossible, whereas isolating the zero in the mathematics example is possible. This same lifelong reader may have come from a home where lots of books and magazines were available to read, or his work of several years may demand that he read the newspaper every day, even though he had not read the newspaper regularly before. These two factors may also have contributed to this individual being a lifelong reader. The cause-and-effect relationships that one studies in education necessarily involve contributory, or probable, causes.

Synonyms for cause include the following:

reason   agent

factor   source

Synonyms for effect include the following:

result   consequence

As you study cause-and-effect relationships, be alert for *terms of qualification,* or words and phrases that make a cause-effect relation contributory, or probable. The most common terms of qualification are the following:

it appears	it seems	apparently
one can assume	perhaps	probably
likely	one can safely say	one can say with reservation
may	might	possibly
perhaps		there seems to be a relationship

In courses dealing with human behavior, be alert for these terms of qualification. Be skeptical of those studies and statements that do not use these terms. You would be correct to question the following conclusion in an educational study:

The cause of poor readers is not being read to as a child.

You could justifiably ask if not being read to as a child is the only cause, or merely a probable cause. This statement could be rephrased in the following way:

Not being read to as a child is one probable cause for a child's reading difficulties in school.

You also should use these terms of qualification when you write about human behavior.

Study the following cause-and-effect paragraph on free reading and reading success in which terms of qualification are carefully used:

> Free reading *may* help a child to become a successful reader. *It is likely that* a young reader learns vocabulary and sentence structure from the interesting reading that she has chosen. Reading is *often* seen as a series of skills that a young reader must learn. *It seems* as if these reading skills can be mastered when a young reader is pleasure reading.

The terms of qualification "may," "it is likely that," "often," and "it seems" suggest that this argument is probable and is supported by contributory causes.

You may now want to read paragraph 11 of Selection 3 on pages 43–44. See if you can determine the contributory causes for the changes in behavior of young people today.

COMPARISON AND CONTRAST

The pattern of comparison and contrast is found in several disciplines. In the *comparison-and-contrast* structure, you read or write about two or more topics that are either similar or different. You could be contrasting two characters in a short story or comparing five reading theories in your writing. When you compare, you attempt to find similarities; when you contrast, you attempt to show differences.

The pattern of comparison and contrast is an important rhetorical structure for you to learn and use, especially as a writing tool. You will often be asked in college to compare and contrast ideas from several works, determining which are similar or different, better or worse. At first this pattern may seem difficult because you will be considering more than one topic at a time.

The following are some common transitions used in the comparison-and-contrast organizational pattern. If used at the beginning of a sentence, many of these transitions are set off with commas.

Contrast

but	on the other hand	although	opposed
however	on the one hand	while	opposing
yet	contrary	different from	conversely
nevertheless	on the contrary	differently	whereas
at variance	in contrast	oppositely	
otherwise	rather	opposite	

Comparison

and	similarly	resembling	exactly like
also	as if	parallel to	analogous to
like	as	much the same as	analogously
similar	just as	comparable	

Study the following two paragraphs on the differences between the old-fashioned system of teaching reading and the modern, technological method. In these paragraphs, you will see how the compare-and-contrast pattern works. In this case, the argument for the traditional method is presented in the first paragraph; then the argument for the modern method is presented second:

> Traditional ways of teaching reading have proven successful to get children to read. Children must be read to, and they must have many types of reading around them. When young, they must have adults willing to read to them. When they are older and able to read, they must have lots of printed material available to them—magazines, comic books, paperbacks, and encyclopedias. Furthermore, they must be introduced to their library early and regularly check books and magazines out. *In contrast to* reading on the computer, traditional methods give readers a lifelong love for the printed word.
>
> *Contrary to* those who say that children learn to read by merely reading books, the proponents of the computer method of reading say that children are much more comfortable with the computer than they are with books. Computer reading teachers realize that children today would rather turn on the computer or play a computer game than open a book. Advocates of computer teaching of reading say that children will learn to read if they see reading as a kind of computer game.

Note the two transitions of contrast used in these paragraphs: "in contrast" and "contrary."

There are two ways to organize comparison and contrast information. This first way compares topics *subject to subject,* as in the previous two paragraphs. Traditional reading methods are discussed; then the computer reading method is addressed. Their differences emerge from this subject-to-subject organization. The second way to organize compare-and-contrast material is to discuss the similarities and differences *point by point.* In the preceding example, a point-by-point comparison and contrast would individually compare traditional and computer teaching methods to the topics that they share: what children read, who reads to them, and where they find reading material. This point-by-point essay would be divided into three separate parts— traditional and computer teaching in regard to (1) what students read (books or computer screens), (2) who reads to them (people or computers), and (3) where they read (library or on the computer screen).

In the next chapter, you will be introduced to three additional organizational patterns: sequence of events, narration and description, and definition and classification. These three patterns complete the six major rhetorical structures you will rely on in much of your college reading and writing.

You may want to quickly read paragraph 12 of Selection 3 on page 44. What transition of contrast is used? Can you determine what this transition of contrast is comparing?

Summary

1. Organizational patterns are structures in reading and writing that allow you to predict what you will read and shape what you write.
2. The thesis-support pattern is a common structure that presents an argument and evidence to support it. Students often are asked to follow this pattern in college, especially in their writing.
3. The cause-and-effect pattern has two parts: the first introduces the cause or reason; the second, the effect or result. The two kinds of causes are direct and contributory. Contributory causes require terms of qualification to be accurate.
4. The comparison-and-contrast pattern is used often in college writing assignments. When students compare topics, they find similarities. When they contrast, they find differences between or among topics. In the compare-and-contrast organizational pattern, two or more topics are studied to determine how they are similar and how they differ.

SELECTION 3: "FINDING MODERN WAYS TO TEACH TODAY'S YOUTH" BY SHARON CURCIO

This article concerns the ways in which today's young people learn through our new visual technology, such as computer games, CD-ROMs, and so on. Sharon Curcio contrasts the technological ways of gathering information to the traditional reading of printed material, which Curcio has found bores most of her students.

Curcio devotes much of her discussion to how imprisoned youths learn, but she contends that many of her conclusions effectively relate to young adult learners in public and private schools today.

BEFORE YOU READ

Before reading this selection, answer these questions in a free-writing journal or in class discussion:

1. Do you remember the ways you learned to read in elementary school?
2. Do you have children or relatives who are in elementary school today? How are they learning to read?

PREVIEWING

Preview the following selection. Read the first and last paragraph. Then read a few sentences, words, and phrases in the middle paragraphs. Before you begin critically reading, write what you believe is the thesis of Curcio's article.

Thesis of the article:

_____

_____

_____

_____

_____

READING CRITICALLY

Now critically read the selection and complete the following outline as you read or after you finish. You may want to make this outline into a visual cluster of the important information.

Sharon Curcio

Finding Modern Ways to Teach Today's Youth

1 Education shouldn't have to compete with the entertainment industry. But whether we like it or not, the entertainment industry is setting the standard for what today's youth find important and will pay attention to. It effectively reaches teens and sells billions of dollars worth of goods and culture to them. "Edutainment" has made education's traditional print-oriented teaching methods **woefully obsolete.**

Recent Findings

2   A U.S. Department of Education study, "Young Adult Literacy and Schooling," revealed that less than 4 percent of non-high school graduates had the literacy level needed to comprehend a bus schedule. Given that 40 percent of those currently in the federal and state correctional system did not finish high school, it is no wonder that teens and adults leave the criminal justice system without improved life skills or literacy. They go from a structured world where not much but compliance is expected to them into the "real" world where there's competition for jobs and where self-reliant and responsible behavior is expected. Lacking preparedness, released inmates fail at real world necessities like finding and keeping a job. So these young adults quickly end up back in the juvenile justice or criminal justice system. The problem is not so much that people or institutions are failing; it's that we have failed to update the learning tools young adults need.

3   In a recent survey of 157 prison wardens, 93 percent indicated that illiteracy was a problem for many youths in detention. As a former educator, I have talked to a lot of high school students and **adjudicated** youths about what they thought of reading. This generated some interesting comments. Overwhelmingly, though, I heard students say they thought reading was slow and boring. From those who could read well to those who struggled with reading, there were complaints about the difficulty of the English vocabulary ("too many strange, big words") and the tedium of learning new vocabulary words. Trying to read through an article with too many new words is frustrating—the student eventually just gives up.

4   Non-native English speakers have an even harder time. Spanish-speaking students said that spelling in English is insane. They complained that English rules are not easy to grasp, and most said they had to memorize spelling to pass quizzes. For many of them memorization wasn't an interesting task, so they simply refused to put in the time to do it.

5   All the students, from the better readers to the struggling, preferred to get information from television. They perceived reading as "slow, painful and torturous," while TV was described as fast and exciting, with changing visuals and colors that kept them awake. I couldn't agree with them more. The unchanging landscapes of black and white print in a book can be pretty boring unless the reader reads fast and comprehends well. It took half of forever for many of my students to read one page, word by painful word. Compare this to watching TV. The television watcher stands to comprehend 123 words in 30 seconds. The words are supported by TV's visuals, which serve to drive a point home. But for a struggling reader, it can take five or 10 minutes to get through a 50-word paragraph.

6   The complaint that "reading is slow" is not surprising among a population constantly timed in to the fast-moving, split-second images of its

generation's visual media. For teaching methods to effectively impart any kind of literacy, or to bring the **preliterate** and today's visually literate kids to print literacy, teaching methods are going to have to get competitive and visual.

7   Literacy is a funny concept. In our culture it has to do with the ability to read and write. One can learn a language with a good ear and become **articulate,** but remain illiterate (unable to read and write) in that language. I've noticed that a lot of the marginal or nonreaders understand questions delivered to them verbally in English but cannot respond to the same question written on a piece of paper.

8   The fascinating part about teaching the TV and Nintendo generation is witnessing students learning visually. If a bus schedule were read aloud in an animated 60-second TV commercial, you would probably have a roomful of illiterate students correctly reading the bus schedule a few minutes later. I am convinced, after teaching preliterate students, that modern kids don't learn by taking little logic bits and then stringing or weaving these bits into a picture. They're graphic. They use whole pictures and spoken language to convey a technique or an idea. They have to see a picture first; then a teacher can tear apart the picture into components and test students on their ability to rebuild the picture.

Technology and Literacy

9   Knowing that young adults respond to visuals more than print and tend to have short attention spans (sometimes only seconds), it would seem that technology would have some useful solutions for institutions trying to impart either life skills or literacy to teen and adult inmates. For example, multimedia curricula are TV-like and visual and provide hours of playing time on CD-ROM. These media are hardy and easy to secure, and workstations are becoming less expensive. Users can replay a lesson or segment as many times as needed to grasp an idea, acquire a skill or pass a test. In some ways, computers are endlessly patient, and programming allows a lesson to be given over and reexplained in a variety of ways so the student will be able to grasp one of several explanatory approaches.

10   Turn-key systems can be developed that require little staff time and are as easy to use as checking out a library book. Although I haven't yet seen private industry develop such learning systems for prisons, prison wardens could use their considerable **clout** and bring innovative learning systems to prisons.

11   A lot of people think today's kids are different from those of previous generations, especially kids in the juvenile justice system. But the difference we see is not in the kids themselves; it comes from the change in our culture. Our culture has undergone an enormous and shocking change in the past five decades. Family bonds, religious beliefs and cultural values have eroded while economic instability and the pervasive

influence of the media–from radio and TV to computers and those **ubiq-uitous** Nintendos–have given us teens who learn in ways we barely understand.

12   There is still controversy about how to reach and teach young adults in the criminal justice system, especially how to impart literacy and life skills to non-native speakers, disadvantaged learners and those with learning disabilities. But the visual effects and tempo seen in music videos combined with the learning systems that are possible with state-of-the-art, computerized multimedia curricula certainly can further education for today's youth.

SOURCE: *Corrections Today* 57, no. 2 (April 1995), p. 28.

OUTLINING/CLUSTERING

  I. Thesis of the Curcio article

_____

 II. Interesting facts on prisoners and literacy

     A. _____

     B. _____

III. Young people's general attitude toward reading

     A. _____

     B. _____

IV. Cultural and economic changes today's young adults face

     A. _____

     B. _____

     C. _____

 V. Curcio's solution to helping today's literacy problem among young adults

_____

woefully obsolete: sadly out of date; **adjudicated:** a case heard and decided on; **preliterate:** having no knowledge of reading and writing; **articulate:** expressing oneself clearly; **clout:** influence; **ubiquitous:** present everywhere

A SECOND READING

Reread the Curcio selection and answer the following questions as you read. Before answering these questions, you may want to write in your reading journal about any questions or comments you have about the selection.

1. Reread paragraph 2. In a sentence, summarize the argument that Curcio is presenting here.
2. Reread paragraph 5. Identify the organizational pattern that structures this paragraph.
3. Paraphrase the following sentence in paragraph 6: "For teaching methods to effectively impart any kind of literacy, or to bring the preliterate and today's visually literate kids to print literacy, teaching methods are going to have to get competitive and visual."
4. Reread paragraph 8. Describe the importance of the picture in teaching the "TV and Nintendo generation."
5. Reread paragraph 9. List several of the most important features of the computer that make it helpful to learning.

READING/WRITING FEATURE: FACTS AND FIGURES

In Selection 1, you were introduced to the importance of using accurate and clear evidence. In this Curcio article, you are presented with some evidence on the reading and learning problems of today's youth. This evidence comes in the form of facts and figures, in large part, from a U.S. Department of Education study.

You will be using evidence from studies in many of your college courses. Your ongoing task is to determine if the facts and figures from such studies are to be trusted, or *reputable*. Questions that can help you determine whether the evidence from such studies is reputable are as follows:

1. Is the evidence believable?

   Usually studies that come from universities or research institutions are to be trusted. Often the results of these studies are printed in respected publications like the *Chronicle of Higher Education* or *Journal of the American Medical Association*. These publications add further believability to the study because you assume that the editors of these publications have carefully examined the study's results. In this selection, we learn that some of the statistics that Curcio quotes come from a federal education study titled "Young Adult Literacy and Schooling." This background information suggests that Curcio's evidence comes from a generally respected source–the U.S. Department of Education.

2. Is the evidence accurate?

The only way that you can be sure that the results of a study are accurate is to have another respected group do the same study and come upon similar results. As you continue to study in college, you will learn about the correct ways to do research in particular fields. See if these accepted procedures are being used in the study you are citing.

3. Is the evidence from a large sample?

Usually a study of a large group is more accurate than a study relying on a small group. So you can be more comfortable with results of educational studies using hundreds or thousands of students rather than just a few students.

Now reread the beginning of paragraph 3, which begins this way:

In a recent survey of 157 prison wardens, 93 percent indicated that illiteracy was a problem for many youths in detention. . . .

Studying 157 prison wardens seems to be a fairly large sample, and the percentage–93–is an impressive response, suggesting that literacy is a major concern in prisons that incarcerate youth. Yet, to be even more certain about the reliability of these figures, you would need to know how many prison wardens there are in the entire country and if the wardens in the study were interviewed from several areas of the United States.

When you read about facts and figures, or when you use facts and figures in your writing, be sure to keep these three factors in mind: Is the evidence believable, accurate, and extensive?

BEFORE YOU WRITE

Before selecting a writing topic, you may want to study sentence fragments with adverbial clauses and complete Practice A3 (pages 208–209) and study ways to write clear introductions and complete Practice B3 (pages 256–257) of the handbook.

WRITING TOPICS

Choose a writing topic from the following questions. Be sure to follow the suggestions for completing your essay on the inside front cover.

Writing about the Reading

1. "Finding Modern Ways to Teach Today's Youth" presents an interesting argument about technology and learning. Summarize Sharon

Curcio's argument. Then present the most important evidence that she uses to support this argument. Finally, do you agree? You may want to describe the ways that you learn as evidence for or against her argument.

Writing from Experience

2. This article discusses reading methods in high schools. In an essay, describe your high school experiences. What stands out in your mind as the three or four most memorable learning events? Be detailed about these experiences and about why they are memorable to you as a learner.

3. If you cannot remember your high school years well, describe how a child you know—son or daughter, brother, sister, or young friend—is learning how to read. Be as detailed as you can and see if the way this child is learning to read is traditional, is using technology to assist the child's reading development, or is using both traditional techniques and technology.

RESPONDING TO STUDENT WRITING

Use some or all of these questions to respond to your draft or to that of your classmate. Read carefully for meaning and make your comments specific.

1. Read the beginning of the draft. What does the writer say he or she plans to do? Is the beginning too long or too short? Are any parts of the introduction unclear to you?

2. In the middle or body of the draft, which paragraph seems most organized to you? Say why.

3. In the middle or body of the draft, which paragraph seems the least organized? How could you revise this paragraph to improve its organization?

4. What pattern or patterns of organization does this draft seem to rely on? Does it effectively use transitions? Where can additional transitions be used effectively?

5. Edit for obvious errors, such as spelling, referring to the title of the article or referring to the author of the article. See if you can find sentence fragments. Correct them if you can. Ask your instructor for help before you mark any sentence that you are not sure is in error.

CHAPTER 4

MORE TYPES OF READING AND WRITING

In Chapter 3, you learned about the first three organizational patterns: (1) thesis support, (2) cause and effect, and (3) comparison and contrast. In this chapter, you learn about ways to read and write with the next three rhetorical structures:

4. Sequence of events

5. Description and narration

6. Definition and classification

In learning about these three patterns and applying them to your work in college, you will be able to read more efficiently and write with a clearer focus.

SEQUENCE OF EVENTS

Sequence of events is perhaps the most natural organizational pattern for students to follow. All people seem to easily understand how events are laid out in time. In the *sequence-of-events* pattern, also sometimes called the *process* pattern, events are set up chronologically or consecutively. You will come across this pattern in several college courses, such as in a history class where you list the events that lead to an important moment in history, in a beginning chemistry course where you learn the steps to follow in performing a laboratory experiment, or in a computer science class where you are told the steps to apply in making a computer program work. In the chemistry and computer science courses, you are following steps in a process rather than events in history.

You can rely on the sequence-of-events pattern to form an argument in your writing. For example, in a report on the scientific method in your chemistry class, your argument could be as follows:

There are five necessary steps to follow in using the scientific method.

Each of the five steps can be used as evidence for this argument. For example, as evidence for your fourth step, you could say:

The fourth step explores the hypothesis that explains the data.

Although listing examples in a particular order is not essential, the steps in a process or those leading to a historical event must be discussed in a specific order. For example, you would be incorrect to place Step 2 of the scientific method, collecting data, before Step 1: asking the right question.

In reading and writing material requiring steps, you must keep the correct sequence in mind. Transitions that are helpful in keeping these steps in order include the following:

first	second	third (and so on)
last	now	next
later	then	before
soon	finally	at the end

When writing a sentence that begins with one of these transitions, you may want to set it off with a comma, as in this sentence: "At the end, you come to your conclusion."

Look at how the following paragraph on the scientific method is structured:

There are five basic steps to follow when you use the scientific method. *First,* a scientist must be a systematic observer. *Then,* from these observations, she needs to explain precisely the problem she sees. *Third,* she sets up a hypothesis. *Then,* she collects and organizes all of the results. *Finally,* she generalizes from these results to determine if they support her hypothesis.

See how the transition words (first, then, third, finally) introduce each step. Note how each step is logically linked to the others.

DESCRIPTION AND NARRATION

In some ways, description and narration are similar to the organizational pattern of sequence of events. *Narration* is a pattern that retells a series of events that are either real or imagined. Fiction and nonfiction fall under this pattern–a story is told from beginning to end. Like sequence of events, the story follows a series of steps, usually from its start to its conclusion. Selection 4 follows the narrative pattern in that Malcolm X takes his reader through the steps he took to learn how to read in prison. This piece organizes the narration *chronologically,* or in a time sequence.

Closely attached to most narrations is the organizational pattern of *description*–the pattern that attempts to record an experience in words. It does not teach or persuade; rather, description recreates a particular moment in time. Like narration, description is found in fiction and nonfiction–in a novel and in a history book. Unlike narration, description does not move the reader from past to present but generally attempts to capture a particular moment. The patterns of narration and description often work together in works of fiction and nonfiction. A character is described, and then the writer relates what he or she does during a period of time.

Unlike the previous organizational patterns, description does not need a general statement supported by specifics. Rather, description often focuses on details, and the main idea is inferred. (You studied ways to make inferences in Selection 2 on Melannie Svoboda's writing development.)

What main idea can you infer from the following descriptive details of a college professor?

> Professor Thomas often preferred to sit rather than stand when he lectured. He spoke hesitantly but quickly and rarely looked his students in the eye. As he spoke, he would unconsciously take his glasses on and off. But when he read something that excited him–a piece of literature like a poem or short story–he changed. Then he would speak powerfully and confidently.

Nowhere in this description does the writer say that Professor Thomas is shy and uncomfortable around his students. Yet a careful reader infers these characteristics from the details. He sits instead of stands, fiddles with his glasses, and talks quickly. A thoughtful reader of this description also infers that Professor Thomas loves literature because he becomes more commanding when he reads an excerpt from literature to the class.

Do you also see in this description that dividing up information into general and specific is not helpful? What you read here is a series of thoughtfully considered details about Professor Thomas. A writer of description re-creates a moment in time with carefully worded details. She leaves the general comments about these details up to her reader.

In college literature courses, you will come upon the patterns or narration and description in what you read and in what you are asked to write. If you take a course in creative writing, you will even be asked to write descriptions and narrations. In some writing assignments in composition courses, you will be asked to describe and narrate particular moments in your life.

Read paragraph 8 in Selection 4 on page 54. Does it seem more descriptive or narrative?

DEFINITION AND CLASSIFICATION

You will come upon definitions in almost every course that you take in college. Definitions are the building blocks for any study. The organizational pattern of *definition* attempts to accurately explain a word usually by dividing it into two parts: a larger category and a more specific one.

Look at how "oral reading" is defined in the following statement:

> Oral reading is the act of repeating aloud the words of printed or written matter.

Note in this definition of oral reading that the general category is the "repeating aloud" and the specific materials of this activity are "printed or written matter."

You will often read material that uses several definitions and organizes them in a particular way. This type of organizational pattern is known as *classification*. As you study material organized under this pattern, you will find that you must know the definitions of each term well and know how these terms relate to each other. These relationships are known as *categories*. The following paragraph explains how narratives are classified into two types:

> A narrative is a story that is either recited aloud or written down. A narrative that recounts the actual events that occurred at a particular time and place is known as nonfiction writing. Histories and autobiographies are considered nonfiction. If a narrative does not rely on an actual set of events, then it is known as fiction. Novels and short stories are the most often cited examples of fictional writing.

Note how the term *narrative* is the more general definition under which nonfiction and fiction are classified and under which histories, autobiographies, novels, and short stories are classified even further.

Before you read or write about any material using the classification organizational pattern, you must know the definitions of your terms well so that you can accurately divide the words along the lines of what is similar and what is different among them. Furthermore, you need to be careful in choosing the right category under which the terms you are comparing can all fall.

You will find that classifications are most often used in the sciences like biology, chemistry, and physics, for which exact relationships among words are necessary.

Writing acceptable definitions and classifications is difficult because you must select the exact words and establish careful, logical relationships. Similarly, reading material of definition and classification is taxing because you must reread this material to see how terms fit into particular categories.

As you use all six organizational patterns, you will often notice overlap among these organizational patterns. For example, you may begin to write a piece that follows the thesis-support pattern but presents evidence through steps and effects. Similarly, in cause-and-effect writing, you may want to compare and contrast your effects.

Be flexible with the ways in which you use these six organizational patterns. Let them help you understand what you read and help organize what you write. Do not expect to write an essay or read a selection that conforms perfectly to just one organizational pattern.

Summary

1. The sequence-of-events pattern is used in writing that presents events in chronological order or steps in a process. Much history and science material relies on this pattern.

2. The organizational pattern of narration accurately recounts the events in a fictional or nonfictional story.

3. The organizational pattern of description re-creates a moment in time through careful word choice.

4. Most works of fiction and nonfiction rely on both the organizational patterns of narration and description.

5. The organizational pattern of definition accurately explains a word by dividing it into its general and specific parts.

6. The organizational pattern of classification organizes several definitions in a particular way.

7. In your reading and writing, you will find a great deal of overlap among these six organizational patterns. Use these patterns to help you read and write more efficiently.

SELECTION 4: "SAVED" BY MALCOLM X AND ALEX HALEY

This excerpt describes how Malcolm X learned to read while he was in prison. Malcolm X was an African-American political leader in the sixties who embraced the Black Muslim faith. He was assassinated in 1964.

In this true story, Malcolm X talks about how his years in prison gave him the chance to teach himself to read. In this selection, Malcolm X shows how powerful a learning tool reading became for him.

BEFORE YOU READ

Before reading this selection, answer these questions in a free-writing journal or in class discussion:

1. Do you remember how you learned to read?
2. Do you believe that reading is one of the most important ways to learn?

PREVIEWING

Preview the following selection. Read the first and last paragraph. Then read a few sentences, words, and phrases in the middle paragraphs. Before you begin critically reading, write a few sentences on what Malcolm X read in prison.

Malcolm X's prison reading:

_____

_____

_____

_____

_____

READING CRITICALLY

Now critically read the selection, and complete the following outline as you read or after you finish. You may want to make this outline into a visual cluster of the important information.

Malcolm X and Alex Haley

Saved

1   Many who today hear me somewhere in person, or on television, or those who read something I've said, will think I went to school far beyond the eighth grade. This impression is due entirely to my prison studies.

2   It had really begun back in the Charlestown Prison, when Bimbi first made me feel envy of his stock of knowledge. Bimbi had always taken charge of any conversation he was in, and I had tried to **emulate** him. But every book I picked up had few sentences which didn't contain anywhere from one to nearly all of the words that might as well have been in Chinese. When I just skipped those words, of course, I really ended up with little idea of what the book said. So I had come to the Norfolk Prison

Colony still going through only book-reading motions. Pretty soon, I would have quit even these motions, unless I had received the motivation that I did.

3   I saw that the best thing I could do was get hold of a dictionary–to study, to learn some words. I was lucky enough to reason also that I should try to improve my penmanship. It was sad. I couldn't even write in a straight line. It was both ideas together that moved me to request a dictionary along with some tablets and pencils from the Norfolk Prison Colony school.

4   I spent two days just **riffling** uncertainly through the dictionary's pages. I'd never realized so many words existed! I didn't know *which* words I needed to learn. Finally, just to start some kind of action, I began copying.

5   In my slow, painstaking, ragged handwriting, I copied into my tablet everything printed on that first page, down to the punctuation marks.

6   I believe it took me a day. Then, aloud, I read back, to myself, everything I'd written on the tablet. Over and over, aloud, to myself, I read my own handwriting.

7   I woke up the next morning, thinking about those words–immensely proud to realize that not only had I written so much at one time, but I'd written words that I never knew were in the world. Moreover, with a little effort, I also could remember what many of these words meant. I reviewed the words whose meanings I didn't remember. Funny thing, from the dictionary first page right now, that "aardvark" springs to my mind. The dictionary had a picture of it, a long-tailed, long-eared, burrowing African mammal, which lives off termites caught by sticking out its tongue as an anteater does for ants.

8   I was so fascinated that I went on–I copied the dictionary's next page. And the same experience came when I studied that. With every succeeding page, I also learned of people and places and events from history. Actually the dictionary is like a miniature encyclopedia. Finally the dictionary's A section had filled a whole tablet–and I went on into the B's. That was the way I started copying what eventually became the entire dictionary. It went a lot faster after so much practice helped me to pick up handwriting speed. Between what I wrote in my tablet, and writing letters, during the rest of my time in prison I would guess I wrote a million words.

9   I suppose it was inevitable that as my word-base broadened, I could for the first time pick up a book and read and now begin to understand what the book was saying. Anyone who has read a great deal can imagine the new world that opened. Let me tell you something: from then until I left that prison, in every free moment I had, if I was not reading in the library, I was reading on my bunk. You couldn't have gotten me out of books with a wedge. Between Mr. Muhammad's teachings, my correspondence, my visitors–usually Ella and Reginald–and my reading of books, months passed without my even thinking about being imprisoned. In fact, up to then, I never had been so truly free in my life.

10   The Norfolk Prison Colony's library was in the school building. A variety of classes was taught there by instructors who came from such paces as Harvard and Boston universities. The weekly debates between inmate teams were also held in the school building. You would be astonished to know how worked up convict debaters and audiences would get over subjects like "Should Babies Be Fed Milk?"

11   Available on the prison library's shelves were books on just about every general subject. Much of the big private collection that Parkhurst had willed to the prison was still in crates and boxes in the back of the library—thousands of old books. Some of them looked ancient: covers faded, old-time parchment-looking binding. Parkhurst, I've mentioned, seemed to have been principally interested in history and religion. He had the money and the special interest to have a lot of books that you wouldn't have in general circulation. Any college library would have been lucky to get that collection.

12   As you can imagine, especially in a prison where there was heavy emphasis on **rehabilitation,** an inmate was smiled upon if he demonstrated an unusually intense interest in books. There was a sizable number of well-read inmates, especially the popular debaters. Some were said by many to be practically walking encyclopedias. They were almost celebrities. No university would ask any student to devour literature as I did when this new world opened to me, of being able to read and *understand.*

13   I read more in my room than in the library itself. An inmate who was known to read a lot could check out more than the permitted maximum number of books. I preferred reading in the total isolation of my own room.

14   When I had progressed to really serious reading, every night at about ten P.M. I would be outraged with the "lights out." It always seemed to catch me right in the middle of something engrossing.

15   Fortunately, right outside my door was a corridor light that cast a glow into my room. The glow was enough to read by, once my eyes adjusted to it. So when "lights out" came, I would sit on the floor where I could continue reading in that glow.

16   At one-hour intervals the night guards paced past every room. Each time I heard the approaching footsteps, I jumped into bed and feigned sleep. And as soon as the guard passed, I got back out of bed onto the floor area of that light-glow, where I would read for another fifty-eight minutes—until the guard approached again. That went on until three or four every morning. Three or four hours of sleep a night was enough for me. Often in the years in the streets I had slept less than that.

17   The teachings of Mr. Muhammad stressed how history had been "whitened"—when white men had written history books, the black man simply had been left out. Mr. Muhammad couldn't have said anything that would have struck me much harder. I had never forgotten how when my class, me and all of those whites, had studied seventh-grade United States history back in Mason, the history of the Negro had been covered

in one paragraph, and the teacher had gotten a big laugh with his joke, "Negroes' feet are so big that when they walk, they leave a hole in the ground."

18   This is one reason why Mr. Muhammad's teachings spread so swiftly all over the United States, among *all* Negroes, whether or not they became followers of Mr. Muhammad. The teachings ring true–to every Negro. You can hardly show me a black adult in America–or a white one, for that matter–who knows from the history books anything like the truth about the black man's role. In my own case, once I heard of the "glorious history of the black man," I took special pains to hunt in the library for books that would inform me on details about black history.

19   I can remember accurately the very first set of books that really impressed me. I have since bought that set of books and have it at home for my children to read as they grow up. It's called *Wonders of the World*. It's full of pictures of archeological finds, statues that depict, usually, non-European people.

20   I found books like Will Durant's *Story of Civilization.* I read H. G. Wells' *Outline of History. Souls of Black Folk* by W. E. B. Du Bois gave me a glimpse into the black people's history before they came to this country. Carter G. Woodson's *Negro History* opened my eyes about black empires before the black slave was brought to the United States, and the early Negro struggles for freedom.

21   J. A. Rogers' three volumes of *Sex and Race* told about race-mixing before Christ's time; about Aesop being a black man who told fables; about Egypt's Pharaohs; about the great **Coptic** Christian Empires; about Ethiopia, the earth's oldest continuous black civilization, as China is the oldest continuous civilization.

22   Mr. Muhammad's teaching about how the white man had been created led me to *Findings in Genetics* by Gregor Mendel. (The dictionary's G section was where I had learned what "genetics" meant.) I really studied this book by the Austrian monk. Reading it over and over, especially certain sections, helped me to understand that if you started with a black man, a white man could be produced; but starting with a white man, you never could produce a black man–because the white chromosome is recessive. And since no one disputes that there was but one Original Man, the conclusion is clear.

23   During the last year or so, in the *New York Times,* Arnold Toynbee used the word "bleached" in describing the white man. (His words were: "White (i.e. bleached) human beings of North European origin. . . .") Toynbee also referred to the European geographic area as only a peninsula of Asia. He said there is no such thing as Europe. And if you look at the glove, you will see for yourself that America is only an extension of Asia. (But at the same time Toynbee is among those who have helped to bleach history. He has written that Africa was the only continent that

produced no history. He won't write that again. Every day now, the truth is coming to light.)

24   I never will forget how shocked I was when I began reading about slavery's total horror. It made such an impact upon me that it later became one of my favorite subjects when I became a minister of Mr. Muhammad's. The world's most monstrous crime, the sin and the blood on the white man's hands, are almost impossible to believe. Books like the one by Frederick Olmstead opened my eyes to the horrors suffered when the slave was landed in the United States. The European woman, Fannie Kimball, who had married a Southern white slaveowner, described how human beings were degraded. Of course I read *Uncle Tom's Cabin*. In fact, I believe that's the only novel I have ever read since I started serious reading.

25   Parkhurst's collection also contained some bound pamphlets of the **Abolitionist** Anti-Slavery Society of New England. I read descriptions of **atrocities,** saw those illustrations of black slave women tied up and flogged with whips; of black mothers watching their babies being dragged off, never to be seen by their mothers again; of dogs after slaves, and of the fugitive slave catchers, evil white men with whips and clubs and chains and guns. I read about the slave preacher Nat Turner, who put the fear of God into the white slavemaster. Nat Turner wasn't going around preaching pie-in-the-sky and "non-violent" freedom for the black man. There in Virginia one night in 1831, Nat and seven other slaves started out at his master's home and through the night they went from one plantation "big house" to the next, killing, until by the next morning 57 white people were dead and Nat had about 70 slaves following him. White people, terrified for their lives, fled from their homes, locked themselves up in public buildings, hid in the woods, and some even left the state. A small army of soldiers took two months to catch and hang Nat Turner. Somewhere I have read where Nat Turner's example is said to have inspired John Brown to invade Virginia and attack Harpers Ferry nearly thirty years later, with thirteen white men and five Negroes.

26   I read Herodotus, "the father of History," or, rather, I read about him. And I read the histories of various nations, which opened my eyes gradually, then wider and wider, to how the whole world's white men had indeed acted like devils, pillaging and raping and bleeding and draining the whole world's non-white people. I remember, for instance, books such as Will Durant's story of Oriental civilization, and Mahatma Gandhi's accounts of the struggle to drive the British out of India.

27   Book after book showed me how the white man had brought upon the world's black, brown, red, and yellow peoples every variety of the sufferings of exploitation. I saw how since the sixteenth century, the so-called "Christian trader" white man began to ply the seas in his lust for Asian and African empires, and plunder, and power. I read, I saw how the white man never has gone among the non-white peoples bearing the Cross in the true manner and spirit of Christ's teachings—meek, humble, and Christ-like.

28   I perceived, as I read, how the collective white man had been actually nothing but a piratical opportunist who used **Faustian machinations** to make his own Christianity his initial wedge in criminal conquests. First, always "religiously," he branded "heathen" and "pagan" labels upon ancient non-white cultures and civilizations. The stage thus set, he then turned upon his non-white victims his weapons of war.

SOURCE: From *The Autobiography of Malcolm X*, Malcolm X and Alex Haley (New York: Ballantine Books, 1964), pp. 171–176.

OUTLINING/CLUSTERING

I. Ways Malcolm X learns to read

A. _____

B. _____

C. _____

D. _____

II. Malcolm X's reading schedule and reading style

A. _____

B. _____

III. Malcolm X's reading interests and some of the books he read

A. _____

B. _____

C. _____

D. _____

E. _____

emulate: imitate; **riffling:** leafing quickly through;
inevitable: unavoidable; **rehabilitation:** treatment to restore normal activity; **Coptic:** pertaining to the native Christian church of Egypt and Ethiopia; **abolitionist:** nineteenth century American opposed to slavery; **atrocities:** extreme cruelties; **Faustian machinations:** devilish schemes

A SECOND READING

Reread the Malcolm X selection and answer the following questions as you read. Before answering these questions, you may want to write in your reading journal about any questions or comments you have about the selection.

1. In paragraph 2, Malcolm X refers to his reading as "book reading motions." What do you think he means by this phrase?
2. Paraphrase the following sentence from paragraph 9: "I suppose it was inevitable that as my word base broadened, I could for the first time pick up a book and read and now begin to understand what the book was saying."
3. At the end of paragraph 9, Malcolm X says, "In fact, up to then, I never had been so truly free in my life." What makes Malcolm X feel this way even though he is in prison?
4. In paragraph 17, Malcolm X refers to how "history had been 'whitened'. . . ." What do you think he means?
5. Reread paragraph 22 on genetics. Summarize Malcolm X's argument here.

READING/WRITING FEATURE: CONCLUSIONS

In Chapter 2, you learned that the conclusions you will write will likely be conclusions of summary or conclusions of synthesis. When you restate what you have written, you are writing a conclusion of summary. When you come upon a new idea from the details you have examined and the argument you have put forth, you are writing a conclusion of synthesis.

In an essay discussing the important points of this Malcolm X selection, see how this writer ended with a conclusion of summary:

In this selection, Malcolm X has shown us the careful, independent ways he learned how to read in prison. Beginning with his copying words from the dictionary, Malcolm X begins reading history. It is no wonder that he focuses on African American history, studying works by W. E. B. Dubois and Harriet Beecher Stowe who wrote *Uncle Tom's Cabin*. These books and others show Malcolm X how the white man has historically mistreated people of color.

You note that these sentences accurately summarize Malcolm X's reading experiences as explained in this selection. They likely summarize what this writer has previously said in more detail in his essay.

In this essay discussing the Malcolm X selection, another writer ended with a conclusion of synthesis:

This excerpt from Malcolm X's *Autobiography* is a very powerful commentary on the necessity to be a critical reader. Malcolm X would never have been able to be such a powerful leader of his people if he had not taught himself to read and question what he read. This is an amazing story about how reading can change lives. Without reading, Malcolm X probably would have wasted away in prison.

In this essay, the writer has come upon a new idea. She has discussed the power of reading to change lives, an argument never directly stated in the selection She has synthesized what Malcolm X narrated about his reading experiences into her new insight that reading can be a life-altering experience.

Both conclusions of summary and synthesis are acceptable ways to end your essays. The conclusion of synthesis merely shows your reader that you have thought deeply about what you have read and have placed it in a framework that you and, perhaps your reader, had not likely considered before.

BEFORE YOU WRITE

Before selecting a writing topic, you may want to study run-on sentences as comma splices and complete Practice A4 (pages 210–211) and study the writing of effective topic sentences and complete Practice B4 (pages 258–259) of the handbook.

WRITING TOPICS

Choose a writing topic from the following questions. Follow the steps in the writing process in the inside front cover as you complete your drafts.

Writing about the Reading

1. Write an essay carefully describing how Malcolm X learns to read. Go through the stages of his reading development logically. Determine what it is about Malcolm X's character and intelligence that allowed him to become such a successful reader. Is Malcolm X's reading story exceptional, or is it one that others could also follow?

Writing from Experience

2. Write an essay that describes the book(s) or person(s) that had the greatest impact on your reading development. Be as detailed as you can to describe how you were introduced to this book or person and what specifically you learned that made an important difference in your life.

3. Because this is the last selection on reading and writing, you may now have many ideas about how people learn to read and write. Assume you are the director of a school (preschool, elementary school, high school, or adult school) that plans to open its doors very soon. Write an essay explaining how you would structure a learning environment so that your students could successfully learn to read and write.

RESPONDING TO STUDENT WRITING

Use some or all of these questions to respond to your draft or that of your classmate. Read carefully for meaning and make your comments specific.

1. Read the beginning of the draft. What do you think this essay will be saying? Is there anything else that you think should be included? Is there anything that you think should be taken out?

2. Study the evidence in the body of the draft. Is the evidence clear? Is it accurate? Where specifically could these paragraphs use more or better evidence?

3. Choose a paragraph from the body of the draft that you particularly like either for its details or for the argument it makes. What is so successful about this paragraph?

4. How does this draft end? Are you satisfied with it? Would you suggest adding anything or taking anything out?

5. Edit for obvious errors in spelling and punctuation. See whether you can correct any sentence fragments or comma splices. If you are unsure about how to correct a fragment or a comma splice, ask your instructor for help.

FOLLOW-UP

Now that you have read four introductory chapters and four selections on ways to read and write, answer the following questions either in a free-writing journal or in discussion.

1. What do you now think are some of the most effective ways to read and write in college?

2. Which reading selection had the greatest impact on you? Why?

PART II

Reading Selections and Writing Topics

BREAKING THE LAW: SELECTIONS 5–8

In the following four reading selections, you will consider the issue of breaking the law. Some writers see society as the cause of crime, whereas others blame the family structure, and still others cannot pinpoint one single cause. By the end of these readings, you will have enough information to formulate your own answers to this issue.

The four selections are titled:

Selection 5: "La Vida Loca (The Crazy Life): Two Generations of Gang Members" by Luis Rodriguez
Selection 6: from "Childhoods of Violence" by Robert K. Ressler and Tom Shachtman
Selection 7: "Look Back in Anger" by Thomas Powers
Selection 8: "The Columbine Tragedy: Countering the Hysteria" by Barbara Dority

As you read these selections, you will also learn about the following aspects of reading and writing:

READING/WRITING FEATURES	GRAMMAR/USAGE	WRITING CONVENTIONS
Selection 5 Voice	Run-ons	Topic Sentences
Selection 6 Coherence	Subject-Verb Agreement	Commenting on Quotes

Selection 7 Word Choice   Compound Sentences   General Evidence

Selection 8 Connotations   Adverbial Clauses   Organizing the
             of Words   Body

READING/WRITING PREP

You may want to answer the following questions in a free-writing journal or in discussion before you begin reading these four selections. Answering these questions should help you determine how much you know and don't know about breaking the law:

1. What are some ways to solve the gang problem in America?
2. Who breaks the law in America?
3. What are some of the reasons why people break the law?
4. Do you think young people are more prone to violence today than they were in the past?

SELECTION 5: "*LA VIDA LOCA* (THE CRAZY LIFE): TWO GENERATIONS OF GANG MEMBERS" BY LUIS RODRIGUEZ

Luis Rodriguez has written an autobiography about his gang life experiences in East Los Angeles titled *Always Running*. This selection is a summary in which Rodriguez describes his history as a gang member and the emerging gang life of his son Ramiro.

Three organizational patterns work together in this selection: description, narration, and cause and effect. Rodriguez describes him and his son, narrates important events in their lives, and uses this information to determine the causes of gang activity in the United States.

READING/WRITING PREP

Before reading this selection, answer the following questions in a free-writing journal or discussion:

1. Why do you think gangs currently exist in the United States?
2. What makes young people join gangs?

PREVIEWING

Preview the following selection. Read the first and last few paragraphs. Then read a few sentences, words, and phrases in the middle paragraphs. Before you read critically, write a few sentences describing Luis and Ramiro.

Description of Luis and Ramiro:

_____

_____

_____

_____

_____

READING CRITICALLY

Now critically read the selection and complete the following outline as you read or after you finish. You may want to make this outline into a visual cluster of the important information.

Luis J. Rodriguez

La Vida Loca (The Crazy Life): Two Generations of Gang Members

1   Late winter Chicago, 1991: The once-white snow that fell in December has turned into a dark scum, an **admixture** of salt, car oil and decay; icicles hang from rooftops and window sills like the whiskers of old men. The bone-chilling temperatures force my family to stay inside a one-and-a-half bedroom apartment in a three-flat building in Humboldt Park. My third wife, Trini, our child Ruben and my 15-year-old son Ramiro from a previous marriage huddle around the television set. Tensions build up like a fever.

2   One evening, words of anger bounce back and forth between the walls of our gray-stone flat. Two-year-old Ruben, confused and afraid, crawls up to my leg and hugs it. Trini and I had jumped on Ramiro's case for coming in late following weeks of trouble: Ramiro had joined the Insane Campbell Boys, a group of Puerto Rican and Mexican youth allied with the Spanish Cobras and Dragons.

3   Within moments, Ramiro runs out of the house, entering the freezing Chicago night. I go after him, sprinting down the gangway leading to a debris-strewn alley. I see Ramiro's fleeing figure, his breath rising in quickly dissipating clouds.

4   I follow him toward Division Street, the neighborhood's main drag. People yell out of windows and doorways: ***"¿Que pasa, hombre?"*** This is not an unfamiliar sight—a father or mother chasing some child down the street.

5   Watching my son's escape, it is as though he enters the waters of a distant time, back to my youth, back to when I ran, to when I jumped over fences, fleeing ***vato locos,*** the police or my own shadow, in some drug-induced hysteria.

6   As Ramiro speeds off, I see my body enter the mouth of darkness, my breath cut the frigid flesh of night—my voice crack open the night sky.

7   We are a second-generation gang family. I was involved in gangs in Los Angeles in the late 1960s and early 1970s. When I was 2 years old, in 1956, my family emigrated from Mexico to Watts. I spent my teen years in a barrio called Las Lomas, east of Los Angeles.

8   I was arrested on charges ranging from theft, assaulting an officer to attempted murder. As a teenager, I did some time. I began using drugs at age 12—including pills, weed and heroin. I had a near-death experience at 16 from sniffing toxic spray. After being kicked out of three high schools, I dropped out at 15.

9   By the time I turned 18, some 25 friends had been killed by rival gangs, the police, overdoses, car crashes and suicides.

10   Three years ago, I brought Ramiro to Chicago to escape the violence. If I barely survived all this, it appeared unlikely my son would make it. But in Chicago, we found kindred conditions.

11   I had to cut Ramiro's bloodline to the street before it became too late. I had to begin the long, intense struggle to save his life from the gathering storm of street violence—some 20 years after I had sneaked out of the 'hood in the dark of night and removed myself from the death fires of *La Vida Loca.*

12   What to do with those whom society cannot accommodate? Criminalize them. Outlaw their actions and creations. Declare them the enemy, then wage war. Emphasize the differences—the shade of skin, the accent or manner of clothes. Like the **scapegoat** of the Bible, place society's ills on them, then "stone them" in **absolution.** It's convenient, it's logical.

13   It doesn't work.

14   Gangs are not alien powers. They begin as unstructured groupings, our children who desire the same as any young person. Respect. A sense of belonging. Protection. This is no different than the YMCA, Little League or the Boy Scouts. It wasn't any more than what I wanted.

15   When I entered 109th Street School in Watts, I spoke perfect Spanish. But teachers punished me for speaking it on the playground. I peed in my pants a few times because I was unable to say in English that I had to go. One teacher banished me to a corner, to build blocks for a year. I learned to be silent within the walls of my body.

16   The older boys who lived on 103rd Street would take my money or food. They chased me through alleys and side streets. Fear compelled my actions.

17   The police, I learned years later, had a strategy: They picked up as many 7-year-old boys as they could—for loitering, throwing dirt clods, curfew—whatever. By the time a boy turned 13, and had been popped for something like stealing, he had accumulated a detention record, and was bound for "juvey."

18   One felt besieged, under intense scrutiny. If you spoke out, dared to resist, you were given a "jacket" of troublemaker; I'd tried many times to take it off, but somebody always put it back on.

19   Soon after my family moved to South San Gabriel, a local group, Thee Mystics, rampaged through the school. They carried bats, chains, pipes and homemade zip guns. They terrorized teachers and students alike. I was 12.

20   I froze as the head stomping came dangerously my way. But I was intrigued. I wanted this power. I wanted to be able to bring a whole school to its knees. All my school life until then had been poised against me. I was broken and shy. I wanted what Thee Mystics had. I wanted to hurt somebody.

21   Police sirens broke the spell. Thee Mystics scattered in all directions. But they had done their damage. They had left their mark on the school—and on me.

22   Gangs flourish when there's a lack of social recreation, decent education or employment. Today, many young people will never know what it is to work. They can only satisfy their needs through collective strength—against the police, who hold the power of life and death, against poverty, against idleness, against their impotence in society.

23   Without definitive solutions, it's easy to throw blame. George Bush and Dan Quayle, for example, say the lack of family values is behind our problems.

24   But "family" is a farce among the propertyless and **disenfranchised.** Too many families are wrenched apart, as even children are forced to supplement meager incomes. At age 9, my mother walked me to the door and, in effect, told me: Now go forth and work.

25   People can't just consume; they have to sell something, including their ability to work. If so-called legitimate work is unavailable, people will do the next best thing—sell sex or dope.

26   You'll find people who don't care about whom they hurt, but nobody I know *wants* to sell death to their children, their neighbors, friends. If there was a viable, productive alternative, they would stop.

27   At 18, I had grown tired. I felt like a war veteran with a kind of **post-traumatic syndrome.** I had seen too many dead across the pavement; I'd walk the aisles in the church wakes as if in a daze; I'd often watched my mother's weary face in hospital corridors, outside of courtrooms and cells, refusing, finally, to have anything to do with me.

28   In addition, I had fallen through the cracks of two languages; unable to communicate well in any.

29   I wanted the pain to end, the self-consuming hate to wither in the sunlight. With the help of those who saw potential in me, perhaps for some poetry, I got out: No more heroin, spray or pills; no more jails; no more trying to hurt somebody until I stopped hurting–which never seemed to pass.

30   There is an aspect of suicide in gang involvement for those whose options have been cut off. They stand on street corners, flash hand signs and invite the bullets. It's life as stance, as bravado. They say "You can't touch this," but "Come kill me," is the inner cry. It's either *la torcida* or death, a warrior's path, where even self-preservation doesn't make a play. If they murder, the targets are the ones who look like them, walk like them, those closest to who they are–the mirror reflection. They murder and they are killing themselves, over and over.

31   Ramiro stayed away for two weeks the day he ran off. When he returned, we entered him into a psychotherapy hospital. After three months, he was back home. Since then, I've had to pull everyone into the battle for my son. I've spent hours with teachers. I've involved therapists, social workers, the police.

32   We all have some responsibility: Schools, the law, parents. But at the same time, there are factors beyond our control. It's not a simple matter of "good" or "bad" values, or even of choices. If we all had a choice, I'm convinced nobody would choose *la vida loca*, the "insane nation"–to gangbang. But it's going to take collective action and a plan.

33   Recently, Ramiro got up at a Chicago poetry event and read a piece about being physically abused by a stepfather. It stopped everyone cold. He later read the poem at Chicago's Poetry Festival. Its title: "Running Away."

34   The best way to deal with your children is to help construct the conditions for free and healthy development of all, but it's also true you can't be for all children if you can't be for your own.

35   There's a small but intense fire burning in my son. Ramiro has just turned 17; he's made it thus far, but it's day by day. Now I tell him: You have an innate value outside of your job, outside the "jacket" imposed on you since birth. Draw on your expressive powers.

36   Stop running.

SOURCE: "*La Vida Loca* (The Crazy Life): Two Generations of Gang Members," by Luis Rodriguez. *Los Angeles Times.* Section M. June 21, 1992. Reprinted by permission.

---

admixture: a compound of substances mixed together; *¿Que pasa, hombre?:* What's happening, man?; *vato locos:* crazy guys; **scapegoat:** a person who gets blamed for another's crime; **absolution:** the act of freeing someone from his or her sins; **disenfranchised:** unfree; **post-traumatic syndrome:** an emotional and physical condition that one has after prolonged stress; *la torcida:* crookedness, deceit

OUTLINING/CLUSTERING

  I. Description of Luis and Ramiro

     A. Luis _____

     B. Ramiro _____

  II. Painful moments in Luis's childhood

     A. _____

     B. _____

     C. _____

     D. _____

     E. _____

     F. _____

 III. Luis's definition of gangs

     _____

  IV. Luis's suggestions to solve the gang problem

     A. _____

     B. _____

     C. _____

A SECOND READING

Reread the Rodriguez selection and answer the following questions as you read. Before answering these questions, write in your reading journal about any questions or comments you have about the selection.

1. What does Rodriguez mean when he says that "gangs are not alien powers" (paragraph 14)?

2. According to Rodriguez, why do the police pick up seven-year-old children?

3. Paraphrase this sentence in paragraph 24: "But 'family' is a farce among the propertyless and the disenfranchised."

4. How does Luis get out of gang life (paragraph 29)? How does Luis's way out suggest a way to solve the gang problem?

5. What advice is Luis giving to his son Ramiro when he says, "Draw on your expressive powers" (paragraph 35)?

READING/WRITING FEATURE: VOICE

Every piece of writing has a unique sound to it. This is the person you create as you read or write a work. Another way of describing this constructed person is voice. Every work has a voice. Voice is closely connected to your appreciation and understanding of a particular work.

When you read a moving narrative, such as this Rodriguez selection, you will be hearing a personal voice, one that wants to speak directly to you, the reader. In contrast, when you read scientific material or a chapter in your college textbook, you will likely be hearing an *impersonal* voice, one that places more value on the information in the selection than on its writer.

Other word pairs that are often used to describe a voice you read or create in writing include *strong or weak, clear or unclear, impassioned or distant, sincere or dishonest.*

Some of the ways you can begin to identify voice in a work you are reading or create a voice in your writing is to consider the following questions:

1. Are personal pronouns like *I* and *we* used?

   These pronouns automatically make the voice personal. Sentences without personal pronouns attached to them help make the voice impersonal.

2. Are strong words used or emotional experiences related?

   When Rodriguez talks about his use of drugs as a "drug-induced hysteria" (paragraph 5), or when he mentions that 25 of his friends has been killed by the time he was 18 (paragraph 9), you get a sense for a writing voice that is impassioned, for one that is showing the seriousness of the gang problem he describes. Of course, if Rodriguez had merely stated that he had taken drugs and that some of his friends had died, you would be hearing a voice that is much less involved with the gang problem.

3. Are the incidents in the narrative consistent?

   If the details in a piece of writing agree with each other, then you can assume that the voice creating the work is honest. All of the details in the Rodriguez piece, for example, support each other. It is likely that Luis, who was involved in gangs, would have a son also interested in gangs. Also, the fact that Ramiro was raised by an abusive stepfather would encourage him to join a gang. These facts make you believe the voice relating this narrative. In contrast, if you read details in a narrative that are not consistent, then you would be right to question the sincerity of the writer's voice.

Reread paragraph 7 of the Rodriguez selection for voice:

We are a second-generation gang family. I was involved in gangs in Los Angeles in the late 1960s and early 1970s. When I was 2 years old, in 1956, my family emigrated from Mexico to Watts. I spent my teen years in a barrio called Las Lomas, east of Los Angeles.

Note how Rodriguez uses a personal pronoun in each sentence–"we" or "I." Note the details concerning dates and ages–1960s, 1970s, 1956, two years old, teen years. Finally, note the geographic details–Mexico, Watts, Las Lomas, East Los Angeles. By talking about himself and presenting ample detail from his life, Rodriguez creates a personal and sincere voice in this selection. As readers, we listen to what he is saying because we sense that Rodriguez's painful experiences have something to tell us about gang life.

Begin being sensitive to voice in the writing you read and in that which you write. Note that you can create several voices. At times, you may want to be personal and impassioned like Rodriguez if you are writing a particularly emotional narrative. At other times, you may choose to create a more impersonal voice, especially when you are summarizing material from your textbook or writing a laboratory report in your science class.

BEFORE YOU WRITE

Before you select a writing topic, you may want to study run-ons as fused sentences and complete Practice A5 (pages 211–212) and study effective topic sentences and complete Practice B5 (pages 259–260) of the handbook.

WRITING TOPICS

Choose an essay topic from the following questions. Follow the steps of the writing process summarized on the inside front cover as you complete your drafts.

Writing about the Reading
1. From this reading, you can conclude that Luis Rodriguez experienced a life-threatening childhood and adolescence. Describe Luis's troubled life up to the age of eighteen. Then show how these experiences led him to gangs. Do you agree that experiences like these make one a gang member? Or do you think there are other factors that lead one to gang life?

Writing from Experience
2. Describe someone you have known, seen on the news, or read about who broke the law. Describe his or her childhood or adolescent experiences with as much detail as you can. Did these experiences encourage the criminal activity? If they did not, how do you explain this person's behavior?

RESPONDING TO STUDENT WRITING

Use some or all of these questions to respond to your draft or to that of your classmate. Read carefully for meaning and make your comments specific.

1. How does this draft begin? Is it clear? Do you have a sense for where this draft is going? If not, what would you like explained further in this beginning part of the draft?

2. (For question 1) How is the material from the Rodriguez selection being used in the middle paragraphs? Are the details accurate? Should the Rodriguez evidence be explained further?

3. Choose a paragraph in which the details are used effectively. Say why this paragraph is so effective.

4. What is your overall reaction to the draft? Provide at least two suggestions for revising it.

5. Edit for obvious errors in spelling and paragraphing. Edit for sentence fragments and run-ons. If you are unsure of a sentence error, ask your instructor for help.

SELECTION 6: FROM "CHILDHOODS OF VIOLENCE" BY ROBERT K. RESSLER AND TOM SHACHTMAN

This selection is part of a chapter from a full-length book titled *Whoever Fights Monsters*. The author, Robert K. Ressler, was an FBI agent who spent twenty years tracking down serial killers. With the assistance of Tom Shachtman, Ressler wrote a study on several aspects of serial killers–their background, their behavior, and their responses to their lives and their crimes.

This chapter, "Childhoods of Violence," studies the early years of various serial killers. It relies on cause-effect, narrative, and descriptive organizational patterns to make its points about these killers' behavior. In this excerpt, you will learn about the similar childhoods that many serial murderers experienced.

READING/WRITING PREP

Before reading this selection, answer the following questions in a free-writing journal or discussion:

1. Who are some of the serial killers that you remember from the news?

2. What sorts of childhoods do you think these serial killers experienced?

PREVIEWING

Preview the following selection. Read the first and last paragraph. Then read a few sentences, words, and phrases in the middle paragraphs. Before you read critically, determine what seems to be the purpose of Ressler's study.

Purpose of Ressler's study:

_____

_____

_____

_____

_____

READING CRITICALLY

Now critically read the selection and complete the following outline as you read or after you finish. You may want to make this outline into a visual cluster of the important information.

Robert K. Ressler and Tom Shachtman

From "Childhoods of Violence"

1   "Where do we come from? Who are we? Where are we going?" These three great questions from Gauguin's triptych were the real subject of the prison interviews of murderers I had started on my own in the late 1970s. I wanted to know what made these people tick, to understand better the mind of the murderer. Shortly, my curiosity became systematized and the interviews brought under the umbrella of the Bureau; they became the core of the Criminal Personality Research Project, partially funded by the Justice Department, and involving Dr. Ann Burgess of Boston University, and other academics, with myself as principal investigator. Using a research protocol of some fifty-seven pages, we interviewed thirty-six individual incarcerated murderers, concentrating on their histories, their motives and fantasies, their specific actions. Eventually, we were able to discern important patterns in their lives and learn something about their developing motivation to murder.

2   In the opinion of a number of experts, our study was the largest, most rigorous, and most complete investigation of multiple murderers ever undertaken, one that included the greatest percentage of the living, incarcerated multiple murderers. In a 1986 article, forensic psychiatrists Drs. Katie Bush and James L. Cavanaugh, Jr., of Chicago's Isaac Ray

Center called the research "exemplary" because of its breadth, and said that "its conclusions warrant evaluation in great detail."

3   Before going into the details of who these murders are and how they became murderers, let me state **unequivocally** that there is no such thing as the person who at age thirty-five suddenly changes from being perfectly normal and erupts into totally evil, disruptive, murderous behavior. The behaviors that are precursors to murder have been present and developing in that person's life for a long, long time–since childhood.

4   A common myth is that murderers come from broken, impoverished homes. Our sample showed that this wasn't really true. Many of the murderers started life in a family that was not desperately poor, where family income was stable. More than half lived initially in a family that appeared to be intact, where the mother and father lived together with their son. These were, on the whole, intelligent children. Though seven of the thirty-six had IQ scores below 90, most were in the normal range, and eleven had scores in the superior range, above 120.

5   Nonetheless, though the homes seemed to outward appearances to be normal, they were in fact dysfunctional. Half of our subjects had mental illness in their immediate family. Half had parents who had been involved in criminal activities. Nearly 70 percent had a familial history of alcohol or drug abuse. All the murderers–every single one–were subjected to serious *emotional* abuse during their childhoods. And all of them developed into what psychiatrists label as sexually dysfunctional adults, unable to sustain a mature, consensual relationship with another adult.

6   From birth to age six or seven, studies have shown, the most important adult figure in a child's life is the mother, and it is in this time period that the child learns what love is. Relationships between our subjects and their mothers were uniformly cool, distant, unloving, neglectful. There was very little touching, emotional warmth, or training in the ways in which normal human beings cherish one another and demonstrate their affection and interdependence. These children were deprived of something more important than money–love. They ended up paying for that deprivation during the remainder of their lives, and society suffered, too, because their crimes removed many people from the world and their assaultive behavior left alive equally as many victims who remain permanently scarred.

7   The abuse that the children endured was both physical and mental. Society has understood somewhat that physical abuse is a precursor to violence, but the emotional component may be as important. One woman propped her infant son in a cardboard box in front of the television set, and left for work; later, she'd put him a playpen, toss in some food, and let the TV set be the baby-sitter until she came home again. A second man reported to us that he had been confined to his room during his childhood evenings; when he wandered into the living room at such

times, he was shooed away and told that evening was the time when his mother and father wanted to be alone together; he grew up believing he was an unwanted boarder in his own home.

8   These children grew up in an environment in which their own actions were ignored, and in which there were no limits set on their behavior. It is part of the task of parenting to teach children what is right and wrong; these were the children who managed to grow up without being taught that poking something into a puppy's eye is harmful and should not be done, or that destroying property is against the rules. The task of the first half-dozen years of life is socialization, of teaching children to understand that they live in a world that encompasses other people as well as themselves, and that proper interaction with other people is essential. The children who grow up to murder never truly comprehend the world in other than **egocentric** terms, because their teachers—principally their mothers—do not train them properly in this important matter.

9   Richard Chase, the "vampire killer" discussed in the first chapter of this book, killed a half-dozen people before he was apprehended. According to psychiatric interviews conducted in conjunction with Chase's sentencing, Chase's mother was a schizophrenic, emotionally unable to concentrate on the task of socializing her son or to care for him in a loving way. The mothers of nine more subjects of the study also had major psychiatric problems. Even those mothers whose problems did not reach the level where they came to the attention of a mental-health professional could be considered dysfunctional in other ways; for instance, many were alcoholic. Neglect has many faces. Ted Bundy summed it up when he reminded an interviewer that he had not come from a "Leave it to Beaver" home. He had been brought up by a woman who he thought was his sister but was actually his mother, and although there was no neglect or abuse pinpointed in that relationship, there were strong indications that Bundy was physically and sexually abused by other members of his family.

10   Sometimes the mother, even when nurturing, cannot balance out or offset the destructive behavior of the father. One murderer came from a family in which the father was in the Navy, was often away on assignments, and was present only occasionally; the children went into a panic when he did come home, because he would then beat up his wife and the children, and sexually abuse the son, who later became a murderer. Over 40 percent of the murderers reported being physically beaten and abused in their childhoods. More than 70 percent said they had witnessed or been part of sexually stressful events when young—a percentage many times greater than that usually found in the general population. "I slept with my mother as a young child," said one; "I was abused by my father from age fourteen," said another; "My stepmother tried to rape me," reported a third; "I got picked up downtown one night by some guy when I was around seven or eight," said a fourth man.

11   The quality of a child's attachments to others in the family is considered the most important factor in how he or she eventually relates to and values nonfamily members of society. Relationships with siblings and other family members, which might make up for a parent's coolness in these situations, were similarly deficient in the murderers' families. These children, nurtured on inadequate relationships in their earliest years, had no one to whom they could easily turn, were unable to form attachments to those closest to them, and grew up increasingly lonely and isolated.

12   It is true that most children who come from dysfunctional early childhoods don't go on to murder or to commit other violent antisocial acts. As far as we could see, the reason for this is that the majority are rescued by strong hands in the next phase of childhood, that of preadolescence–but our subjects were definitely not saved from drowning; they were pushed further under in this phase of their lives. From the ages of eight to twelve, all the negative tendencies present in their early childhoods were **exacerbated** and reinforced. In this period, a male child really needs a father, and it was in just this time period that the fathers of half the subjects disappeared in one way or another. Some fathers died, some were incarcerated, most just left through divorce or abandonment; other fathers, while physically present, drifted away emotionally. John Gacy killed thirty-three young men and buried them beneath his home before he was caught. In Gacy's youth, his father used to come home, go down into the basement, sit in a stuffed chair, and drink; when anyone approached, the father would chase them away; later, drunk, he'd come up for dinner and pick fights and beat his wife and children.

13   John Joubert killed three boys before he was caught. John's mother and father divorced when he was a preadolescent, and when John wanted to see his father, his natural mother refused to take him to the father's residence or provide money for his trip. That's abuse, too, in a manner psychologists call passive-aggressive. Now, divorce in the United States is a very common occurrence, and hundreds of thousands of children grow up in single-parent homes. Only a handful of them go on to commit murder. I'm not impugning single-parent homes; rather, I am recognizing the fact that the preponderance of murders in our study came from dysfunctional settings, many of which were rendered dysfunctional by divorce.

14   Monte Ralph Rissell raped a dozen women, and killed five of them, before he was nineteen. His parents had divorced when he was seven, after which his mother moved with her three children from Virginia to California. Monte was the youngest, and he cried all the way across the country in the car. When I interviewed him in prison, years later, Monte told me that if he had been allowed to go with his father instead of his mother at the time of the divorce, he would have been in law school now, not in a penitentiary for life. His conclusion is debatable, though the sentiment is real. In any event, he'd had quite a childhood.

15   Monte began life as an Rh baby who required a complete blood transfusion, but was afterward healthy, though always small for his age. His parents fought for several years before they divorced. He claims he was exposed to marijuana and alcohol by his older siblings before he was seven. His first recorded antisocial behavior came at age nine, when he and several other boys were caught by the school principal while writing obscene words on the sidewalk. There were problems in the home, as well. His mother and new stepfather were spending a lot of time by themselves, leaving the children to supervise one another, and then arbitrarily punishing them if something went wrong. In our interview, Monte repeatedly claimed that his stepfather didn't know how to raise children, having been away in the military for much of his adult life. He would buy things for his new stepchildren, attempting to purchase their love, but did not know how to relate to them in other ways. Monte was still just nine years old when he took out his early anger on a cousin, shooting at him with a BB gun that his stepfather had bought for him. After the incident, his stepfather smashed the gun and then beat Monte with the barrel. Monte felt he and his sister were responsible for the breakup of his mother's second marriage, which came when he was twelve. That year, back in Virginia, he broke into an apartment and stole some property; at age thirteen, he was charged by the police with driving without a license; and at fourteen, with burglary, larceny, car theft, and two rapes. Monte Rissell was quite advanced in his deviant behavior by his early teens, but the escalation of this behavior replicates the development of many murderers.

16   Another murderer of women had antisocial tendencies that surfaced early. Premature at birth, the man was the last of four children of a Mobile, Alabama, family that was both poor and abusive. The story of his having been in an incubator for nine days became a family legend, as did the tale of an apparent seizure a few months later, during which the man believed he "died and was revived." During his first six years, he slept in the same bed with his mother, and for twelve years after that, he slept in the same room with his mother, in a separate bed. This was done, the mother later claimed, to protect her from the advances of the alcoholic father. She treated her son as if he was quite special–but also abused him. She was strict with her four children, at times hitting them with an electrical cord; additionally, she left them daily in the care of her mother, who beat the children if they disobeyed. The man's two older brothers quickly left the family when they graduated from high school, and after they were gone, the mother, the grandmother, and the sister used the man to ward off the drunken father, encouraging the boy to hit the father to keep him away from the mother.

17   In school, the boy's performance was spotty, and a principal wrote in a report that he was often "lost in fantasy," a description seconded by his sister. At puberty, he gained and then lost thirty pounds, and was openly

vitriolic toward his mother. She reports that he would become violent because he wanted two hot dogs instead of one, or because he was unable to have chocolate syrup on his ice cream. He stole female underwear, and spied on his sister in the bathroom. In a later autobiographical statement, the murderer wrote, "I was a freak in others' eyes. . . . I chose to swallow the insults. . . . I was a dog who got petted when I used the paper." At age thirteen, he started to snatch purses and became involved in gang fights. His family continued to protect him, however. At age sixteen, he was charged with snatching the purse of an elderly blind woman and attempting to assault and rape her fourteen-year-old niece. During the time that these charges were being investigated, another elderly woman in the community who talked to the boy about his "wrongdoing" was shot in the head and killed. The physical evidence pointed to this boy, but the father lied about his whereabouts at the time of the murder and the mother hired a lawyer, and he got all the charges dismissed. (Many years later, after conviction on other murder charges, the killer admitted that he had shot the woman.)

18   Two years after these incidents, the killer completed high school and enlisted in the military, in effect leaving parental supervision and intervention behind him. Within a month of his induction, he was charged with the attempted murder of a young woman, convicted, and sentenced to twenty years in military prison. While in that system, he again received support from his mother, who instigated appeals to congressmen and attempts to reverse the conviction on technical grounds. After serving seven years, and over the objection of some mental-health professionals who had tried to treat him and were rebuffed, he was paroled in the care of his mother.

19   He soon married a divorced woman with several children, who reported that relations between them were somewhat normal at first, though marred by strange incidents. When she said she was depressed over the actions of her ex-husband and wanted to commit suicide, the new husband said he would kill her and started to suffocate her with a pillow. At other times, especially when he had been drinking, he would threaten to crush her skull if she did not leave him alone. She also noted, with horror, that he had killed a pet rabbit by bashing it against a post, covering himself with blood. The turning point in their relationship was the birth of a daughter, after which his behavior became erratic and he isolated himself from his wife and their child. Shortly thereafter, and within two years of having been paroled, he began a series of rapes, murders, and mutilations of several women, choosing those who were clerks in convenience stores.

SOURCE: Robert K. Ressler and Tom Shachtman, *Whoever Fights Monsters* (New York: St. Martin's Paperbacks, 1992), pp. 82–88.

---

unequivocally: clearly; **egocentric:** dwelling inscessantly on oneself; **exacerbated:** much worse; **vitriolic:** sharp and bitter

OUTLINING/CLUSTERING

I. Purpose of the study

_____

II. Similar patterns in families of serial killers

A. _____

B. _____

C. _____

D. _____

E. _____

F. _____

III. Revealing experiences in Monte Ralph Rissell's life

A. _____

B. _____

C. _____

D. _____

E. _____

A SECOND READING

Reread the Ressler selection and answer the following questions as you read. Before answering these questions, write in your reading journal about any questions or comments you have about the selection.

1. In paragraph 2, Ressler talks about the importance of his study. Why does Ressler believe that the study his team conducted is different from others?

2. What are some of the myths that Ressler dispels about serial killers in paragraph 4?

3. In paragraph 5, Ressler describes the kinds of dysfunctional homes these serial killers come from. What is the nature of the problems in their homes?

4. How would you describe the typical mother of a serial killer as described in paragraph 6?

5. Reread paragraph 12. What factor is responsible for the majority of children from dysfunctional families not becoming serial murderers?

READING/WRITING FEATURE: COHERENCE

A consistent feature of good writing is that it is carefully organized so that sentences follow logically from one to the next and the ideas in one paragraph move smoothly into the concepts developed in the next paragraphs. Sentences and paragraphs that move smoothly and logically from one part of a piece of writing to the next are said to have *coherence.*

You achieve coherence in your writing not just by writing careful topic sentences and detail sentences that support them. A coherent piece of writing also moves the reader every step of the way to a greater understanding of your topic. One sentence further explains the point made in the previous sentence, and one paragraph provides a deeper understanding of a point you have made earlier.

Look at how Ressler achieves coherence in paragraph 7 of the selection:

> The abuse that the children endured was both physical and mental. Society has understood somewhat that physical abuse is a precursor to violence, but the emotional component may be as important. One woman propped her infant son in a cardboard box in front of the television set, and left for work; later, she'd put him in a playpen, toss in some food, and let the TV set be the baby-sitter until she came home again. A second man reported to us that he had been confined to his room during his childhood evenings; when he wandered into the living room at such times, he was shooed away and told that evening was the time when his mother and father wanted to be alone together; he grew up believing he was an unwanted boarder in his own home.

The argument of this paragraph is that emotional abuse has serious effects on a child, as serious as physical violence. Many of us know what physical violence entails, but it is harder to pinpoint emotional violence. Ressler has provided revealing examples from the childhoods of his serial killers to describe just what emotional violence involves. The infant child placed in a cardboard box set in front of a television and being tossed food in a playpen is a vivid and revealing account of emotional cruelty to an infant. The second example of emotional abuse is different from the previous, but it is equally powerful. A child is regularly told to stay in his room during evenings because his parents want to be alone. Ressler nicely summarizes this child's plight as being an "unwanted boarder in his own home."

Ressler thus makes his description of emotional abuse powerful by presenting two different but complementary examples. Both of these examples move nicely into his summary of "unwanted boarders" who eventually spill their anger out on others. The two examples cohere because both support the thesis of the paragraph that emotional violence can help create a serial killer who flees his home because he feels alienated.

Ressler and Shachtman are professional writers, so clearly you are not expected to write sentences and paragraphs that cohere as nicely as theirs. However, coherence is a writing standard that you can strive for. As you revise each paragraph, see how one sentence follows logically to the next. Also look to see how a paragraph coming later in your writing more fully explains what you stated in a previous paragraph.

You will find that the more you research and understand a topic, the more coherent your writing becomes because you have a wide range of material to select for your arguments, allowing you to speak with more authority about the points you are making.

BEFORE YOU WRITE

Before selecting a writing topic, you may want to study ways to edit for subject-verb agreement errors and complete Practice A6 (pages 213–214); then study ways to comment on quoted material and complete Practice B6 (pages 241–242) of the handbook.

WRITING TOPICS

Choose an essay topic from the following questions. Follow the steps of the writing process summarized on the inside front cover as you complete your drafts.

Writing about the Reading

1. Discuss the typical childhoods of serial murderers, as described by Ressler and Shachtman, focusing on the reasons why they turned to murder. Then apply these causes to one of the case studies in the selection. How do these causes help explain the case study you chose?

Writing from Experience

2. You have read Ressler's reasons for how serial killers are created. Write an essay in which you present your reasons why serial murderers commit these murders. These reasons may come from theories and beliefs you have read in newspapers or magazines, seen on the news, or thought of on your own.

3. Describe a person who does good deeds, someone opposite in character to the killers you have read about. Carefully describe the good this person does and trace the causes for why you believe this person does good. Be as specific as you can to describe this individual and to explain the causes that make this individual do good.

RESPONDING TO STUDENT WRITING

Use some or all of these questions to respond to your draft or to that of your classmate. Read carefully for meaning and make your comments specific.

1. Read the introduction carefully. Do you think it is too short or too long? Would you suggest that anything be added or taken out?

2. Locate a paragraph in the body that you think needs more detail. Suggest ways to revise it.

3. Locate a paragraph in the body that you think is well organized and carefully argued. State why you think this paragraph shows coherence.

4. What is your overall reaction to the draft? What suggestions would you give to help revise it?

5. Edit for obvious errors in spelling and verb tense. Edit carefully for fragments, run-ons, and subject-verb agreement. If you are unsure about a particular error, ask your instructor for help before you make the correction.

SELECTION 7: "LOOK BACK IN ANGER" BY THOMAS POWERS

In this selection, Thomas Powers describes the profile of the Unabomber, Theodore (Ted) Kaczynski, and discusses his motivations for the murders that he was finally convicted of committing.

   As with the other selections in this part, you will notice the ways in which Powers relies on the organizational patterns of description and cause and effect. Powers wants to put Kaczynski into a larger social framework, so he also discusses the nature of terrorist crimes in America and abroad.

READING/WRITING PREP

Before reading this selection, answer the following questions in a free-writing journal or discussion:

   1. What do you already know about the Unabomber?

   2. What are some of the reasons why some people are dissatisfied with the American government?

PREVIEWING

Preview the following selection. Read the first and last paragraph. Then read a few sentences, words, and phrases in the middle paragraphs.

Before you read critically, write a few sentences that describe Ted Kaczynski.

Description of Ted Kaczynski:

_____

_____

_____

_____

_____

READING CRITICALLY

Now critically read the selection and complete the following outline as you read or after you finish. You may want to make this outline into a visual cluster of the important information.

Thomas Powers

Look Back in Anger

1   Something important is missing from the personal history of the man the FBI claims is the Unabomber. The bombs were **meticulously** crafted, ingeniously disguised. The targets implied an obsession with computers, technology, airlines, corporate "enemies" of the environment. The 18-year span of the bomber's lethal campaign suggests a deeply rooted anger that could not be **assuaged.** What's missing is the source of that rage.

2   Photos of the FBI's suspect, Theodore J. (Ted) Kaczynski, beginning with a high-school photo in 1958, show the aging of a proud, tight-lipped man whose glare seems to hold the world at a distance. The last in the series, Kaczynski's FBI mug shot after his arrest in April, has a wild, sullen look, as if the anger that drove him had coarsened over the years. It is the set of the jaw that arrests our gaze, teeth clenched, as if challenging the world to drag out the words that explain his acts.

3   Murder, like anger, is as old as **Cain,** but technology gives modern killers the power to kill on a scale far exceeding the reach of one man with his hands on the throat of another. This is bad news for a society where the level of anger is both high and rising—not just personal anger of the sort that begins to fester in childhood, but social anger, where the injury may be inflicted by impersonal forces or some item on the news. Timothy McVeigh, charged with the Oklahoma City bombing that killed 168 people, allegedly picked the date of his attack to commemorate the **immolation** of David Koresh and his followers in Waco, Tex.

4   Kaczynski and his lawyer both say he is not the Unabomber, and federal prosecutors will have to prove their case in court. But the evidence discovered in Kaczynski's cabin—notebooks filled with diagrams for bombs, materials for making bombs, an assembled bomb, the typewriter that apparently typed the manuscript of the Unabomber's **manifesto**—strongly suggests the public career of the Unabomber is at an end.

5   While the FBI was searching for the culprit, they put together a psychological portrait with a hazy focus, missing as much as it spotted. A few things were right on the money—for example, that he came from or had lived in Chicago and Berkeley. On some points, the FBI psychologists were plain wrong—they thought he was only a high-school graduate; he has a Harvard BA and PhD in math from the University of Michigan. Vaguest of all was the FBI's guess at the core of the Unabomber's soul; they figured he was a loner with a grudge. Well, yes—but a grudge about what?

6   Psychology is, at best, an inexact science, but it makes some fundamental assumptions: one is that you can't get something from nothing. If anger is what comes out, then at some point anger went in. There has been plenty of anger on the front pages lately, personal anger that comes out of personal history. In Scotland, a man with a history of what social workers call an "inappropriate" interest in children burst into a school and shot 16 children to death before turning the gun on himself. In Oakland, a 6-year-old boy is charged with attempted murder after allegedly tipping a month-old baby out of its bassinet and kicking and stomping it before stealing a tricycle. In Australia, a young man with a history of "mental problems" went on a shooting spree that left 35 dead. In Middlebury, Vt., an hour from my house, a man shot two people and then himself in an episode that made little impression beyond the range of local papers because the nature of the case has grown so (distressingly) routine.

7   In each of these cases, the motive for murder appears to have come solely from the killer's (or aspirant killer's) personal history. What horrifies is the ferocity of the response to some purely private hurt.

8   Literary critics have long debated what lies at the root of the poisonous insinuations of Iago in William Shakespeare's "Othello." A jealous rage, artfully encouraged by Iago, prompts Othello to murder his beloved Desdemona, then kill himself—a pattern of sexual murder increasingly common on police blotters. The mystery in the play is what drives Iago; **"motiveless malignity"**—the trait theologians once called "evil"—is how some critics have described it. The killers in Scotland and Australia and the monstrous 6-year-old all seem to share Iago's desire to inflict pain for its own sake, for no reason, but blindly, out of their own nature, as the wind howls.

9   What distinguishes the Unabomber—Kaczynski, if it's he—from these other compulsive killers is that he claims to be driven by social anger, moral and intellectual rejection of the basic premise of Western democratic society: that technology gives everybody more, and more is good. The Unabomber's views on this were spelled out in the 35,000-word

manifesto he persuaded the New York Times and Washington Post to print last year. There, he said flatly: "The Industrial Revolution and its consequences have been a disaster for the human race. . . . The single overriding goal must be the elimination of modern technology."

10   This sounds odd coming from a man skilled in the use of computers; a meticulous fabricator of highly sophisticated explosive devices; a man who called a plywood cabin home and sponged on his brother whenever he needed money. Much about Kaczynski's life suggests human isolation rather than political rebellion; his windowless cabin did not place him in nature as much as it sealed him off from the world. In 1978, he began harassing a woman who spurned a relationship, forcing his brother to fire him from one of the few jobs he ever held, and a dozen years later he refused to attend his father's funeral. But, at the same time, in letters to a Mexican farmer, he complained of loneliness and wished for a wife and family. There is plenty of evidence of a tortured inner life.

11   But the Unabomber's manifesto says his goal is a kind of revolution in reverse, and he killed three men and wounded 23 others in a crazy attempt to shock the U.S. public into rethinking its dependence on technology. This is what 19th-century bomb-throwing **anarchists,** who invented the strategy, called "propaganda of the deed," and like the Oklahoma City bombing a year ago, it was intended, and should be seen, as a political act.

12   Modern political terrorism had its roots in the aftermath of World War II in Palestine, where Arab and Jewish underground groups attacked the British and each other. Succeeding waves of terrorism have since touched every corner of the globe, with one exception. The United States, both the most violent and most heavily armed civilized country on Earth, has been largely spared the terror campaigns that have swept France, Ireland, Italy and the Middle East. In the 1960s, white racist groups in the South bombed black churches, and in the 1970s, white radical groups set off a few bombs to prove all was not serene in the homeland of capitalism. But real terror was missing.

13   Now that may be changing. The Unabomber claimed to speak in the name of an organized movement—but investigators were apparently right in their guess that he plotted alone. But they were wrong when they guessed his bombing was the result of a grudge, meaning a desire for revenge of a personal slight. The Unabomber's grudge, if grudge it can be called, is on the grand scale, directed against an entire society—and in this he is far from alone. The so-called freemen holed up in Montana, the hundreds of militia groups arming for **Armageddon,** the **Aryan** white supremacists and gun fanatics who think they're being followed by the Bureau of Alcohol, Tobacco and Firearms are walking time bombs of social anger waiting to explode.

14   Somewhere in Kaczynski's past, if prosecutors are right, is that primal hurt that gave him what most Americans lack—the ability to kill. Some psychologists suspect the injury occurred in his first year—doctors

isolated him for treatment of an allergy at a stage of infancy when fundamental bonds of human connection are forged in the eye contact and touching between mother and child.

15   But we should not forget the Unabomber's manifesto, burning with passionate resentment of the material world built by American finance and industry. If what you hate is urban sprawl, parking lots, factories like football fields, dammed rivers, power lines, multilane highways shouldering aside mountains and multiengine jets streaking the **pristine** sky over dwindling pockets of wilderness, then there is plenty to hate. Add the traditional American genius for mechanical tinkering, the obsession with guns and violence, the dislike of foreigners and distrust of government, and we have assembled, at last, the ingredients for home-grown terrorism. Bombs are not much good for pressing complex political agendas, but they are ideal for expressing anger.

SOURCE: *Los Angeles Times,* May 5, 1996, pp. M1 and M6.

OUTLINING/CLUSTERING

   I. Kaczynski's facial expressions: _____

   _____

   II. Reason for Kaczynski's anger: _____

   _____

   III. Examples of Kaczynski's isolation

      A. _____

      B. _____

      C. _____

   IV. Reason for political terrorism: _____

   _____

---

meticulously: in an extremely careful manner; **assuaged:** soothed; **Cain:** Old Testament son of Adam and Eve who killed his brother Abel; **immolation:** the act of killing in a ritualistic sacrifice; **manifesto:** public declaration of intentions; **"motiveless malignity":** intense ill-will without a definite reason; **anarchists:** believers in lawlessness; **Armageddon:** biblical reference to where the last battle between good and evil will be fought; **Aryan:** term used by Nazis to refer to Caucasians of non-Jewish descent; **pristine:** pure, untouched

V. Other angry social groups in the United States

A. _____

B. _____

A SECOND READING

Reread the Powers selection and answer the following questions as you read. Before answering these questions, you may want to write in your reading journal about any questions or comments you have about the selection.

1. Reread paragraph 3. How has technology changed the ways people commit crimes today?
2. What is the "fundamental assumption" that psychology makes? What is the point Powers is making in paragraph 6?
3. What is Kaczynski's quarrel with technology as Powers explains it in paragraph 9?
4. Review paragraph 10. What is ironic about Kaczynski's anger toward technology?
5. What is the reason that Powers gives for Kaczynski becoming a killer in paragraph 14? How does this explanation differ from the more traditional reasons psychologists give for criminal behavior?

READING/WRITING FEATURE: WORD CHOICE

You have learned about the importance of providing details to support what you say in your writing. Details are made real by the words you choose. In composition, word choice is often referred to as diction. A successful writer chooses words that are exact and that create a clear picture in the reader's mind.

Powers' writing is nicely detailed. We have a sense for who Ted Kaczynski is and for his world by the careful descriptions that Powers creates. This exact diction helps make this selection enjoyable to read. Consider the first part of paragraph 15 to see how Powers brings to life the unattractive aspects of the material world in America:

> But we should not forget the Unabomber's manifesto, burning with passionate resentment of the material world built by American finance and industry. If what you hate is urban sprawl, parking lots, factories like football fields, dammed rivers, power lines, multilane highways shouldering aside mountains and multiengine jets streaking the pristine sky over dwindling pockets of wilderness, then there is plenty to hate.

Note how Powers carefully describes the highways as multilane roads that destroy mountain ranges and the jets as multiengines that pollute the sky and the contracting wilderness. These details give some powerful reasons for disliking technology. With such specific descriptions, Powers allows his readers to enter into Kaczynski's mind, to begin to see the depth of his anger toward technology.

Powers is a professional writer, so no one expects you to write such detailed prose at this point in your writing development. However, as you write details in your narratives and descriptions, as well as in your expository and persuasive essays, consider the following questions:

1. Can my reader visualize what I am describing?
2. Are there any other words that I can use to more clearly express my description?
3. Do these details enhance the argument or feeling that I am trying to create?

As you revise your drafts, look at your details with these questions in mind.

BEFORE YOU WRITE

Before selecting a writing topic, you may want to study the compound sentence and complete Practice A7 (pages 214–215) and study when evidence is too general and complete Practice B7 (pages 242–243) of the handbook.

WRITING TOPICS

Choose an essay topic from the following questions. Follow the steps of the writing process summarized on the inside front cover as you complete your drafts.

Writing about the Reading

1. Describe Ted Kaczynski from the details presented by Thomas Powers in this selection. Then summarize the reasons that Powers gives for why Kaczynski committed the violent murders. Quote from the selection, providing some of the revealing details that Powers uses and comment on the quotes you choose.

Writing from Experience

2. The major argument in this selection is that Ted Kaczynski, like many other Americans, is unhappy with the way the federal government treats its citizens. Write an essay in which you present some of the reasons why you believe people are unhappy with our government. You may use evidence from your own experience or from what you have read or seen on the news.

RESPONDING TO STUDENT WRITING

Use some or all of these questions to respond to your draft or to that of your classmate.

1. How many paragraphs make up the beginning, or introduction, of the draft? Is enough information included? Is there anything else you would like to add?

2. (For question 1) What are the major characteristics in the profile of Ted Kaczynski that are presented in the body of the draft? Are these characteristics specific or general? Are there any that you would like to add, take out, or revise?

3. Are there any sections of the draft that you think speak too generally? Identify these paragraphs and suggest how they can be made more detailed.

4. How does the draft end? Does it end abruptly? Would you want to add or take anything out in this paragraph?

5. Edit for obvious errors in spelling and punctuation. Edit for fragments, run-ons, and correct punctuation of compound sentences. If you are unsure about how a sentence should be punctuated or if you are unsure whether you have correctly identified a fragment, ask your instructor for help.

SELECTION 8: "THE COLUMBINE TRAGEDY: COUNTERING THE HYSTERIA" BY BARBARA DORITY

This selection is longer than the previous three. It addresses an issue that has gripped our nation: teenage violence in schools. As the title suggests, Barbara Dority wants to stop some of the hysteria and easy blaming that she observed right after the Columbine High School shootings in Littleton, Colorado. This article is a strong thesis-support argument, with Dority clearly introducing her argument and providing several pieces of evidence to support her contention.

You learned about causes—direct, indirect, and contributory—in Chapter 3. Dority introduces a new term related to the cause-effect structure: *correlation.* A correlation is a relation that exists between two topics. Sometimes this relationship shows cause and effect, sometimes not. At an elementary school, for example, taller students generally score higher on reading tests than shorter students. Yet height is not the cause of reading development; age is. A correlation is, therefore, not always as certain as a cause-effect relationship, yet often readers misunderstand this distinction and assume that a correlation is a synonym for a cause-effect relation.

READING/WRITING PREP

Before reading this selection, answer the following questions in a free-writing journal or discussion:

1. What do you think are the causes for violence in the high schools today?
2. How should high schools be prepared for the possibility of violence on their campuses?

PREVIEWING

Preview the following selection. Read the first few and last few paragraphs. Then read a few sentences, words, and phrases in the middle paragraphs. Before you read critically, write a few sentences summarizing Dority's argument.

Summary of Dority's argument:

_____

_____

_____

_____

_____

READING CRITICALLY

Now critically read the selection and complete the following outline as you read or after you finish. You may want to make this outline into a visual cluster of the important information.

Barbara Dority

The Columbine Tragedy: Countering the Hysteria

1 Columbine High School is an open, attractive, sprawling campus in the middle of a relatively safe suburban **enclave** in Littleton, Colorado. The school was a showplace when it opened, distinguishing itself in academics, music, drama, and athletics. Thus it was an unlikely setting for a tragedy of the magnitude that took place on April 20, 1999, when witnesses say at least two students–eighteen-year-old Eric Harris and seventeen-year-old Dylan Klebold–killed thirteen people and wounded twenty-three others before shooting themselves.

2   Fellow students later said the group Harris and Klebold belonged to, self-proclaimed the Trench Coat Mafia, had been a target of derision for at least four years. Members were picked on, harassed, and excluded— "always on the outside looking in." Most of the time, the members appeared to like it that way. As many cliques of young people do, the members played up their differentness. They wore army gear, black trench coats, and Nazi symbols. They spoke German to each other and were quite vocal about their fascination with Hitler and World War II.

3   Membership in such groups is just one of a remarkable assortment of "explanations" and assignments of blame that panicked overreaction to this tragedy has produced, accompanied by an onslaught of repressive "solutions" allegedly designed to prevent recurrences. We are witnessing the institution of a **myriad** of alarming civil-liberties violations, most aimed at obstructing the basic rights of young people—an already heavily restricted group of U.S. citizens.

4   This is a classic **scenario:** particularly shocking incidents of violence, especially those involving young people, lead to mass hysteria and are invariably used to justify repressive government intervention. Fred Medway, psychology professor at the University of South Carolina, says, "People feel much more comfortable overreacting than underreacting. It makes them feel they've done something to prevent a potentially negative thing from happening."

5   It is in the midst of just such frightening and dangerous times that this tendency to overreact must be most forcefully resisted. A few reality checks can be the first step in countering panic and assisting us in putting the situation into a realistic perspective:

- According to information from the National School Safety Center, killings are the exception, not the rule, at schools across the United States, and suburban and rural schools remain safer than their inner-city counterparts.
- The number of violent deaths in both urban and suburban neighborhoods has dropped dramatically since 1992. More than 95 percent of children are never involved in a violent crime.
- Not one of the mass school shootings of the past two and a half years has occurred in an inner-city area, and nearly all victims have been white.
- A 1998 report by the U.S. Departments of Justice and Education says children have more chance of getting killed by lightning than suffering a violent death on campus—which boils down to less than one chance in a million.
- The current generation of teenagers is less likely to use drugs, more sexually conservative, and less likely to be caught up in school violence than the one of twenty years ago.

- It's not unusual for young males, especially students at large suburban schools, to make videos of shootings and robberies in video-production classes (as Harris and Klebold are said to have done); in fact, nearly half do so.
- In a recent survey of 900 fourth- through eighth-grade students, almost half said their favorite video games involve simulated violence.
- High-profile school violence isn't new. Similar incidents have occurred at least as early as the 1950s.

6   But despite all these facts, we're being told that the primary cause of the Columbine and similar tragedies is violence on network television and in cartoons, comic books, music, and movies. As usual, Hollywood is to blame. Next in line are various "violent" games, especially "killing" video games and "violent" toys.

7   And, of course, we must not forget that wildly dangerous and insidious corruptor of American youth: the Internet—where Harris and Klebold are said to have gotten their bomb-making knowledge. It must be noted, however, that such terrorist know-how, complete with illustrated instructions for making bombs, is also frequently available in military manuals at surplus stores as well as in numerous mail-order civilian manuals, which are available through some public libraries. Are proponents of censoring this information advocating that we somehow locate, remove, and destroy all these sources?

8   Nation columnist Alexander Cockburn addresses a closely related aspect of public reaction in the magazine's May 17 issue:

> Commentators have fastened onto the fact that one of the youths had a personal Web site "espousing an addled philosophy of violence." Those were the words of the *New York Times'* [editorial team, the same people] who espoused an addled philosophy of violence a few days earlier when they suggested that NATO intensify the bombing of Serbia. Perhaps . . . it wasn't a personal Web site the kid had in his computer but nytimes.com.

9   I'm not, of course, insinuating that the war in Yugoslavia caused the Columbine tragedy or any other instances of domestic crime. I am, however, appalled at the hypocrisy of those who blame such incidents on the media and popular culture while simultaneously ignoring violence perpetrated by our own government.

10   They ignore, too, that the institution most adept at putting guns into the hands of youngsters (many of them troubled) and training them to kill their fellow human beings is, of course, the U.S. military—which also insists on the right to accept teenagers at an age younger than most other nations. It is amazing that those who are now blaming media violence for the Columbine tragedy—President Clinton among them—can completely exclude sanctioned, even glorified violence of this magnitude from their

analysis. Yet, clearly they can and do fail to realize that, in order to maintain consistency and credibility, they must equally condemn all violence. This incredible feat of **dissociation** by government officials and the American public is so complete that no one noticed the appalling irony when the air force sent F-16s over the funerals for those killed in Littleton.

11   In reality, and contrary to thousands of news sources, absolutely no causal link has been established between simulated violence in media and actual real-life violence. Just one example of how the media blatantly misrepresents this issue can be found in an Associated Press story that appeared a few days after the Littleton incident. It was picked up by most major newspapers under various versions of the headline, "Scores of studies link media and youth violence." The story opens by referring to a bill in Congress to require the U.S. surgeon general to conduct a comprehensive study of the effects of media violence on American youths, then immediately goes on to state that "the evidence already exists." Finally, five paragraphs into the story, we read that "a few scholars object to this research, saying the links do not prove cause and effect."

12   Among those who object is Jonathan Freedman, professor of psychology at the University of Toronto. He points out that correlative links could come from many factors, including the likelihood that children who watch a lot of violent television are often those least supervised by responsible adults. Freedman tries repeatedly to make the simple point most researchers recognize: that correlations don't establish causal links.

13   Harvard psychiatrist James Gilligan, who spent years interviewing murderers in Massachusetts, has concluded, "Nothing stimulates violence as powerfully as the experience of being shamed and humiliated."

14   Still, one after another, congressional representatives continue to pronounce that simulated violence produced by Hollywood is to blame for violence in our society. They then threaten government intervention to curb violence in movies, video games, and music if this is not done "voluntarily." Republican Senator Orrin Hatch of Utah and Democratic Senator Joseph Lieberman of Connecticut have likened the content of popular entertainment to a vice industry, claiming that, like tobacco, it requires special attention on public-safety grounds.

15   The April 28 edition of *20/20* presented a particularly shameless and **sensationalistic** feature about a "violent movement" spreading across America to which Harris and Klebold supposedly belonged. The followers of this new movement, Sam Donaldson grimly reported, call themselves "Goths." This feature then proceeded to demonize and place blame for violence on the Gothic American subculture. Parents were told that "warning signs" include being "attracted to a very strange group of people and listening to very alternative music." Diane Sawyer then haphazardly lumped together music groups with very little in common. As was the case with many of the music groups that various news sources connected with the Columbine suspects, most of them don't even fit the Goth

mold. In fact, the boys themselves didn't fit any known Goth mold. Neither did their lifestyles.

16   And never mind that the modern Goth lifestyle dates back to the 1970s. "What they're thinking," warned the Denver Police Department's Steve Rickard in the *20/20* report, "is totally irrelevant to a normal person's thoughts." What does this say about the many thousands of young professionals who grew up listening to Goth music, who solved video games like Doom and Quake years ago, and who once participated in the grandfather of all supposedly mind-warping games, Dungeons and Dragons? If *20/20* is to be believed, most of us are surrounded by ticking time bombs.

17   The obvious appeal of "very alternative" music, like many other forms of pop music, is that it gives voice to feelings of loneliness or anger shared by many young people and usually serves as an outlet for these feelings. Out-of-the-mainstream lifestyles, complete with music, provide a vital form of release. Many other seemingly anti-social behaviors are part of the rebellion we've come to accept as a normal and healthy part of the maturation process. Usually kids outgrow its self-destructive and counterproductive aspects. Similarly, although many video games do feature virtual guns and **carnage,** for all but a tiny percentage of young people they serve as a means of blowing off steam, certainly not as a blueprint for actual killing.

18   In the past twenty years, the Goth subculture has become its own culture, generating many subcultures within itself. I am acquainted with several young people who are part of this. They share my concern at the media's portrayal of Harris and Klebold as Goths. Several have been harassed on the street since the Columbine incident. Yet the truth is that violence is **anathema** to most gothic lifestyles. And Nazism is not glorified by Goths. How could it be, my friends ask, when Goths would be among the first persecuted by Nazis today? They fear for younger "quiet freaks" still in high school "who wear black, tint their hair, have multiple piercings, write dark poetry—and aren't ever going to hurt anyone." So do I.

19   My Goth friends also point out that there are many more computer and video game players in much of Asia than in the United States, and we don't hear about similar incidents in that part of the world. Video games, they say, are fun, and they're just games: "It's what we do for entertainment, what we like, and that's all it is."

20   On the front page of my May 2 newspaper was an eight-by-ten-inch color photograph of four police officers in the main foyer of a local high school. Some are seen talking to students, others are standing guard, and so on. Certainly I've no problem with students meeting and relating to police officers. But students becoming used to seeing police constantly monitoring their normal daily activities? How will this experience affect their perceptions and expectations of privacy? Many are so frightened they welcome this police presence, but what are the implications of creating

citizens who feel safe only when directly watched over and protected by law enforcement personnel?

21   We're also instituting SWAT training in schools; installing metal detectors; conducting random locker searches (these have been mandated for all schools in the Seattle, Washington, school district, along with metal-detector checks in classrooms and at sports events); supplying teachers with walkie-talkies; banning black clothing, symbols of any kind, and any type of trench coat; **mandating** school uniforms; searching students' backpacks, purses, and such; banning the production of "gruesome" videos in school video classes; and conducting "lock-down drills."

22   One proposed "solution" to the school violence problem that is enjoying a surge of support is the concept of prosecuting parents for teenagers' crimes (which does seem particularly ridiculous when in most states, until now, any eighteen-year-old could purchase a gun-show pistol immediately). Twenty-three states have extended some form of legal sanctions against parents whose children commit crimes, although rarely are these enforced. Thirteen states now have laws making parents criminally responsible for failing to supervise delinquent children–but, again, rarely are such charges brought. Five states have adopted laws threatening parents with fines or imprisonment for negligent parenting, although some have been struck down by the courts.

23   All these simplistic solutions avoid confronting the much more difficult problems affecting children, like reducing poverty, improving child-rearing skills, and funding child-care services. Bruce Shapiro, writing in the May 17 *Nation,* states that "only a broadly conceived community safety net–derided as bleeding-heart social work by those now rushing to blame the culture–can catch such children as they fall."

24   Finally, there is one particular aspect of the American public's reaction to this tragedy that cries out for rational evaluation by freethinkers, as it is rooted in the irrationality of religion. We are subjected to pronouncements that the cause of Columbine and other violent episodes in schools is "Godless parenting" and "America's spiritual drift." Syndicated columnist Donna Britt actually wrote, "Kids grounded in God often have more spiritual weapons with which to fight darkness." The beliefs of Christian kids, she maintains, "get media attention only when awfulness is done in His name."

25   When I opened my newspaper on April 27 to the headline "Deaths seen through prism of Christianity," I felt a chill. "How much worse can it get?" I asked myself. I discovered that several of the murdered students were eulogized at funerals and memorial services as "Christian martyrs." Friends and family were quoted expressing how glad they were that these "strong Christians" had the privilege of dying for their belief in Jesus Christ. This is almost incomprehensible.

26   Unflinchingly facing reality has never been more critical. There is no evidence that Christians or those who believed in God were selectively

murdered. The Reverend Barry Palser, minister at the church of one of these Christian martyrs, was quoted as saying, "Inside that school library, they knew what they were doing. They knew what they were going after. That's what Hitler did." What planet are we on here? If these murderers had been adherents of Hitler's doctrines, they would have embraced Christianity and murdered only Jews, atheists, and others outside their faith.

27   Christians are certainly free to comfort themselves with the fantasy that some of these youngsters were "Christians who died for their beliefs" and to "thank God" they got to go out as "martyrs." But it's just another **delusion** to avoid dealing with the simple truth: twelve beautiful young people and their teacher were in the wrong place at the wrong time, died tragically and needlessly, and are gone forever.

28   The even less appealing truth is that we don't know why the murderers did what they did. We don't know why other incidents of school violence have occurred. We don't know if any one incident is meaningfully related to any other, or which incidents, if any, are related to which of a variety of factors in our society. Nor do we know how to prevent future incidents. We certainly can and should continue sincere efforts to learn as much as we can, but we're a long way from any definitive answers. As we await further information from law enforcement officials, it is our task–indeed, our duty as citizens–to resist panicked responses and stand in opposition to such tragedies being used to rationalize **draconian** violations of young peoples' civil liberties.

SOURCE: *The Humanist*, 59, no. 4 (July 1999), p. 7.

OUTLINING/CLUSTERING

I. Dority's argument

_____

II. Some facts about teenage crime

A. _____

B. _____

C. _____

D. _____

enclave: foreign territory surrounded by a specified country; **myriad:** an indefinitely large number; **scenario:** an outline of an event; **dissociation:** separation; **sensationalistic:** describing that which is intended to shock; **carnage:** slaughter; **anathema:** anything greatly detested; **mandating:** ordering by written statement; **delusion:** false belief; **draconian:** severe

III. Reasons why some people listen to alternative music

    A. _____

    B. _____

IV. Arguments against the assumption that computer games lead to violence

    A. _____

    B. _____

V. Some social problems that must be addressed in our society to help curb violence

    A. _____

    B. _____

    C. _____

A SECOND READING

Reread the Dority selection and answer the following questions as you read. Before answering these questions, write in your reading journal about any questions or comments you have about the selection.

1. Reread paragraph 8. What is the purpose of Dority quoting the Alexander Cockburn column?

2. Reread paragraphs 11 and 12. How does Dority call into question the supposed cause-effect relationship between viewing media violence and acting violently?

3. Paraphrase the following sentence in paragraph 17: ". . . although many video games do feature virtual guns and carnage, for all but a tiny percentage of young people they serve as a means of blowing off steam, certainly not as a blueprint for actual killing."

4. Reread paragraph 18. Summarize why Dority believes that the Goth subculture should not be blamed for the violence at Columbine High School.

5. In paragraph 28, Dority expresses her understanding of why there is school violence. Summarize this paragraph.

READING/WRITING FEATURE: CONNOTATIONS OF WORDS

You have previously learned about diction in Selection 7 and making inferences in Selection 1. Both of these concepts will help you understand connotations. Readers generally have an emotional response to the words they read. This response may either be *positive* or *negative,* and in a few cases the reader has no response, or a *neutral* reaction. The *connotation* of a word is its positive, negative, or neutral suggestion.

To understand a word's connotation as you read is to better appreciate the writer's intent. If a writer wants to show a positive, negative, or neutral feelings for a particular issue, he or she can do so in part by selecting words that suggest similar feelings.

Barbara Dority wants to show that the public's response to the Columbine incident was extreme, so the diction she chooses to describe this response is harsh. Look at the negative diction that Dority uses in this excerpt from paragraph 4:

> This is a classic scenario: particularly shocking incidents of violence, especially involving young people, lead to mass *hysteria* and are invariably used to justify *repressive* government *intervention.* . . .

Study the italicized words in the above excerpt. Note how they all suggest extreme emotion ("hysteria") and hostility ("repressive" and "intervention"). Dority wants to show how emotional responses to tragedy only lead to unreasoned responses from the government. As a critical reader, you can infer Dority's negative attitude to unreasoned actions.

Oppositely, note how Dority describes Columbine High School in paragraph 1:

> Columbine High School is an *open, attractive, sprawling* campus in the middle of a relatively safe suburban enclave in Littleton, Colorado.

Notice how these italicized words paint a very pleasant picture of this high school, through the positive connotations of "open," "attractive," and "sprawling." Dority wants to show the contrast between the campus's physical beauty and the violence hidden in some of its students. Again, a critical reader can study Dority's language to make this inference.

As a reader, learn to be sensitive to the connotations of words, for they help you understand the author's attitude toward his or her subject. As a writer, begin to select more carefully words with positive and negative connotations as you revise your drafts to find through your diction another way to support your argument.

Start asking the following questions about what you read and write:

1. What is the writer's or my attitude toward the topic?
2. How does my or the writer's language help to support this attitude?
3. Are the connotations of the words generally positive, negative, or neutral?

BEFORE YOU WRITE

Before selecting a writing topic, you may want to study ways to punctuate adverbial clauses and complete Practice A8 (page 215) and study ways to organize the middle of your essay and complete Practice B8 (pages 243–244) of the handbook.

WRITING TOPICS

Choose an essay topic from the following questions. Follow the steps of the writing process summarized on the inside front cover as you complete your drafts.

Writing about the Reading

1. In an expository essay, summarize the argument that Barbara Dority presents in "The Columbine Tragedy: Countering the Hysteria." Then select and analyze at least five pieces of evidence that she uses to support this argument. Do you find her argument convincing, or do you have a different opinion regarding why violence occurred at Columbine High School?

2. You have now read several selections concerning why people break the law. In a compare-and-contrast essay, select two or more of these readings to show how these writers agree and how they disagree about why people become law breakers. Be specific in the comparisons and distinctions you make.

Writing from Experience

3. Think back on your high school experiences to describe the relationship that existed among the students. If you remember any violence that occurred on your campus, describe it carefully and explain why you think this violent act or these violent acts broke out. Another option: If you have a child or relative of high school age and are familiar with his or her high school, you may want to describe what you know about the high school environment today, describing how students seem to get along and whether violent acts have occurred on campus. Provide as much detail as you can.

RESPONDING TO STUDENT WRITING

Use some or all of these questions to respond to your draft or to that of your classmate. Read carefully for meaning and make your comments specific.

1. How does this draft begin? Is it clear? Is there anything that you think should be added?

2. Choose a paragraph in the middle of the draft that is effectively detailed. Why do you think this paragraph is so effective?

3. Choose a paragraph in the middle of the draft that is not as effectively detailed. Why do you think this paragraph is less effective?

4. How does this draft end? Are you satisfied with this conclusion? How would you improve it?

5. Edit for obvious errors in spelling and in introducing a quote. Edit for comma-related errors in punctuating compound sentences and adverbial clauses. If you are unsure of how a comma should be used, ask your instructor for help.

FOLLOW-UP

Now that you have read several selections on why people break the law, answer the following questions either in a free-writing journal or in discussion:

1. Summarize the key points made by the authors that you have read in this part.

2. Which authors do you agree with? Which do you disagree with? Do you have any ideas about crime prevention that were not treated in these selections? If so, explain them.

THE MEDIA — TELEVISION AND MUSIC: SELECTIONS 9–12

In the following four reading selections, you will be examining popular culture in America, particularly as it concerns television and popular music. You will be considering how television has been influenced by technology and how television commercials have evolved to become part of the television programs they sponsor. The last two selections examine rap music and country-and-western music, considering such issues as women in rap and the ways that rap and country-and-western music are similar. By the end of these readings, you should have a keener sense for how popular culture can be seriously studied.

The four selections are titled:

Selection 9: "Taking the Fun out of Watching Television" by Charles Gordon
Selection 10: "Where's the Pitch?" by Paul Brownfield
Selection 11: "Salt-N-Pepa Have a New CD and Newfound Faith" by Veronica Chambers
Selection 12: "Parallel Worlds: The Surprising Similarities (and Differences) of Country-and-Western and Rap" by Denise Noe

As you read these selections, you will also learn about the following aspects of reading and writing:

READING/WRITING FEATURES		GRAMMAR/USAGE	WRITING CONVENTIONS
Selection 9	Audience	Adjective Clauses	Transitions
Selection 10	Analyzing Generalizations	Compound-Complex Sentences	Redundancies
Selection 11	Style	Semicolons	Vague Phrasing
Selection 12	Academic Writing	Colons	Colloquialisms

READING/WRITING PREP

You may want to answer the following questions in a free-writing journal or in discussion before you begin reading these four selections. Answering these questions should help you determine how much you know and don't know about popular culture in television and music:

1. How has television changed over the past fifty years?
2. How have television commercials changed over the past fifty years?
3. What are some of the positive and negative aspects of rap music?
4. How are rap music and country-and-western music similar? How are they different?

SELECTION 9: "TAKING THE FUN OUT OF WATCHING TELEVISION" BY CHARLES GORDON

"Taking the Fun out of Watching Television" in *Maclean's Hunter Magazine* presents an interesting argument about television viewing today. It looks at how television viewers have changed over the past fifty years, particularly how other technologies have eroded the original appeal of television. This article is a cleverly written thesis-support essay. Although short, it provides a thought-provoking and playful introduction to these selections, focusing on popular culture.

READING/WRITING PREP

Before reading this selection, answer the following questions in a free-writing journal or in small or large group discussion:

1. How much television do you watch each day?
2. How have you changed as a television viewer over the past several years?

PREVIEWING

Preview the following selection. Read the fourth and last two paragraphs and a few sentences, words, and phrases in the middle of the article. Before you read critically, write a sentence or two summarizing the article's argument.

The article's argument:

_____

_____

_____

_____

_____

READING CRITICALLY

Now critically read the selection and complete the following outline as you read or after you finish. You may want to make this outline into a visual cluster of the important information.

Charles Gordon

Taking the Fun out of Watching Television

1   After 50 years, TV has become just another appliance, which we can now use as we see fit rather than be controlled by it.

2   You would think we were all obsessed with television. At least, you'd think that from watching television. The talk shows and the entertainment news shows on television are obsessed with television. The _Seinfeld_ final episode was treated as one of the major events in the current millennium.

3   Television is not the only medium to be obsessed with television. Think of the number of trees that died so that newspapers and magazines could do justice—if that is the word—to the final _Seinfeld._ You'd think, to read them, that readers could barely pause in their TV-watching to look at a newspaper or a magazine, that newspapers and magazines see their only role as to convey information about television.

4   Of course, the print media would not want you to think that they are so uncool as to go straightforward gaga over mere television. So they provided the other side, too—tons and tons of ink from people explaining why they would not be watching _Seinfeld._ The fact that they felt a need to make such declarations only reinforces the notion of a people gone mad over television.

5   What then to make of the fact that nobody actually seems to be watching television all that much any more? In fact, we are now watching $1\frac{1}{2}$ hours less per week than a decade ago. How to reconcile all the

media attention given to television with the impression that television plays a far less important role in our lives?

6   The most obvious way of explaining the media attention is to say that the number of media outlets–magazines, television networks, on-line thingamajigs–has grown significantly and they need subject matter. Entertainment fits the bill. It is now almost impossible for a television program to begin, or a new movie to open, without massive media coverage preceding it.

7   Ordinarily, you would think that would stimulate interest, and it certainly does, for a number of people. For others, though, the advance publicity has the opposite effect. It takes the romance and the surprise out of movies and television. In this era of excessive information, a reader or television viewer has to work to avoid knowing the plots of movies and television programs in advance. Since part of the fun of dramatic programs is not knowing how they will end, their value, in the Information Age, is lowered substantially.

8   The same goes for another of life's little pleasures, the discovery of new stars, new writers, new musicians. That is gone. Actors, musicians and films cannot sneak up on us any more. There is no such thing as a **"sleeper."** Whether it's a song, a movie or a new star, by the time it gets to us, we already know all there is to know, and more than that. For many people, that takes away a lot of the enjoyment.

9   One of the appeals of television, in its early days, was its immediacy. If you missed *Gunsmoke* or *The Milton Berle Show,* you would never see it. Or so you thought, at the time. If you wanted to know what people were talking about at work or at school, you had to watch. That has all changed. First, **syndication** brought repeats, in the late afternoon, of many of the programs you thought you would never see again. Then networks, to cut production costs, began introducing reruns in mid-season. then came the VCR, giving the viewers the ability to capture and replay any show. Now, with the onset of dozens of specialty channels, you don't even need a VCR. Everything that appears on a major network is going to turn up, sooner or later, on a channel devoted to comedy or history or space or just about anything.

10   So why get excited about a television program? Why make a point of staying home for it?

11   Television, after 50 years of it, is just another appliance, which is not all bad. If television is just another appliance, it means we can use it as we see fit, rather than be controlled by it, as earlier generations of viewers were. We can watch a little of this, a little of that, skip this, tape that and not be at the mercy of network programmers.

12   Still, one of the things that makes television just another appliance is the growth in the number of other appliances. When television was big, there were no VCRs. There were no programmable CD players and there were no home computers. People who have all these toys now may be

spending less time with their television sets, but they may be spending just as much time with their other toys, perhaps more.

13   One reason to be encouraged by this is that the new toys are a bit more under our control. The home computer can shoot down pretend enemy space ships, it can indulge in an **orgy** of chat about Celine Dion, or it can write the Great Canadian Novel. It is up to us. The television set has never really been able to do much for us, except entertain. When it tried to do otherwise–to inform, to educate–it usually ran into the reality that other media did those things better. Now, we can use television for our own purposes. Or we can read, or just get out of the house.

14   It is ironic that television's grip is at its weakest when its reach is greatest. There is more cable, there are more channels, more opportunity for television to penetrate more deeply into our lives. Yet the reverse is the case. Faced with 50 channels, instead of the handful we grew up with, we are somehow **demoralized,** unable to choose. Being offered that range of choice dramatizes the idea that there is less choice than we thought, or that none of the choices are what we want.

15   Perhaps, in the end, what we want has nothing to do with what we want to watch. If the multichannel universe forces us into that realization, then it can't be all bad.

SOURCE: *Maclean's* 111, no. 23 (June 8, 1998), p. 11.

OUTLINING/CLUSTERING

I. The article's argument

_____

II. How television shows are publicized today

_____

III. Ways that television differs from what it was in the past

A. _____

B. _____

C. _____

"sleeper": a surprise success; **syndication:** release for airing in a number of television stations; **orgy:** wild, riotous partying; **demoralized:** lowered in morale

IV. Technologies that compete with television today

    A. _____

    B. _____

    C. _____

V. Article's conclusion

_____

A SECOND READING

Reread the Gordon selection and answer the following questions as you read. Before answering these questions, you may want to write in your reading journal about any questions or comments you have about the selection.

1. Reread paragraph 4. What is the contrast that exists today between television viewing and television publicity?

2. Paragraph 8 describes television in the fifties. Summarize how viewers experienced television then.

3. What does the author mean in paragraph 10 that "television is just another appliance"?

4. Explain what is meant in paragraph 12 by "the new toys are a bit more under our control"?

5. Paraphrase the following sentence from paragraph 13: "It is ironic that television's grip is at its weakest when its reach is greatest."

READING/WRITING FEATURE: AUDIENCE

Audience is an essential feature of what you read and a necessary concern of what you write. Like the people watching a play, audience is simply *who is listening*. In written works, the audience is always the reader. When you read, you need to determine early on who the writer's audience apparently is. Is the writer speaking to a general group of readers or to a specific, more informed group?

You can determine the writer's audience by considering the following aspects of the written piece:

1. Its vocabulary. Is the vocabulary general or technical?

2. Its sentence length. Are the sentences long and complicated, or are they short and simple?

3. The allusions it makes. Are you unfamiliar with the names or terms that are mentioned? Or are there very few words whose meanings you do not know?

Consider "Taking the Fun out of Watching Television" from the perspective of the audience. Do you see that the audience is directed at critical viewers of television, those who are interested in how television has changed over the years, and, particularly, how technology has altered television's importance? The author's vocabulary and sentence length are generally readable the first time through. Moreover, it is also a playful article. Note the reference to "the trees that died" in regard to the publicity for the last *Seinfeld* episode (paragraph 2) and to the carefree reference to the Internet as "on-line thingamajigs" (paragraph 5). It is material that you would often find in the popular press, that is, writing that a nonspecialist could read.

The more serious discussion of technology and television suggests that the author is directing his material at a more informed audience. Paragraph 13 has a particularly thought-provoking tone. Here the author presents the interesting paradox: Though television has greatly expanded its audience potential, it seems to have had the opposite effect in that the more choices we have, the fewer television choices we tend to make. As a reader who is drawn into this article with the author's playful vocabulary, you end up considering some complex media questions. Clearly, this author is speaking to a reader who wants to be informed and entertained.

As a writer, you should start carefully considering your audience *before* and *as* you write. An e-mail to a friend usually has a relaxed and conversational voice because your audience is one who you know well and one who is looking for your thoughts at that moment, not deep reflections on a topic. Similarly, the audience for your journal entries is also a more relaxed and less authoritative reader. Yet when you compose a formal essay to hand in to your instructor, you should assume that your audience is more critical and more educated. You need to write in a more complex sentence style and use more exact, careful vocabulary. As you draft your formal essays, you must keep this critical audience at the back of your mind.

Just as you carefully consider the voice that your writing creates, so must you think about the audience for each type of writing. If you consider audience as you draft, your revisions will be more meaningful.

BEFORE YOU WRITE

Before selecting a writing topic, you may want to study the adjective clause and complete Practice A9 (pages 216–217) and study transitions and complete Practice B9 (pages 244–245) of the handbook.

WRITING TOPICS

Choose an essay topic from the following questions. Follow the steps of the writing process summarized on the inside front cover as you complete your drafts.

Writing about the Reading

1. "Taking the Fun out of Watching Television" introduces a very interesting argument. In an organized essay, explain Charles Gordon's argument; then present the most important details that are used to support this argument. Conclude by analyzing this argument and determining whether you agree with it. Be specific in saying why you agree or disagree with the article's premise.

Writing from Experience

2. Describe the ways in which you use television. You may want to note how you watch television over several days. Consider the following three questions: What do you watch? When do you watch? Why do you watch? Or do you use other forms of technology instead of television: Internet, CDs, video games, and so on? Or do you read when you have spare time? Do you even have spare time? Be as detailed as you can to create a picture of yourself as a contemporary television viewer.

RESPONDING TO STUDENT WRITING

Use some or all of these questions to respond to your draft or that of your classmate. Read carefully for meaning and make your comments specific.

1. How does the draft begin? Is it clear? Do you have a sense for where this draft is going? If not, what would you like explained further in the beginning part of this draft?

2. (For questions 1) How is the material from the Gordon selection being used in the middle paragraphs? Is the material that is used here accurate? Should any part of the Gordon material be explained further?

3. Choose a paragraph in which the evidence is used effectively. Explain why the use of evidence here is effective.

4. Provide at least two suggestions for revising the entire draft.

5. Edit for obvious errors in spelling and paragraphing. Edit for errors in correctly using commas, as well as for fragments and run-ons. Ask your instructor for help with any comma-related errors if you are not sure.

SELECTION 10: "WHERE'S THE PITCH?"
BY PAUL BROWNFIELD

In this selection, Paul Brownfield explores the current world of television commercials. He presents an interesting argument with examples to support his thesis from recent commercials and commentary from advertising executives.

This selection is nicely structured along the thesis-support pattern. After a lead-in, Brownfield presents his thesis and then goes about supporting this argument.

READING/WRITING PREP

Before reading this selection, answer the following questions in a freewriting journal or in small or large group discussion:

1. Can you fully describe a particularly interesting commercial that you have recently seen on television?
2. In what ways are television commercials like the programs that they sponsor?

PREVIEWING

Preview the following selection. Read through the first several paragraphs until you reach the argument of the article. Then read a few sentences, words, and phrases in the middle paragraphs. Before you read critically, put into your own words Brownfield's argument.

Thesis of the selection:

_____

_____

_____

_____

_____

READING CRITICALLY

Now critically read the selection and complete the following outline as you read or after you finish. You may want to make this outline a visual cluster of the important information.

Paul Brownfield

Where's the Pitch?

1 The new breed of TV commercial is so cool they wouldn't *dream* of screaming slogans–they know what that remote is for. But it can be hard to tell where the programs stop and the ads begin.

2   Jerry Seinfeld is onstage in London, and he's bombing.

3 "... so I got off the elevator, cut in line and said, 'What is this, the seventh inning stretch?'"

4 Silence. The trouble isn't his jokes, Seinfeld thinks, it's the language barrier. Why not hang out a bit, spend some time with the British people, get to know the local expressions?

5 Adventures ensue. Riding in a cab, Jerry thinks he sees the Queen Mother. He herds sheep. He plays cricket. He eats too much sausage. But by the end of it all, he's speaking like an honest-to-God Brit, and back onstage his jokes kill, even though he's saying them in a dialect he himself doesn't understand.

6 Is it "Seinfeld" the show or "Seinfeld" the ad? Because the story only takes 30 seconds to tell, the answer is Seinfeld the ad. But who can tell anymore, the way commercials look like music videos, dramatic series, sit-coms, feature film previews—look, in other words, like anything but commercials.

7 In fact, while "Seinfeld" the series is set to leave the air May 14, "Seinfeld" the commercials will continue at least into the summer, as the comedian shoots new spots for American Express.

8 Cloaking a hard-sell message in the soothing image of a celebrity is a tactic as old as TV advertising itself, but the making of the Seinfeld ads reveals how much the line is blurring between the TV commercial and the TV program. In the age of the cable boom and the multi-channel viewer, commercials strive to be part of a **seamless** mix of seductive and slick images—an attempt, in effect, to eliminate the traditionally jarring experience of the commercial break.

9 "I often say that it's a mistake to think you are just competing with other commercials," says David Apicella, creative director at Ogilvy & Mather, the New York ad agency that does the Seinfeld American Express ads. "I think you're competing with everything else on television."

10 To that end, advertising agencies are hauling out every gimmick they can think of—recurring lizards playing out-of-work actors (Budweiser), Claymation baseball heroes (Babe Ruth and Reggie Jackson in a Lipton Brisk ad) and sometimes, as in the case of Seinfeld, characters lifted fully formed from their popular sitcoms—to condition viewers to see commercials as part of the programming mosaic.

11 Not only does Seinfeld have final script approval of the American Express commercials, but he conducts story meetings and pitch sessions, Apicella says.

12 "We do it sort of the way his show is done," Apicella says. "We pitch concepts to him and then we settle on a half dozen and we write those with him."

13 On the one hand, Seinfeld's involvement is testimony to his interest in the advertising field (in a recent *Vanity Fair* profile, he even floated the idea of opening his own boutique agency). But it also shows how much ad-making has come to resemble the process of making network TV.

14   A September 1997 *Los Angeles Times* poll underscored the mandate for advertisers: In the survey, four in 10 men said they always or frequently change channels when a commercial comes on; 28% of women said they did too.

15   And so, commercials have adopted the look and feel of the shows themselves, trying to create what Clay Williams, a creative director at the Venice ad agency TBWA-Chiat/Day, calls "a seamless transition between the stuff you're tuning into to watch and the commercial."

16   Commercials for ESPN's "SportsCenter" resemble the **parodying** tone of Saturday Night Live" skits. A dancing baby goes from Internet icon to Ally McBeal's imagination to pitch-infant for Blockbuster Video. Nike uses "Bittersweet Symphony," a popular song by the rock group the Verve, to turn a shoe commercial into a music video. An ad campaign for Levi's jeans bears a striking resemblance to MTV's Generation X docudrama "The Real World."

17   Any wonder, then, that the Academy of Television Arts & Sciences inaugurated an Emmy for commercials last year, with the first winner an HBO spot in which chimpanzees spoke lines from classic films including "The Godfather" and Network"?

18   To be sure, the viewing audience is still bombarded by commercials done earnestly–straightforward, consumer-oriented pitches for deodorant, nasal spray and medical care.

19   And some products may be parody-proof: The day of the tongue-in-cheek feminine hygiene product ad is, blessedly, light years away.

20   But advertising agencies that do things the old way are confronting a new reality. As generations of young people enter the prized 18-to 49-year-old **demographic,** commercials will have to adapt to the way they receive information through television.

21   "A lot of it has to do with the fact that they don't have the same kind of linear way of receiving advertising [as older people]," says Brian Bacino, creative director at the San Francisco-based ad agency Foote, Cone and Belding, which experimented recently with a six-part, mini-film ad campaign for Levi's jeans.

22   "It's more of a collage approach, and they fill in the blanks. If you don't have something that gets them involved, they'll get bored with it."

23   Even the most entertaining commercials used to sound and look like advertising. The cutesy jingle, for instance, is now considered an **anachronism** in many ad circles. Better to use a classic rock ballad (i.e. Bob Seger's "Like a Rock," which since 1991 has been Chevy's jingle of choice) or something more **au currant** (i.e. Nike's use of the Verve's "Bittersweet Symphony").

24   The Leo Burnett Company in Chicago–long a pillar of tradition, the people who brought you the "Ho-ho-ho" of the Jolly Green Giant and the giggling Pillsbury doughboy–was knocked back on its heels recently when it lost the United Airlines account, reportedly because the "Come

Fly the Friendly Skies" approach was deemed out of touch with today's savvier, more cynical consumer.

25   The **paradigm** for today's jingle? Last year's commercial for the Volkswagen Golf, in which two guys wander city streets aimlessly in their VW, pick up a couch, drive some more, then drop off the couch because it smells bad. Providing background is an **innocuous** but hypnotic pop song by the German band Trio, with the refrain "Da da da."

26   Arnold Communications, the Boston ad agency that created the commercial, is also behind the new Volkswagen Beetle ads, which are short on text, long on texture. In one spot, a fuzzy, almost psychedelic yellow daisy twirls at the viewer, until the image reveals itself as seven conjoined Beetle cars.

27   "There was a time when viewers were a captive audience because there was no place else to go," says Bob Garfield, who reviews new commercials for the industry trade magazine *Advertising Age*. "You could say, 'Ring around the collar' really loud and they wouldn't go anywhere."

28   Now, people will go somewhere. And fast. So fast you're better off entertaining them than providing the kind of useful information normally associated with a product pitch.

29   A new ad for Gatorade has an immediate visual hook, one that's liable to stay **burnished** in the viewer's memory while the product itself is glimpsed and quickly forgotten. It features the **requisite** athletes, only this time they're in black and white, while their blood, sweat and tears are in vivid purples and blues.

30   Depending on your point of view, ads such as these are either indicative of a medium getting more sophisticated or more **insidious.**

31   Put media critic Mark Crispin Miller in the latter camp. "[Commercials] are all trying desperately to be interesting, but that massive effort to attract us is in itself extremely monotonous," says Miller.

32   But others argue that the commercial-as-mass-entertainment is getting some long-deserved recognition.

33   "Commercials are setting a sophisticated trend," says Kinka Usher, a veteran director whose recent work includes a Mountain Dew spot in which track star Michael Johnson goes back in time by sprinting around the world. "I think TV programs are trying to emulate *them.*"

34   Left out of this discussion, of course, is whether a slick, well-made ad actually does Job One–sell the product.

35   Such memorable campaigns as the Wendy's "Where's the Beef?" spots and Alka Seltzer's "I Can't Believe I Ate the Whole Thing," both done in the 1980s, failed to jolt sales.

36   "Good advertising and bad advertising work approximately [the same], which is why what I do for a living is largely irrelevant," jokes *Ad Age* critic Garfield.

37   In a recent review of the new Volkswagen Beetle spots, Garfield wrote: "The advertising introducing the new Beetle . . . is bright, clever,

eye-catching, product-centered. . . . It is also very nearly beside the point—because this car is the right product at the right moment."

38   Can the same be said for the Gordita?

39   Clay Williams and Chuck Bennett, the Chiat/Day creative team charged with promoting Taco Bell's new taco, have created a buzz—if not identifiable sales results—with a talking Chihuahua ("Yo Quiero Taco Bell").

40   The Chihuahua, which began appearing on TV screens late last year, will reappear in new ads set to run around Memorial Day to coincide with the opening of the movie "Godzilla" (Taco Bell has a merchandising tie-in with the film).

41   Asked to explain the appeal of the dog, Williams and Bennett come up with some high-minded explanations (the Chihuahua is a kind of anti-hero—small, rodent-like, but ultimately lovable), then Williams finally admits: "You know, there's no architecture for this."

42   For all of the supposed separation between ads and programming, it's remarkable how much the two have in common. TV shows are measured by ratings; commercials by sales figures. TV shows are quickly canceled when they don't show immediate numbers; commercials can be pulled and accounts canceled when a product's sales figures don't improve.

43   Interviewed in a lounge at Chiat/Day's headquarters (a binocular-shaped, Frank Gehry-designed building), Williams and Bennett, 35 and 44, respectively, **exude** the future of TV advertising. They're young, driven, media-savvy, dressed in jeans and comfortable shirts, sneakers. And they enthusiastically admit they can't do straightforward ad campaigns. A laxative spot? Forget it. If the two have a creative point of view, it's that they feel the viewer's pain about lousy commercials.

44   "As an advertiser, the more you can break down the barrier between the ad and the entertainment, the more chance you'll have to get under people's skins," says Williams. "People are super savvy to being sold, and they turn off to it."

45   "Basically, commercials are an intrusion into your viewing," Bennett interjects. ". . . You have to immediately disarm people with something that interests them."

46   Even though they didn't do them, both are high on the Beetle ads, saying they manage to be compelling but spare—good to look at, organic to the sales pitch, not overdone.

47   "At the same time that computers and special effects allow us to do amazing things, they're also a trap," Bennett says. "You start getting into a 'because we can' thing. I think it's refreshing to find work that's based on an idea, executed very purely and very simply."

48   But when clever ads go wrong, they can be maddeningly obtuse, self-conscious attempts to be above the sell.

49   Witness the "They Go On" campaign for Levi's jeans, which began running last summer.

50   Bacino, of Foote, Cone and Belding, thought his team had come up with just the sort of fresh idea that would attract people to Levi's.

51   Designed as a six-month campaign under the tag line "They Go On," the series of commercials followed the adventures of an unrelated cast of urban Generation X-ers, their only link the fact that they were wearing Levi's jeans.

52   "We were trying to convey that Levi's are for people who live life their own way, on their own terms," says Bacino.

53   The ads began running in the summer, but by the end of the year Levi-Strauss had canceled the ads and pulled its $90-million account.

54   "Like TV networks, advertisers can be impatient for success," Bacino says. "But when you have a company looking for immediate results, that's when you see the least interesting advertising.

55   "How many times have you been in your living room, seen a commercial, and thought, 'I've gotta go buy that tomorrow'? For an image to stay in the consumer's mind set, you have to do something interesting and provocative."

56   Certainly, viewers can count on a higher class of ad during the May 14 final episode of "Seinfeld."

57   NBC set a record when several companies, including Anheuser Busch, Fuji Film and MasterCard International, bought in at the rate of $1.8 million per 30-second commercial.

58   That exceeds even the Super Bowl. And in this case, presumably, the game won't turn dull and tedious, chasing viewers away.

SOURCE: *Los Angeles Times*, May 3, 1998, pp. 6 and 96.

OUTLINING/CLUSTERING

I. Thesis of article (relationship between television commercials and programming)

_____

II. Examples of ads that show this relationship

A. _____

B. _____

C. _____

seamless: smooth, without interruption or division; **parody:** artful imitation of the style of another work; **demographic:** relating to the study of populations; **anachronism:** anything out of its proper historical time; **au currant:** French phrase for fashionable; **paradigm:** pattern, example, or model; **innocuous:** harmless; **burnished:** bright; **requisite:** necessary; **insidious:** tricky or deceitful; **exude:** ooze

III. How young viewers respond to television commercials

    A. _____

    B. _____

IV. Williams' and Bennetts' approach to creating commercials

    A. _____

    B. _____

    C. _____

A SECOND READING

Reread the Brownfield selection, and answer the following questions as you read. Before answering these questions, write in your reading journal about any questions or comments you have about the selection.

1. Paraphrase the following sentence in paragraph 6: "In the age of the cable boom and the multi-channel viewer, commercials strive to be part of a seamless mix of seductive and slick images—an attempt, in effect, to eliminate the traditionally jarring experience of the commercial break."

2. Reread the statistics in paragraph 12. What do these percentages suggest about men and women who view television commercials?

3. Reread paragraphs 19 and 20. Summarize the ways young people process television commercials.

4. In paragraph 23, Brownfield describes a recent Beetle television commercial. Why does this commercial seem so successful for today's television viewer?

5. There is an irony to the fact stated in paragraph 34. Put this puzzling conclusion about advertising in your own words.

READING/WRITING FEATURE: ANALYZING GENERALIZATIONS

In Chapter 3, you were introduced to terms of qualification when you studied the organizational pattern of cause-effect (pages 36–38). Here you learned that certain statements needed to be revised with words like "may or perhaps" to ensure that the statement was not misleading.

    When you *generalize*, you make a statement that is true a part or all of the time. In one sense, a generalization can be said to be an accurate summary of several details. Effective writing is careful to qualify the generalizations it makes. Responsible writing avoids making sweeping statements that cannot be adequately supported.

Notice the careful generalizations made in the Brownfield selection:

"The cutesy jingle, for instance, is now considered an anachronism in many ad circles. (paragraph 21)

Brownfield wants to show how ads have changed from the jingle to the complex story line. Yet he does not want to say that all ads avoid the jingle, so he includes the qualifier "many" in the phrase "in many ad circles."

Note the use of "can" in the following statement that Brownfield makes about ads:

". . . commercials can be pulled and accounts canceled when a product's sales figures don't improve." (paragraph 40)

Brownfield is unwilling to say that commercials are always dropped when sales go down because he knows of exceptions. In using the qualifier "can," Brownfield makes his statement more accurate.

When you make a statement drawn from many details or read a statement built on several bits of evidence, ask yourself the following questions:

1. Is the generalization always true?
2. What are the exceptions?
3. How frequent are the exceptions?
4. What qualifier should be used to make the statement accurate?

Most statements about popular culture, or about human behavior in general, are almost always qualified because exceptions occur when people's actions are studied. As you revise your drafts, include qualifiers like *most, some, perhaps, it seems, often,* or *rarely* to add accuracy to your statements. Writing qualified generalizations tells your audience that you have studied the material you are writing about and are coming to responsible conclusions. Critical readers tend to believe the qualified generalization over the *sweeping generalization*–the statement that is said to be always true, allowing no exceptions.

Similarly, when you read a selection, note the types of generalizations that are made and determine if they can be supported by the evidence that the writer presents. Look carefully for the presence or absence of terms of qualifications in these generalizations. As a reader, you can determine how responsible a writer is by studying how accurate the generalizations are.

BEFORE YOU WRITE

Before selecting a writing topic, you may want to study the compound-complex sentence and complete Practice A10 (pages 217–219) and study redundancies and complete Practice B10 (pages 245–249) of the handbook.

WRITING TOPICS

Choose an essay topic from the following questions. Follow the steps of the writing process summarized on the inside front cover as you complete your drafts.

Writing about the Reading

1. Summarize the thesis of "Where's the Pitch?" Then find four separate pieces of evidence in the selection that support this argument. Be sure to discuss the evidence accurately and completely. Finally, at the end of your essay, discuss whether you agree with the argument that Paul Brownfield presents. Give specific reasons for why you agree or disagree.

2. In "Where's the Pitch?" Paul Brownfield describes several "successful" and several "unsuccessful" television commercials, at least for today's viewers. Discuss, from Brownfield's point of view, what television viewers expect from a commercial today. Then show how several of the commercials that he introduces either conform or do not conform to today's viewing standards.

Writing from Experience

3. Choose a television commercial that you particularly enjoy. Discuss it in detail and analyze why you think it is effective. Determine if the commercial you chose conforms to Brownfield's standards of a successful commercial. You may want to videotape your commercial so you can study it carefully.

4. Choose a television commercial that you find particularly unsuccessful. Discuss it in detail and analyze why you think it does not succeed. Then determine if this commercial conforms to today's standards for an unsuccessful commercial. If you can, videotape the commercial so you can review it carefully.

RESPONDING TO STUDENT WRITING

Use some or all of these questions to respond to your draft or to that of your classmate. Read carefully for meaning and make your comments specific.

1. Is Brownfield's argument about commercials and television stated somewhere in the first few paragraphs? Would you add anything to make this explanation clearer?

2. (For questions 1 and 2) Are the commercials discussed by Brownfield clearly analyzed in the body of the draft? Would you suggest that any details be added or deleted in this part of the draft?

3. (For questions 3 and 4) Are the details of the television commercial selected for the draft clearly presented? Do you think that any other information needs to be included about this commercial?

4. Which paragraph is most clearly organized and supported with convincing detail? Explain why.

5. Edit for obvious errors in spelling and punctuation. Edit also for sentence errors, punctuation errors, and generalizations that are not accurately worded. If you are unsure about how to punctuate or how to revise a generalization, ask your instructor for help.

SELECTION 11: "SALT-N-PEPA HAVE A NEW CD AND NEWFOUND FAITH" BY VERONICA CHAMBERS

This selection is an informative description of the successful female rap group Salt-N-Pepa. Veronica Chambers carefully focuses on how this group has made room for women in rap. In so doing, she describes the ways in which female rappers differ from their male counterparts.

This selection fits nicely into the organizational pattern of description. The article is rich in detail concerning the musical lives of the three women making up this group. The reader learns about their beliefs, their close relationship to each other, and their understanding of rap.

READING/WRITING PREP

Before reading this selection, answer the following questions in a freewriting journal or in small or large group discussion:

1. What is your attitude toward rap music?
2. Why do you think rap music is so popular?

PREVIEWING

Preview the following selection. Read the first and last paragraph and a few words, phrases, and sentences in the body. Before you read critically, write out what you believe sets Salt-N-Pepa apart from other rap groups.

What sets Salt-N-Pepa apart from other rap groups:

_____

_____

_____

_____

_____

READING CRITICALLY

Now critically read the selection and complete the following outline as you read or after you read. You may want to make this outline a visual cluster of the important information.

Veronica Chambers

Salt-N-Pepa Have a New CD and Newfound Faith

1 It's 4 o'clock on a rainy Wednesday afternoon at the MTV Studios in New York, and Cheryl (Salt) James and Sandi (Pepa) Denton are quietly making their way through wardrobe and makeup. The group's deejay, Dee Dee (Spinderella) Roper, is taking a nap in the greenroom. This week, the Queens of Rap will release their first album in four years, appropriately titled "Brand New." But here in the tiresome round of publicity and promotion, it's just the same ol' same ol'.

2 Salt-N-Pepa's low-key manner **belies** what a major moment this is for the Grammy-winning rap group. "Brand New" is the first album that the women have written and produced on their own, without Hurby Azor, the producer who formed the group and the man whom James has called a **"Svengali."** More than another bumpin' collection of **female-centric** rap songs, "Brand New" is Salt-N-Pepa's declaration of independence.

3 The group also faced a creative crisis on "Brand New," as James's newfound faith in Christianity deepened. Could she perpetuate the sexy girl-rapper **persona** she'd helped to pioneer? After she performed on last summer's gospel rap hit "Stomp" with Kirk Franklin and God's Property, rumors began to spread that "Brand New" would be Salt-N-Pepa's last album together and that James was interested only in recording inspirational music.

4 James believes that there's a way to be sexual without losing the focus on her faith. "I can look sexy, have a good time and still be praising God," she says. "Holier-than-thou church folk won't encourage it, but my spirituality is personal." After all, Salt-N-Pepa have always been about playful sexual **allegory** rather than the explicit lyrics of a Foxy Brown or Lil' Kim. And she plans to do more gospel, but won't abandon the group: "Salt-N-Pepa is my purpose in life."

5 It's been more than 13 years since Salt-N-Pepa broke the gender barrier in rap music. Each of their four previous albums has gone platinum or multiplatinum, a rare feat for any rap artist, doubly so because the artists are female. Although the group members are only in their late 20s (they never give their ages), Salt-N-Pepa are the godmothers of rap,

young women who opened the door for such acts as Queen Latifah, Lil' Kim and Da Brat.

6   Few groups survive without infighting and jealousy, so the close friendship among the women of Salt-N-Pepa is legendary. All three are single mothers, and it was Salt who paired up with Pepa in Lamaze classes and helped deliver her best friend's baby. "This business will throw a lot of bricks your way. Our foundation is that we are a sisterhood, not just a group," says Roper. "We take business very seriously, but we're friends first."

7   Part of the enduring popularity of Salt-N-Pepa is that they can always be counted on for two things: a good time and an uplifting message. "Brand New" will not disappoint their core fans, though it attempts to broaden their fan base. The first single, "R U Ready?," a fun party song, is already in heavy rotation on MTV. Sheryl Crow collaborates with the group on an anti-racism song called "Imagine." James continues her path of music ministry with another Kirk Franklin duet called "Hold On." "We listen to all kinds of music," says James. "This is Salt-N-Pepa being really honest. We are rock and roll. We are alternative. We are gospel. We enjoy all these things, and this album is letting you into our world."

8   The biggest surprise on "Brand New" is the emergence of Roper as a full-fledged member of the group. In the '80s, no self-respecting rap group traveled without a deejay who could spin vinyl while the rappers freestyled lyrics. It was James and Denton's idea to hire a female deejay, a Spinderella, to back the group. In 1987 they chose 17-year-old Dee Dee Roper, a high-school senior, from an open audition.

9   In the early '90s, as digital audiotapes replaced deejays, Roper's role began to shrink. She appeared in all the videos, rapped a few lines here and there, but over time Spinderella became the Tito Jackson of the group. Now that the women have full creative control over their music, Roper's role has been beefed up. "Brand New" features the deejay taking center stage on almost half the songs. The occasional gospel track may not be enough to keep James wedded to Salt-N-Pepa forever, but for now she's sticking around. She and Denton have already begun working on their next project, a solo album for Roper. The title? "Spinderella's Ball."

SOURCE: *Newsweek,* 130, no. 17 (October 27, 1997): p. 72.

belies: disguises; **Svengali:** a hypnotist known for a cruel domination of his subjects; **female centric:** focused solely on women; **persona:** character; **allegory:** a work in which people, things, and events have another meaning

OUTLINING/ CLUSTERING

   I. General description of Salt-N-Pepa

  II. Characteristics of the new album "Brand New"

     A. _____

     B. _____

 III. The beliefs of Cheryl James

     A. _____

     B. _____

  IV. A description of the group

     A. _____

     B. _____

   V. The new features of "Brand New"

     A. _____

     B. _____

     C. _____

A SECOND READING

Reread the Chambers selection and answer the following questions as you read. Before answering these questions, you may want to write in your reading journal about any questions or comments that you may have about the selection.

1. Reread paragraph 2. According to Chambers, what seems to make Salt-N-Pepa unique?

2. Paraphrase the following sentence from paragraph 4: "After all, Salt-N-Pepa have always been about playful sexual allegory rather than the explicit lyrics of a Foxy Brown or Lil' Kim."

3. Reread paragraph 6. What does Chambers suggest is the key to the group's longevity?

4. Reread paragraph 7. In a sentence or two, summarize what Chambers believes is the type of rap Salt-N-Pepa create.

5. In paragraph 9, Chambers describes Dee Dee Roper's expanded duties. Why does she suggest that this was an artistic decision that a woman could more easily make?

READING/WRITING FEATURE: STYLE

Now, at the halfway point in this textbook, you have been introduced to several reading/writing features: voice, coherence, word choice, connotations, and audience, to name just a few. These are some of the many tools that a writer has. *Style* is the sense of individuality that exists in every piece of writing, so we can say that each writer has his or her own style. Style is the result of the combination of all the tools that a writer can use.

Some of the types of style you will read and write are formal and informal, serious and playful, and complicated and clear. A formal writing style is the kind you have likely written in your college essays, whereas an informal style is the sort you write in your journal entries, e-mails, and letters to friends. A serious style is found often in writing that deals with critical topics like capital punishment or alcoholism. A more playful style often accompanies a less serious topic like vacationing or entertaining your friends. Finally, clear styles often are expressed in direct subject-verb-object sentences, whereas complicated styles are characterized by longer sentences with many modifiers and qualifiers. Writing in a clear style is not always the appropriate choice. Some topics are complicated, so your sentence structure is shaped by the complexity of your topic. Yet you should always strive for clarity in your writing. Sometimes clarity is best expressed in a direct-sentence structure, and at other times, it is best achieved with complicated sentences.

How can you identify a particular style–in your writing or in the writing that you read? Consider the following suggestions:

1. Determine the audience. Is the piece written for specialists in a field, educated people, educated and uneducated people, or friends? Here you can determine early on the sort of style that the writing should follow.

2. Look through the writing for sentence structure and vocabulary. Are they advanced or easy to read?

3. Determine if the vocabulary and sentence structure are consistent throughout the writing. Or does the writing begin in a complicated way and end simply?

4. After reading the material critically, see if you can characterize it with one of the words described earlier, such as formal, informal, and so on.

5. Determine if the style you have identified is appropriate for the subject that the writing examines.

Take a moment to review the Chambers article. Did you note that the vocabulary is both colloquial and formal: "just the same ol' same ol'" (paragraph 1) as opposed to "playful sexual allegory" and "explicit lyrics" (paragraph 4)? Did you also see that many of the sentences are long, but some are short? Also, did you notice that when colloquial words are used, like "same ol' same ol'" or "bumpin' collection" (paragraph 2), they are not put in quotes to suggest that the colloquial language is just as natural as the formal? This is a national magazine piece that successfully explains the urban rap world in both formal and colloquial terms.

Given these aspects to Chamber's writing, you can conclude that this article is written both in a formal and colloquial style to examine the unique features of female rap music as a type of expression and as an industry. You can thus conclude that it is a magazine piece that seriously explains those aspects of female rap music that most readers of *Newsweek* have likely not considered.

You can use the five suggestions stated previously as you revise the drafts of your various essays. Ask yourself: What style or styles are appropriate for the writing topic? Then use the various sentence structure and vocabulary tools to make your writing consistent with that particular style or styles.

Your style develops throughout your writing career. As a beginning college writer, you are still working to establish the sorts of styles you are comfortable with. Feel free to experiment with several writing styles to discover which ones most effectively express what you want to say in writing.

BEFORE YOU WRITE

Before selecting a writing topic, you may want to study semicolons and complete Practice A11 (pages 219–221) and study vague phrasing and complete Practice B11 (pages 248–249) of the handbook.

WRITING TOPICS

Choose any topic from the following questions. Follow the steps of the writing process summarized on the inside front cover.

Writing about the Reading

1. Describe the uniqueness of the group Salt-N-Pepa. Focus on how Veronica Chambers describes the three performers in the group. Examine especially their musical beliefs as female rap artists and how they have forged an independence from their male rap counterparts. Finally, determine the ways that Salt-N-Pepa have transformed the genre of African-American rap music.

Writing from Experience

2. Describe any rap artist or rap lyric that you find especially powerful. What message is this lyric or artist sending? Why is it so effective?

3. Select any form of popular American music (blues, jazz, rock and roll, country-and-western, and so on) and describe why you find it so

appealing. You may describe this form of popular music, a particular performer, or a particular song, or several of these features together. What is it about this music that is so powerful? To what type of listener is this music speaking?

RESPONDING TO STUDENT WRITING

Use some or all of these questions to respond to your draft or to that of your classmate. Read carefully for meaning and make your comments specific.

1. How does this draft begin? Is it clear? What would you like to be explained further in the first part of the draft?

2. (For question 1) Is appropriate evidence used to explain the argument? Is the evidence accurately explained? How could this evidence be revised?

3. (For questions 2 and 3) Are appropriate details presented about the lyric, performer, or popular music form? Should more detail be included here? If so, what types of detail?

4. Which paragraph seems to be the most effective? Explain why.

5. Edit for obvious errors in spelling and organization. Then, edit for sentence errors and comma errors. Finally, revise for vague phrasing. Ask your instructor for help with any errors in sentences, commas, and word choice.

SELECTION 12: "PARALLEL WORLDS: THE SURPRISING SIMILARITIES (AND DIFFERENCES) OF COUNTRY-AND-WESTERN AND RAP" BY DENISE NOE

Denise Noe writes a revealing article comparing two very popular expressions of American popular culture—rap and country-and-western (C&W) music. Her question is one that few of us have considered: How do these two musical expressions differ, and how are they similar?

This article follows very carefully the organizational pattern of thesis support. Early on, Noe presents her argument and painstakingly supports this argument with ample evidence from these two musical worlds. This is a longer selection than the previous three and asks you to stretch some of your critical reading abilities.

READING/WRITING PREP

Before reading the selection, answer the following questions in a free-writing journal or in discussion:

1. Do you believe that any similarities exist between rap and C&W music?

2. What commentary do these two types of music make about America?

PREVIEWING

Preview the following selection. Read the first and last paragraph. Then move quickly through the article to get a sense for the evidence that Noe provides. Before you read critically, put into your own words what you think Noe's argument is.

Noe's argument:

_____

_____

_____

_____

_____

READING CRITICALLY

Now critically read the selection and complete the following outline as you read or after you finish. You may want to make this outline into a visual cluster of the important information.

Denise Noe

Parallel Worlds: The Surprising Similarities (and Differences) of Country-and-Western and Rap

1 In all of popular music today, there are probably no two **genres** that are more apparently dissimilar than country-and-western and rap: the one rural, white, and southern; the other urban, black, and identified with the two coasts ("New York style" versus "L.A. style"). Yet C&W and rap are surprisingly similar in many ways. In both C&W and rap, for example, lyrics are important. Both types of music tell stories, as do folk songs, and the story is much more than frosting for the rhythm and beat.

2   The **ideologies** espoused by these types of music are remarkably similar as well. We frequently stereotype country fans as simple-minded conservatives–"redneck," moralistic super-patriots a la Archie Bunker.

But country music often speaks critically of mainstream American plat-
itudes, especially in such highly charged areas as sexual morality, crime,
and the Protestant work ethic.

3   The sexual **ethos** of C&W and rap are depressingly similar: the men
of both genres are champion **chauvinists.** Country singer Hank
Williams, Jr., declares he's "Going Hunting Tonight," but he doesn't need
a gun since he's hunting the "she-cats" in a singles bar. Male rappers
such as Ice-T, Ice Cube, and Snoop Doggy Dogg are stridently **misogy-
nist,** with "bitches" and "hos" their trademark terms for half of human-
ity; their enthusiastic depictions of women raped and murdered are
terrifying. Indeed, the sexism of rap group NWA (Niggaz with Attitude)
reached a real-life nadir when one member of the group beat up a
woman he thought "dissed" them—and was praised for his brutality by
the other members.

4   On a happier note, both rap and C&W feature strong female voices as
well. Women rappers are strong, confident, and raunchy: "I want a man,
not a boy/to approach me/Your lame game really insults me. . . . I've got
to sit on my feet to come down to your level," taunt lady rappers Entice
and Barbie at Too Short in their duet/duel, "Don't Fight the Feeling,"
Likewise, Loretta Lynn rose to C&W fame with defiant songs like "Don't
Come Home a-Drinkin' with Lovin' on Your Mind" and "Your Squaw Is
on the Warpath Tonight."

5   Country music can be bluntly honest about the realities of sex and
money—in sharp contrast to the "family values" rhetoric of the right. "Son
of Hickory Hollow's Tramp" by Johnny Darrell salutes a mother who
works as a prostitute to support her children. "Fancy" by Bobbie Gentry
(and, more recently, Reba McEntire) describes a poverty-stricken
woman's use of sex for survival and her rise to wealth on the ancient
"gold mine." Both tunes are unapologetic about the **pragmatic** coping
strategies of their heroines.

6   More startling than the resemblances in their male sexism and
"uppity" women are the parallels between C&W and rap in their treatment of criminality. Country-and-western music is very far from a rigid
law-and-order mentality. The criminal's life is celebrated for its excite-
ment and clear-cut rewards—a seemingly promising alternative to the
dull grind of day-to-day labor.

7   "Ain't got no money/Ain't got no job/Let's find a place to rob," sings
a jaunty Ricky Van Shelton in "Crime of Passion." In "I Never Picked
Cotton," Roy Clark is more subdued but still unrepentant when he says:
"I never picked cotton/like my mother did and my sister did and my
brother did/And I'll never die young/working in a coal mine like my
daddy did." Waylon Jennings' "Good Ole Boys" boast gleefully of having
"hot-wired a city truck/turned it over in the mayor's yard."

8   Similarly, rap songs like "Gangsta, Gangsta" and "Dopeman" by
NWA and "Drama" by Ice-T tell of the thrill and easy money offered by a

life of crime. "Drama" records the dizzying high of the thief; "Gangsta, Gangsta," the rush of adrenaline experienced by a murderer making a quick getaway. Of course, both C&W and rap songs do express the idea that in the long run crime doesn't pay. The sad narrator of Merle Haggard's "Mama Tried" "turned 21 in prison/doing life without parole," while the thief of Ice-T's "Drama" is forced to realize that "I wouldn't be here if I'd fed my brain/Got knowledge from schoolbooks/'stead of street crooks/Now all I get is penitentiary hard looks."

9   Though both C&W and rap narrators are often criminals, their attitudes toward law enforcement differ radically. The Irish Rovers' "Wasn't That a Party?" ("that little drag race down on Main Street/was just to see if the cops could run") pokes light-hearted fun at the police, while the Bobby Fuller Four's "I Fought the Law and the Law Won" expresses the most common C&W attitude: an acceptance that criminals must be caught, even if you are one. Neither song displays any anger toward the police, who are, after all, just doing their job.

10   To rappers, on the other hand, cops are the enemy. Two of the most notorious rap songs are Ice-T's "Cop Killer" and NWA's "Fuck tha Police" (which angrily asserts, "Some police think they have the authority to kill a minority"). Despite ample evidence of police brutality in the inner city, "Fuck tha Police" was almost certainly regarded by nonblack America as a paranoid shriek–until the world witnessed the infamous videotape of several of Los Angeles' finest brutally beating Rodney King while a dozen other "peace officers" nonchalantly looked on.

11   Interestingly, although the C&W view of law enforcement naturally sits better with the general public (certainly with the police themselves), the fact remains that country-and-western music contains a good deal of crime, violence, and casual sex. Yet it is easily accepted by white Americans while rap arouses alarm and calls for labeling. Why?

12   I believe there are three major reasons. The first, and simplest, is language. Rappers say "bitch," "ho," "fuck," and "motherfucker"; C&W artists don't. Country singers may say, "I'm in the mood to speak some French tonight" (Mary Chapin-Carpenter, "How Do") or "There's two kinds of cherries/and two kinds of fairies" (Merle Haggard, "My Own Kind of Hat"), but they avoid the bluntest Anglo-Saxon terms.

13   A second reason is race. African-Americans have a unique history of oppression in this country, and rap reflects the inner city African-American experience. Then, too, whites expect angry, frightening messages from blacks and listen for them. Many blacks, on the other hand, hope for uplifting messages–and are dismayed when black artists seem to encourage or glorify the drug abuse and violence in their **beleaguered** communities. Thus, the focus on violence in rap–and the dismissal of same in C&W.

14   While the differing attitudes toward law enforcement are real enough, much of the difference between violence in country-and-western music

and in rap lies not in the songs themselves but in the way they are heard. Thus, when Ice Cube says, "Let the suburbs see a nigga invasion/Point-blank, smoke the Caucasian," many whites interpret that as an incitement to violence. But when Johnny Cash's disgruntled factory worker in "Oney" crows, "Today's the day old Oney gets his," it's merely a joke. Likewise, when Ice Cube raps, "I've got a shotgun and here's the plot/ Taking niggas out with the fire of buckshot" ("Gangsta, Gangsta"), he sends shudders through many African-Americans heartbroken by black-on-black violence; but when Johnny Cash sings of an equally nihilistic killing in "Folsom Prison Blues"–"shot a man in Reno/just to watch him die"–the public taps its feet and hums along. . . . It's just a song, after all.

15   There is a third–and ironic–reason why rap is so widely attacked: rap is actually closer to mainstream American economic ideology than country-and-western is. While C&W complains about the rough life of honest labor for poor and working-class people, rap ignores it almost entirely. "Work your fingers to the bone and what do you get?" asks Hoyt Axton in a satirical C&W song, then answers sardonically with its title: "Bony Fingers." Likewise, Johnny Paycheck's infamous "Take this Job and Shove It" is a blue-collar man's bitter protest against the rough and repetitive nature of his life's work. Work in C&W is hard and meaningless; it keeps one alive, but leaves the worker with little time or energy left to enjoy life.

16   Songs by female country singers reinforce this point in a different way; they insist that love (with sex) is more important than affluence. The heroine of Reba McEntire's "Little Rock" says she'll have to "slip [her wedding ring] off," feeling no loyalty to the workaholic husband who "sure likes his money" but neglects his wife's emotional and physical needs. Jeanne Pruett in "Back to Back" **lampoons** the trappings of wealth and proclaims, "I'd trade this mansion/for a run-down shack/and a man who don't believe in sleeping back to back."

17   Rap's protagonists, on the other hand, are shrewd, materialistic, and rabidly ambitious–although the means to their success are officially proscribed in our society. Not for them a "life that moves at a slower pace" (Alabama, "Down Home"); unlike the languorous hero of country-and-western, "catching these fish like they're going out of style" (Hank Williams, Jr., "Country State of Mind"), rap singers and rap characters alike are imbued with the great American determination to get ahead.

18   Rap's protagonists–drug dealers, burglars, armed robbers, and "gangstas"–live in a society where success is "a fistful of jewelry" (Eazy E, "No More ?s"), "Motorola phones, Sony color TVs" (Ice-T, "Drama"), where "without a BMW you're through" (NWA, "A Bitch Iz a Bitch"). In NWA's "Dopeman," sometimes cited as an anti-drug song, the "Dopeman" is the archetypal American entrepreneur: clever, organized, ruthless, and not ruled by impulse–"To be a dopeman you must qualify/ Don't get high off your own supply."

19   The proximity of rap to our success ethic arouses hostility because America is torn by a deep ideological contradiction: we proudly proclaim ourselves a moral (even religious) nation and tout our capitalist economic system. But the reality of a successful capitalist system is that it undermines conventional morality. A glance at the history books shows how our supposedly moral nation heaped rewards upon the aptly named "robber barons": the Rockefellers, Vanderbilts, Carnegies, and Morgans. The crack dealer is a contemporary version of the bootlegger—at least one of whom, Joe Kennedy, Sr., founded America's most famous political dynasty. (Indeed; I would not be surprised if history repeated itself and the son—or daughter—of a drug lord becomes this country's first African-American president.)

20   Capitalism is unparalleled in its ability to create goods and distribute services, but it is, like the hero of "Drama," "blind to what's wrong." The only real criterion of a person's worth becomes how much money she or he has—a successful crook is treated better than a poor, law-abiding failure.

21   In short, the laid-back anti-materialist of country-and-western can be dismissed with a shrug, but the rapper is attacked for that unforgivable sin: holding a mirror up to unpleasant truths. And one of them is that amoral ambition is as American as apple pie and the Saturday Night Special.

SOURCE: *The Humanist* 55, no. 4 (July-August 1995), p. 20.

OUTLINING/CLUSTERING

I. The ideology of C&W

_____

II. The attitude toward sex in rap and C&W

A. Rap: _____

B. C&W: _____

III. The voices of women in rap and C&W

A. Rap: _____

B. C&W: _____

genres: types of artistic works; **ideologies:** a people's ways of thinking;
ethos: the distinguishing attitudes of a particular group;
chauvinists: persons unreasonably devoted to their race or sex;
misogynists: persons, usually men, who hate women;
pragmatic: practical; **beleaguered:** surrounded with negative
commentary; **lampoons:** strongly criticizes or satirizes

IV. The attitude toward law enforcement in rap and C&W

    A. Rap: _____

    B. C&W: _____

V. Reasons why many people fear rap music

    A. _____

    B. _____

    C. _____

VI. How rap music is an expression of capitalism

_____

A SECOND READING

Reread the Noe selection and answer the following questions as you read. Before answering these questions, you may want to write in your reading journal about any questions or comments you have about the selection.

1. Paraphrase this sentence in paragraph 3: "The ideologies of C&W and rap are depressingly similar: the men of both genres are champion chauvinists."

2. In paragraph 10, Noe refers to Rodney King. What is her purpose for providing this piece of evidence?

3. In paragraph 15, Noe comments on why she believes rap is so "widely attacked." What is she inferring here about American capitalists?

4. Summarize the "deep ideological contradiction" that American capitalists face (paragraph 19).

5. In paragraph 21, Noe refers to "apple pie" and the "Saturday Night Special." Why does she place these two phrases together?

READING/WRITING FEATURE: ACADEMIC WRITING

In college, you will come across several types of writing–autobiographies, works of fiction, journalistic writing, and academic pieces, to name a few. The Noe selection is an example of academic writing: formal writing that represents a specific discipline. Noe is writing from a humanities perspective. Each type of academic writing has a different set of standards. Scientific writing, for example, differs from writing in the humanities or the arts.

All academic writing is known for the particular diction, or word choice, it uses. Each discipline has a specific vocabulary that students in that field know. Denise Noe is a cultural critic, so much of the language in her "Parallel Worlds" comes from the humanities, such as "ideologies" (paragraph 2), "genres" (paragraph 3), "sexual ethos" (paragraph 3), and "protagonists" (paragraph 17). The more you study a particular field, the more familiar you become with its language.

In academic writing, sentences are often longer and more complex than those you would normally see in newspaper and magazine articles. Also, ways of proving a point vary with each discipline. In most of the sciences, experiments are analyzed, and the scientific method is emphasized. In the social sciences, studies are analyzed, and statistics are valued. In the humanities and the arts, evidence and details are carefully interpreted, as seen in the Noe selection.

As a college student, you are not expected to fully understand academic writing when you first study it nor write in the academic voice of that discipline right away. As you continue to study a field and when you select a major, your reading and writing will become more proficient with each course you complete.

When you come upon academic writing, as a reader, you should ask the following questions:

1. Do I understand the vocabulary?
2. If the sentences are long, can I paraphrase them?
3. What type of information (experimental results, statistical studies, interpretation of evidence, etc.) seems important?
4. Can I identify the argument? Can I locate the evidence used to support this argument?

As a writer, do not expect to be proficient in a particular discipline right away. You will develop this academic voice as you continue to study in this field. If you do use the vocabulary of the discipline in your writing, be sure to understand what each term means.

BEFORE YOU WRITE

Before selecting a writing topic, you may want to study the colon and complete Practice A12 (pages 221–222), then study colloquialisms and complete Practice B12 (pages 249–250) of the handbook.

WRITING TOPICS

Choose an essay topic from the following questions. Follow the steps of the writing process on the inside front cover.

Writing about the Reading

1. Using evidence from the Denise Noe selection, compare the ways that rap and C&W music are similar and different in regard to how they

understand sexuality, women, crime, and capitalism. Are there any other similarities or differences that Noe has overlooked? You may want to refer to the organizational pattern of compare-contrast on pages 38–40 as you draft your essay.

2. Denise Noe contends that the American public has a strong dislike for rap music. Examine the argument that she makes for her claim. Do you agree? Or do you believe that rap music is more accepted among Americans than she believes?

Writing from Experience

3. Choose a rap or C&W artist whom you particularly enjoy. Say why you find his or her music particularly appealing and what it says about American society. You may want to examine specific lyrics from the artist's work.

4. Now that you have completed four selections on American popular culture, you may want to reflect on the significance that the media and music have on your life. Write an essay that describes your relationship to the media and music. Talk about the types of media and music that you enjoy and how important or unimportant they are to your daily work and leisure schedule.

RESPONDING TO STUDENT WRITING

Use some or all of these questions to respond to your draft or to that of your classmate. Read carefully for meaning and make your comments specific.

1. Is the introduction to the draft clear? Is Noe's argument or the student's argument about the particular musician clear? Should the argument be revised in any way?

2. (For questions 1 and 2) Is the evidence from the Noe article clearly explained, or is the Noe material not completely understood? If so, how should the explanation of Noe be revised?

3. (For question 3) Is the evidence describing the musician adequate? Do you have a sense for why this musician is successful? What other information do you need?

4. Choose one paragraph that is most successfully argued. Explain why.

5. Edit for obvious errors in spelling and punctuation. Edit carefully for the correct uses of commas. Ask your instructor for help if you are unsure of any comma-related errors.

FOLLOW-UP

Now that you have read several selections on television and popular music, answer the following questions either in a free-writing journal or in discussion:

1. What are the most important points made in these selections about television and television commercials, rap music, and C&W music?

2. Which points about television and popular music do you agree with? Which points do you disagree with? Are there any insights that you have about today's television programming and rap and C&W music that were not mentioned in these selections? If so, explain them.

EXERCISE AND HEALTH: SELECTIONS 13–16

In the following four selections, you will study how exercise relates to your health. You will be introduced to the key terms in fitness medicine and read about studies treating how moderate exercise and strenuous exercise can improve your health. As you study the last two selections, you will learn about how scientific experiments are conducted–which ones are sound and which ones should be questioned. By the end of these four selections, you should know more about what you can do to improve your own fitness program, as well as how to better read and write about scientific material.

The four selections are titled:

Selection 13: From "Introduction to Lifetime Physical Fitness and Wellness" by Werner W. K. Hoeger and Sharon Hoeger
Selection 14: "Can You Be Fit and Fat?" by Jan Sheehan
Selection 15: "How Far Should You Go to Stay Fit?" by Lynn Rosellini
Selection 16: "Burning Calories May Be Easier Than You Think" by Patricia Andersen-Parrado

As you read these selections, you will also learn about the following aspects of reading and writing:

READING/WRITING FEATURES	GRAMMAR/USAGE	WRITING CONVENTIONS
Selection 13 Understanding Scientific Material	Appositives	Sentence Variety
Selection 14 Cause and Effect in Scientific Studies	Dashes	Paraphrases That Are Too Similar
Selection 15 Understanding Scientific Studies	Noun Clauses	Active and Passive Constructions
Selection 16 The Logic of Scientific Writing	There is . . . There are	Sentence Length

READING/WRITING PREP

You may want to answer the following questions in a free-writing journal or in group discussion before you begin reading these four selections. Answering these questions should help you determine how much you know and don't know about exercise and health.

1. How much do you exercise each day? Does it seem to help you keep your weight down?
2. What are some of the qualities that make a person fit today?
3. Do you think joggers tend to be healthier than those who merely walk regularly?
4. How do you think weight is related to your health?

SELECTION 13: FROM "INTRODUCTION TO LIFETIME PHYSICAL FITNESS AND WELLNESS" BY WERNER W. K. HOEGER AND SHARON HOEGER

This excerpt comes from a college health textbook titled *Lifetime Physical Fitness and Wellness*. This selection is part of the first chapter, in which the authors introduce their readers to a series of health terms related to fitness and health that they use throughout their textbook.

This excerpt relies on the organizational pattern of definition. The authors Hoeger and Hoeger introduce key fitness and health terms, then show how these terms relate to each other. This material provides an important introduction to the discussion of fitness and health. You can then use this knowledge as you read the remaining three selections.

READING/WRITING PREP

Before reading this selection, you may want to answer the following questions in a free-writing journal or in group discussion:

1. How would you define physical activity and exercise?
2. How would you define wellness?

PREVIEWING

Preview the following selection to determine which terms the excerpt will discuss. Move quickly through the entire selection. Before you read critically, list the terms that will be explored in this excerpt.

List of terms to be defined:

_____

_____

_____

_____

_____

READING CRITICALLY

Now critically read the selection, and complete the following outline as you read or after you finish. You may want to make this outline into a visual cluster of the important information.

Werner W. K. Hoeger and Sharon Hoeger

From "Introduction to Lifetime Physical Fitness and Wellness"

Physical Activity Versus Exercise

1 Based on the abundance of scientific research on physical activity and exercise over the last three decades, a clear distinction has been established between physical activity and exercise. _Physical activity_ is defined as bodily movement produced by skeletal muscles that requires energy expenditure and produces progressive health benefits.[1] Examples of physical activity are walking to and from work and the store, taking stairs (instead of elevators and escalators), gardening, doing household chores, dancing, and washing the car by hand. Physical inactivity, on the other hand, implies a level of activity that is lower than that required to maintain good health.

2   _Exercise_ is considered a type of physical activity that requires "planned, structured, and repetitive bodily movement done to improve or maintain one or more components of physical fitness."[2] A regular weekly program of walking, jogging, cycling, aerobics, swimming, strength training, or stretching exercises are all examples of exercise.

Surgeon General's Report on Physical Activity and Health

3 A landmark report on the influence of regular physical activity on health was released in July of 1996 by the U.S. Surgeon General.[3] The significance of this historic document cannot be underestimated. Until 1996, only two previous reports had been released by the Surgeon General: one on smoking and health in 1964 and a second one on nutrition and

health in 1988. More than 1,000 scientific studies from the fields of epidemiology, exercise physiology, medicine, and the behavioral sciences are summarized in this document on physical activity and health.

4 The report states that regular moderate physical activity provides substantial benefits in health and well-being for the vast majority of Americans who are not physically active. Among these benefits are a significant reduction in the risk of developing or dying from heart disease, diabetes, colon cancer, and high blood pressure. Regular physical activity is important for health of muscles, bones, and joints. It seems to reduce symptoms of depression and anxiety, improve mood, and enhance the ability to perform daily tasks throughout life. For individuals who are moderately active already, greater health benefits can be achieved by increasing the amount of physical activity.

5 According to the Surgeon General, improving health through physical activity is a serious public health issue that we must meet head-on at once. More than 60% of adults do not achieve the recommended amount of physical activity, and 25% are not physically active at all. Further, almost half of all people between age 12 and 21 are not vigorously active on a regular basis. This report has become a call to nationwide action.

6 Regular moderate physical activity can prevent premature death, unnecessary illness, and disability. It can also help control health care costs and help to maintain a high quality of life into old age. In the report, *moderate physical activity* has been defined as physical activity that uses 150 calories of energy per day, or 1,000 calories per week. People should strive to achieve at least 30 minutes of physical activity per day most days of the week. Examples of moderate physical activity include walking, cycling, playing basketball or volleyball, swimming, water aerobics, dancing fast, pushing a stroller, raking leaves, shoveling snow, washing or waxing a car, washing windows or floors, and gardening.

7 Most people recognize that participating in fitness programs improves their quality of life. In recent years, however, we came to realize that improving physical fitness alone was not always sufficient to lower the risk for disease and ensure better health. For example, individuals who run 3 miles (about 5 km) a day, lift weights regularly, participate in stretching exercises, and watch their body weight can be classified as having good or excellent fitness. If these same people, however, have high blood pressure, smoke, are under constant stress, consume alcohol excessively, and eat too many fatty foods, they are at risk for **cardiovascular** disease and may not be aware of it. These characteristics that predict which people may develop a certain disease are called *risk factors.*

8 One of the best examples that good fitness does not always provide a risk-free guarantee of a healthy and productive life was the tragic death in 1984 of Jim Fixx, author of the best selling book *The Complete Book of Running.* At the time of his death by heart attack, Fixx was 52 years old. He had been running between 60 and 80 miles a week and had believed that people at his high level of fitness could not die from heart disease.

9   At age 36, Jim Fixx smoked two packs of cigarettes per day, weighed about 215 pounds, did not participate in regular physical activity, and had a family history of heart disease. His father, having had a first heart attack at age 35, later died at age 43.

10   Perhaps in an effort to lessen his risk for heart disease, Fixx began to raise his level of fitness. He started to jog, lost 50 pounds, and quit cigarette smoking. On several occasions, though, Fixx declined to have an exercise **electrocardiogram** (ECG) test, which most likely would have revealed his cardiovascular problem. His unfortunate death is a tragic example that exercise programs by themselves will not make high-risk people immune to heart disease, though they may delay the onset of a serious or fatal problem.

11   Good health, therefore, no longer is viewed as simply the absence of illness. The notion of good health has evolved notably in the last few years and continues to change as scientists learn more about lifestyle factors that bring on illness and affect wellness. Once the idea took hold that fitness by itself would not always decrease the risk for disease and ensure better health, a new wellness concept developed in the 1980s.

Wellness

12   *Wellness* is defined as the constant and deliberate effort to stay healthy and achieve the highest potential for well-being. Wellness is an all-inclusive umbrella covering a variety of activities aimed at helping individuals recognize components of lifestyle that are detrimental to their health. Wellness living requires implementing positive programs to change behavior to improve health and quality of life, prolong life, and achieve total well-being.

13   To enjoy a wellness lifestyle, a person needs to practice behaviors that will lead to positive outcomes in the five dimensions of wellness: physical, emotional, intellectual, social, and spiritual. These dimensions are interrelated, and one dimension frequently affects the others. For example, a person who is emotionally down often has no desire to exercise, study, socialize with friends, or attend church.

14   In looking at the five dimensions of wellness, high-level wellness clearly goes beyond the absence of disease and optimal fitness. Wellness incorporates factors such as adequate fitness, proper nutrition, stress management, disease prevention, spirituality, smoking cessation, personal safety, substance abuse control, regular physical examinations, health education, and environmental support.

15   For a wellness way of life, not only must individuals be physically fit and **manifest** no signs of disease, but they also must have no risk factors for disease (such as **hypertension,** cigarette smoking, negative stress, faulty nutrition, careless sex). Even though an individual tested in a fitness center may demonstrate adequate or even excellent fitness, indulgence in unhealthy lifestyle behaviors still will increase the risk for chronic diseases and decrease the person's well-being.

Notes

1. National Institutes of Health, *Consensus Development Conference Statement: Physical Activity and Cardiovascular Health,* Washington, DC, December 18–20, 1995.
2. National Institutes of Health.
3. U. S. Department of Health and Human Services, "Physical Activity and Health: A Report of the Surgeon General," Atlanta, GA: U.S. Department of Health and Human Services, Centers for Disease Control and Prevention, National Center for Chronic Disease Prevention and Health Promotion, 1996.

SOURCE: Werner W.K. Hoeger and Sharon Hoeger. *Lifetime Physical Fitness and Wellness,* Morton, 1998, pp. 2–5.

OUTLINING/CLUSTERING

I. Definition of physical activity

_____

II. Definition of exercise

_____

III. Conclusions of Surgeon General's report

A. _____

B. _____

C. _____

IV. Definition of moderate physical exercise

_____

V. Definition of risk factors

_____

VI. Definition of wellness

_____

A SECOND READING

Reread the Hoeger and Hoeger excerpt and answer the following questions as you read. Before answering these questions, write in your reading journal about any questions or comments you have about the selection.

_____

cardiovascular: relating to the organism's heart and blood vessels; **electrocardiogram:** test used to measure the electrical potential of the heart when it contracts; **manifest:** reveal or show; **hypertension:** high blood pressure

1. How do the terms *"physical activity"* (paragraph 1) and *exercise* (paragraph 2) differ in meaning?

2. Why do the authors find the Surgeon General's report on physical activity so significant?

3. Why do the authors conclude that "good health, therefore, no longer is viewed as simply the absence of illness" (paragraph 11)?

4. Paraphrase this sentence from paragraph 12: "Wellness is an all-inclusive umbrella covering a variety of activities aimed at helping individuals recognize components of lifestyle that are detrimental to their health."

5. Why do Hoeger and Hoeger emphasize that the five dimensions of wellness are interrelated (paragraph 13)?

READING/WRITING FEATURE: UNDERSTANDING SCIENTIFIC MATERIAL

This excerpt is from a health textbook. Health is an applied study, relying to a large degree on the concepts in biology and chemistry. As you read material regarding health, you obtain a sense for how scientific material in biology, chemistry, and the applied sciences is written.

Scientific writing relies heavily on definitions. As you noticed in the fitness selection, the bulk of the writers' discussion centers around terms like *physical activity, exercise, risk factors,* and *wellness.* Each definition is carefully considered, so you should read and reread scientific definitions. You will find that there are no repetitive words and phrases in these definitions. As you read them, study how they compare with others in the discussion. For example, note how the terms *physical activity* and *exercise* are related in that exercise is a type of physical activity; however, note that exercise differs because it is a more intense physical activity that is "planned, structured, and repetitive" (paragraph 2). Note that each of these adjectives describes a different aspect of exercise.

Scientific writing also relies on the organizational pattern of cause and effect. Scientists often ask: How does X influence Y? In fact, so many of their experiments are based on these kinds of cause-effect questions. If you study paragraph 3, wherein the authors discuss the Surgeon General's 1996 report, you will notice that the central question asked is: How does physical activity affect wellness?

Scientific writing is characterized by an exact, concise style. It often presents its thesis, or *hypothesis,* early on and then analyzes the experimental results to prove this hypothesis. The conclusion often summarizes these results as it relates to the hypothesis.

As you read or write about scientific material, be sure that you can accomplish the following:

1. Understand each term that is presented and how one term relates to the other
2. Understand how each experiment was constructed and what it tried to prove
3. Clearly identify in each experiment the various causes and effects that relate to the particular study
4. Accurately summarize the procedures and results in the experiments that are discussed

BEFORE YOU WRITE

Before selecting a writing topic, you may want to study appositives and complete Practice A13 (pages 222–223); then study the use of sentence variety and complete Practice B13 (pages 250–252) of the handbook.

WRITING TOPICS

Choose an essay from the following questions. Follow the steps of the writing process summarized on the inside front cover as you complete your drafts.

Writing about the Reading

1. In an organized essay, define the important health terms in "Introduction to Lifetime Physical Fitness and Wellness." Show how they differ and how they are similar. Be sure the definitions you summarize are accurate.

2. In an organized essay, summarize the exercise history of Jim Fixx (paragraphs 8–10). Then, by using the terminology of this excerpt, show why exercise did not prevent his sudden death.

Writing from Experience

3. Write your own wellness profile. Describe your daily physical activities and your exercise program, if you follow one. Finally, describe your wellness lifestyle using the five dimensions of wellness listed in paragraph 13. Be sure you are using each fitness and wellness term correctly.

RESPONDING TO STUDENT WRITING

Use some or all of these questions to respond to your draft or to that of your classmate. Read carefully for meaning and make your comments specific.

1. How does the draft begin? Do you have a clear idea for where the essay is going? How could the beginning be more directed?

2. Is the material from the Hoeger and Hoeger selection presented accurately? Are there any terms that should be defined more clearly?

3. Choose a paragraph that is the most organized and logical. Explain why.

4. What is your overall reaction to the draft? In what ways is it successful? How can it be improved?

5. Edit for obvious errors in spelling and edit for any errors in the use of commas, semicolons, and colons. If you are unsure of any punctuation errors, ask your instructor for help.

SELECTION 14: "CAN YOU BE FIT AND FAT?" BY JAN SHEEHAN

The article "Can You Be Fit and Fat?" by Jan Sheehan is from a women's fitness magazine. It presents an interesting argument about weight and fitness that relies on recent medical studies.

This article incorporates the thesis-support organizational pattern throughout. Although dealing with several technical medical issues, this article can be read easily by the average reader.

READING/WRITING PREP

Before reading this selection, answer the following questions in a freewriting journal or in group discussion:

1. Do you consider yourself overweight? Why or why not?

2. What do you think it means to be overweight?

PREVIEWING

Preview the following selection. Look over the first and last paragraph to read for the argument. Then quickly move through the rest of the paragraphs to see the kinds of evidence the article uses.

Sheehan's argument:

_____

_____

_____

_____

_____

_____

READING CRITICALLY

Now critically read the selection and complete the following outline as you read or after you finish. You may want to make this outline into a visual cluster of the important information.

Jan Sheehan

Can You Be Fit And Fat?

1 You pound away on the treadmill, churn out endless laps in the pool and avoid all excess calories. These tough workouts and dietary sacrifices are a small price to pay, you tell yourself–if you can just drop two dress sizes, you'll finally be "in shape."

2   It may be time to give yourself a break–new research is **debunking** the notion that being thin equals being fit. In fact, studies show that some heavy people who exercise regularly can be healthier than couch potatoes with lean physiques.

3   "Fit bodies come in all shapes and sizes," says Glenn Gaesser, Ph.D., associate professor of exercise physiology at the University of Virginia in Charlottesville and author of *Big Fat Lies: The Truth About Your Weight and Your Health* (Ballantine, 1998). "An active woman who is 40 pounds overweight will probably stand a better chance of living a long, healthy life than a sedentary, slim woman. When it comes to overall health, it's very clear that fitness matters more than thinness."

Does Weight Really Matter?

4 Obesity (defined as being 20 percent or more over your ideal weight) has long been associated with hypertension, diabetes, **osteoarthritis,** heart disease and certain types of cancer. And public health officials are worried because we keep getting fatter: The percentage of overweight Americans rose from 24.4 percent in the 1960s to 34.8 percent by 1994. Spurred by our growing tubbiness, in 1998 the government set new weight standards using the body Mass Index (BMI). The bad news: A whopping 55 percent of Americans are now overweight.

5   But since then, a growing chorus of experts has begun questioning whether most people put too much emphasis on weight. "We know that the heavier you are, the higher your risk for certain diseases and early death," says Steven Blair, P.E.D., director of research at the Cooper Institute for Aerobics Research in Dallas. "But is the real problem being fat or being unfit?"

6   Until recently, little of the research into weight and health took fitness into account. But the latest findings show that becoming fit is likely to improve your health and prolong your life–no matter what your

weight. In several studies, Blair and his colleagues at the Cooper Institute found that physically fit people, whether tubby or teeny, lived longer than unfit folks. In one groundbreaking study, researchers followed 25,389 men of various weights and fitness levels between 1970 and 1989. (Fitness was measured with treadmill tests.) The results, reported in the *International Journal of Obesity,* showed that death rates among overweight but fit men were 66 percent lower than those among unfit men of normal weight. Similarly, a study of 7,080 women, reported in the *Journal of the American Medical Association,* found that fit women at all weights had death rates almost half those of unfit women.

7   Such findings are putting a new spin on the concept of fitness. "It's possible to be overweight and still be fit," says Blair. "If you're exercising regularly and eating a good diet, I say don't worry too much about your weight."

Finding the Best Size for You

8 For mere mortals, **replicating** the petite butts and flat tummies they see on TV may seem an impossible dream. "Look in the real world: How many people have bodies like models? Yet women are told they can look like that," says Kelly Brownell, Ph.D., director of the Yale University Center for Eating and Weight Disorders in New Haven, Connecticut. "Rather than being crazed about your weight, it's better to concentrate on being active."

9   But just because fat isn't necessarily bad doesn't mean it's good, either. So at what point *should* you become concerned about your weight? That's debatable. The various height and weight tables, such as those published by the Metropolitan Life Insurance Company, are a starting point. Most give ranges of "desirable weight" for small, average and large body frames based on longevity studies.

10   A more precise indication of unsafe weight is probably the BMI, a measure of weight in relation to height issued by the National Institutes of Health. Under the newest guidelines, a body mass of 25 or more is considered too pudgy and over 30 is deemed obese. (To figure your BMI, multiply your weight in pounds by 703. Then divide that number by your height in inches and divide the resulting number by your height in inches again.) However, even the much-touted BMI is not a perfect measure of fatness.

11   "It doesn't reflect fitness levels or body composition," says Lawrence Golding, Ph.D., professor of exercise physiology at the University of Nevada in Las Vegas. "A person can be overweight, but not overfat." In fact, many athletes—such as boxer Evander Holyfield and skier Picabo Street—have BMIs above 25 simply because their muscle mass pushes their body weight up.

12   Looking at past personal battles of the bulge may be a better indication of the healthiest size for you. "The best weight for most adults is simply the lowest they've been able to maintain for a year without struggling too

much," explains Brownell. If you've had to diet constantly and exercise **slavishly** to maintain a particular weight, it's probably too low for you.

How Your Body Type Can Boost Your Health

13   To some degree, your size is beyond your control. "You can defy genetics to a certain extent," says Gaesser. "By sheer **tenacity,** some people can restrict calories and exercise excessively to keep weight off. But that's darn hard to do over the long haul." Plus, it's difficult to alter your basic body shape, says Golding. "You inherit that."

14   Your **predetermined** packaging may be more an aesthetic annoyance than a health hazard, though. Doctors have found that people with pear-shaped physiques (heavier hips, thighs and buttocks) fare better than those with apple shapes (thickness around the middle) healthwise. Surplus belly fat, especially if it's stored around internal organs, can raise cholesterol, blood pressure and blood sugar levels.

15   And believe it or not, pudgy thighs may be healthy. A tantalizing study from the Stanford University School of Medicine found that thigh flab can reduce the risk of cardiovascular disease. The 1991 study involved moderately overweight people (130 women and 133 men) with a BMI in the 24 to 34 range. Those with the most thigh fat were found to have the best blood lipid profiles, according to results published in the journal *Metabolism.*

Healthy Women Don't Need to Lose

16   So is fighting fat pointless? Perhaps—if good health is the goal. To determine if you're healthy at your current size, look at your blood pressure, cholesterol and blood sugar levels, advises Blair. "If those are normal, there's no reason to lose weight," he says.

17   In fact, the health benefits of peeling off pounds may be negligible for women with no health problems. A 1995 study on intentional weight loss by the Centers for Disease Control and Prevention in Atlanta found that shedding weight had no effect on disease risk and mortality in healthy females. Of 43,457 overweight women between the ages of 40 and 64, the healthy ones showed no **mortality** improvement by losing weight— although women with weight-related health problems decreased their risk of early death by 20 percent.

18   Among those women, even small weight losses provided big health gains. The ones who lost between one and 19 pounds benefited as much as those who lost more, according to results published in the *American Journal of Epidemiology.* "That's important," says Gaesser. "If somebody wants to improve her health, it appears that losing a few pounds is just as helpful as losing 20 or more."

19   It's also important to assess your fitness goals. Setting practical strength, flexibility and cardio goals and taking systematic steps toward an improved body every day will enable you to get as fit as personally

possible. The bonus: long-term health and fitness–whether you're a size 6 or 16. "The belief that the perfect body will lead to the perfect job and the perfect life is nonsense," says Blair. "There will always be tall, skinny people and short, stocky people. That's out of our control. What we can do is exercise regularly, follow good health practices and live life to the fullest."

SOURCE: *Fitness*, July 1999, pp. 100–104.

OUTLINING/CLUSTERING

I. Definition of obesity

_____

II. Results of Cooper Institute Study

_____

II. Explanation of BMI

A. _____

B. _____

IV. Body types that seem to affect your health

A. _____

B. _____

V. Results of experiment from the Centers for Disease Control and Prevention

A. _____

B. _____

VI. The conclusions the article draws

A. _____

B. _____

debunking: exposing false claims; **osteoarthritis:** a joint disease worsened by mechanical stress; **replicating:** copying; **slavishly:** in a blindly dependent manner; **tenacity:** persistence; **predetermined:** settled beforehand; **mortality:** death on a large scale

A SECOND READING

Reread the Sheehan selection and answer the following questions as you read. Before answering these questions, write in your reading journal about any questions or comments that you have about the selection.

1. In paragraph 6, Sheehan presents a relationship between weight, fitness, and health. What is she suggesting here?

2. In paragraph 10, Sheehan shows the reader how to determine BMI—the relationship between weight and height. From the directions in this paragraph, determine your own BMI.

3. Paraphrase this first sentence in paragraph 14: "Your predetermined packaging may be more an aesthetic annoyance than a health hazard, though."

4. Summarize the experimental findings in paragraph 6.

5. Summarize the experimental findings in paragraph 17.

READING/WRITING FEATURE: CAUSE AND EFFECT IN SCIENTIFIC STUDIES

As you continue to read experimental results regarding fitness and health, you will note how central the cause-effect relationship is. The researchers on fitness and health usually consider an effect—overweight or wellness—then determine what causes it.

In the article you read, the essential cause-effect relationships concern the relationships between weight and health and fitness and health. That is, how does weight affect health, and how does fitness affect health? Weight and fitness are the causes; health is the effect. In the medical field and in most fields in the health sciences, these questions have no easy answers. So often, in the conclusion to these studies, you will note qualifiers, such as *may, it seems, likely,* or *suggests,* to describe the relationship.

Look at how the experimental results of the Cooper Institute rely on cause and effect (paragraph 6). The results read: ". . . becoming fit is likely to improve your health and prolong your life—no matter what your weight." Note that the qualifier "likely" to suggest that the relationship between fitness and health is not always the case. Health researchers know that illness and wellness are caused by a great number of factors, many of which the researchers themselves cannot identify. So to assume that one factor is the only cause for wellness is an unsound conclusion.

Note also in paragraph 6 how the experiment on fitness and health was conducted. About 25,000 men "of various weights and fitness levels" were studied between 1970 and 1989. The study assumed that fitness could be determined by a treadmill test. The results showed that "the death rates of overweight but fit men were 66 percent lower than those among unfit men of normal weight."

From these results, can we assume that fitness leads to a longer life and that being overweight is not a factor shortening life if the overweight person exercises? Such conclusions are not that easy to draw. All one can conclude is that exercise is a likely factor in extending life and that being overweight may not necessarily shorten one's life. There may be other activities that these overweight, yet fit males shared that were overlooked by the researcher and that contributed to their longer life.

As you read experimental studies in the health sciences, examine the conclusions. Look for qualifiers and question any conclusion that is stated without some qualifier attached to it. As you study the experiment, identify any other factors that may have contributed to the result shown by the experiment.

In all experiments in the health sciences that you come across, be sure that you accomplish the following:

1. Can identify cause and effect
2. Study how the experiment was conducted
3. Study the conclusions
4. Examine how the conclusions are worded

All too often the media presents an experimental result in fitness and health without providing the viewer with the necessary qualifiers. Many viewers thus make unwise life choices that could negatively affect their well-being.

BEFORE YOU WRITE

Before selecting a writing topic, you may want to study the uses of the dash and complete Practice A14 (pages 223–224); then study paraphrases that are too similar to the original and complete Practice B14 (pages 252–253) of the handbook.

WRITING TOPICS

Choose an essay topic from the following questions. Follow the steps of the writing process summarized on the inside front cover as you complete your drafts.

Writing about the Reading

1. Explain the argument that Sheehan presents in the article "Can You Be Fit and Fat?" Then analyze the most important evidence that she presents to support her argument. Is her argument convincing, or is there other evidence that you believe she needs to consider?

2. Analyze the two experiments discussed by Sheehan in her article. Carefully summarize each experiment and its conclusions. How do these experiments support Sheehan's argument? What other kinds of experiments do you think could be constructed to further support her argument?

Writing from Experience

3. Describe your body type as completely as you can. Use some of the terminology mentioned in paragraphs 14 and 15 of the selection. Have you ever dieted to change your body type? What were the results? Be detailed in your description of your diet and its results.

RESPONDING TO STUDENT WRITING

Use some or all of these questions to respond to your draft or to that of your classmate. Read carefully for meaning and make your comments specific.

1. Read the beginning of the draft to see if it has a clear direction. For questions 1 and 2, is Sheehan's argument carefully and clearly explained? If the beginning is not clear, provide suggestions for improving it.

2. Is the evidence used in the middle of the draft clear and accurate? If experiments are mentioned, are they correctly analyzed? What other evidence could be used in the middle of the draft?

3. Select a paragraph that is the least developed. State why and provide suggestions for improving it.

4. Select a paragraph that is the most organized and convincing. Explain why.

5. Edit for obvious errors in spelling and punctuation. Determine if the format for introducing the various quotes is correct. If you are unsure about a particular error, ask your instructor for help.

SELECTION 15: "HOW FAR SHOULD YOU GO TO STAY FIT?" BY LYNN ROSELLINI

This article is from a weekly magazine written for the reader wanting to keep abreast of important news events. Lynn Rosellini explores the question of how much exercise is effective for well-being. It is a bit more technical than the previous two selections.

Following the thesis-support organizational pattern, Rosellini presents her argument and then uses the results from experimental studies to support it. This article carefully analyzes these experiments, examining their strengths and weaknesses.

READING/WRITING PREP

Before reading this selection, answer the following questions in a free-writing journal or in group discussion:

1. How much do you exercise each week?
2. How much do you think you should exercise each week?

PREVIEWING

Preview the following selection. Look carefully at the first and last paragraph and quickly read through the experiments that Rosellini analyzes. Before you read critically, write how you think this article concludes.
Article's conclusion:

_____

_____

_____

_____

_____

READING CRITICALLY

Now critically read the selection and complete the following outline as you read or after you finish. You may want to make this outline into a visual cluster of the important information.

Lynn Rosellini

How Far Should You Go to Stay Fit? The Battle Between Tough and Tame

1 Oh, the horror. OK, so it's not really the final reckoning, but for nine women on black Reebok stationary bikes, it might as well be. Grunting and **grimacing,** they pedal madly in a windowless, mirrored room at the Tenley Sport & Health Club in Washington, D.C. The smell of perspiration hangs in the air, and sweat drips off noses, making handlebars slippery. "Tough it out!" shouts aerobics instructor Jan Wright above the sound of whirring wheels and pounding jazz.

2 Upstairs, a less taxing routine is in progress. Listening to disco music through her earphones, her breathing rate barely elevated, Catalina Rizo strides briskly around the club's rubberized indoor track. "I've read that

walking can be just as effective [as aerobics classes] if you do it at a certain pace," says Rizo, 58, whose pink T-shirt and sweats give her the air of a tourist out for a stroll around the Jefferson Memorial. "They say any exercise is good."

3   That may be the only point exercise experts agree on these days. The contrasting fitness routines on display at the Tenley club illustrate two warring philosophies about how much and what kind of exercise Americans should get.

4   Too good to be true? Wright's cycle class harks back to the dogma of the late 1970s, amplified by exercise **gurus** like Jane Fonda and Jim Fixx: A minimum of 20 minutes of continuous running, cycling, or other vigorous activity at least three times a week is essential to guard against heart disease, high blood pressure, and other diseases.

5   Rizo's workout reflects the revisionist message of a 1993 report from the federal Centers for Disease Control and Prevention and the American College of Sports Medicine. At the time, the new public-health message seemed impossible but delightful, at least to couch potatoes: Just 30 minutes of ordinary activities—like walking, playing with a child, or gardening—most days of the week could enhance cardiovascular health. That half-hour could be pieced together from several shorter bouts of activity, such as a morning walk to the bus stop and an evening stint of lawn mowing.

6   Now it turns out that the government's recommendations may have been too optimistic. A cadre of researchers contend that the panel let public-health advocacy get in the way of good science. "I think it was deliberate on the part of the CDC and ACSM to make their guidelines more **palatable** [to the public]," says Paul D. Thompson, director of preventive cardiology at Hartford Hospital in Connecticut and president-elect of the American College of Sports Medicine. The CDC/ACSM panel "really made those recommendations without solid scientific proof," he says.

7   Risky calculation. Exercise experts are not simply squabbling over details. How much Americans exercise has an enormous impact on public health. The CDC estimates that lack of regular exercise kills as many as 250,000 Americans each year—about 12 percent of the total who die. People who don't exercise have twice as great a risk of coronary heart disease as those who exercise regularly. Middle-aged women are more likely to die of heart disease than breast cancer by a factor of more than 2 to 1. Moderate to strenuous exercise also lowers chances of developing diabetes, osteoporosis, colon cancer, anxiety, and depression.

8   The most roundly criticized aspect of the government's report was the contention that short, intermittent bouts of exercise are as good for health as a solid half-hour workout. The dispute stems partly from the CDC/ACSM panel's interpretation of studies that measured health gains among men who had a variety of weekly exercise routines. The men reported the amount they exercised but did not specify whether the

activity was continuous or intermittent. The panel assumed that the men's workouts were broken up into short segments, although two of the scientists who conducted the studies contend that the nature of some of the activities, such as swimming, indicates that subjects often exercised for sustained periods.

9   Critics also fault the panel's interpretation of the results of other studies, including one by the Cooper Institute for Aerobics Research in Dallas. That 1989 study assigned 13,000 men and women to one of five fitness categories, based on their performances on a treadmill. Over an eight-year period, researchers found that the least fit group had proportionally many more deaths than did those in the next, slightly fitter, group. The Cooper researchers didn't report on their subjects' exercise routines. But from studies showing that people have to exercise only moderately to become as fit as the slightly fitter group, the researchers concluded that moderate physical activity lowered death rates.

10   The main problem with relying on those conclusions, critics say, is that the panel used measures of fitness, not actual physical exercise, to come up with its workout guidelines. Fitness is determined by more than just exercise; another key factor is genetic predisposition, points out Paul Williams, an exercise researcher at Lawrence Berkeley National Laboratory in Berkeley, Calif. "This is the government policy that confused genes with walking shorts," he says.

11   Members of the panel counter that they assessed dozens of studies that, when taken as a whole, show that moderate amounts of exercise can help prevent disease and promote good health. Russell Pate, the lead author of the report and an exercise physiologist at the University of South Carolina, now **concedes** that panel members took their best guess when they asserted that intermittent activity confers the same health benefits as continuous activity, but he says, "I have great confidence in the fundamental conclusions [of the guidelines]."

12   The purpose of those conclusions, supporters of the guidelines say, is to get the public off its duff. Despite all the publicity about the health value of physical activity, some 60 percent of Americans engage in little or no exercise. "The public-health approach is, 'Get them started, something is better than nothing,'" says University of Minnesota epidemiologist Arthur Leon, one of the authors of the report.

13   But in the effort to get people started, critics say, the panel may have set the bar too low. By exaggerating the benefits of moderate exercise, according to Williams, the government may have discouraged some people from the kind of rigorous workouts that yield far greater health benefits.

14   To date, however, the guidelines appear to have done little to alter the way Americans exercise. "There's no data to say with any confidence that anything has changed," says Carl J. Caspersen, a physical activity epidemiologist for the CDC.

15   Despite the controversy over the benefits of low-sweat exercise, the experts have reached a consensus on a couple of basic rules: The more variety you have in an exercise program—mixing running, swimming, and cycling, for instance—the less likely you are to get injured. And, in most cases, the more exercise, the better. Williams's studies of female runners, for instance, show that those who increase their mileage from 10 miles a week to 40 miles a week can expect to decrease their chances of coronary heart disease by 29 percent (while **incurring** a somewhat greater risk of injury as a result of the increased mileage). To him, and to other experts, those taunting mottoes from the '80s—"no pain, no gain," "go for the burn"—were right, after all. Oh, the horror . . .

SOURCE: *US News & World Report* 123, no. 18 (November 10, 1997): p. 95.

OUTLINING/CLUSTERING

   I. 1970's attitude toward exercise

   _____

   II. Revisionist message of 1993 concerning exercise

   _____

   III. Risks of not exercising

      A. _____

      B. _____

      C. _____

   IV. Faults with the government report on exercise

      A. _____

      B. _____

   V. Conclusions regarding exercise

      A. _____

      B. _____

   grimacing: distorting the facial features; **gurus:** spiritual guides; **palatable:** agreeable; **concedes:** admits as true; **incurring:** acquiring or receiving

A SECOND READING

Reread the Rosellini selection and answer the following questions as you read. Before answering these questions, you may want to write in your reading journal about any questions or comments you have about the selection.

1. In paragraph 8, Rosellini refers to two types of exercise: continuous and intermittent. What are these two types of exercise, and how do they differ?

2. In paragraph 10, Rosellini refers to "measures of fitness." What are they, and how do they challenge the experimental conclusions?

3. In paragraph 10, the phrase "genetic predisposition" is introduced. What do you think this phrase means?

4. Paraphrase the following sentence in paragraph 13: "By exaggerating the benefits of moderate exercise, according to Williams, the government may have discouraged some people from the kind of vigorous workouts that yield far greater health benefits."

5. In paragraph 15, Rosellini says that the mottoes from the eighties were correct. Why does she make this statement?

READING/WRITING FEATURE: UNDERSTANDING SCIENTIFIC STUDIES

The scientific studies you have read about in the last three selections all tend to follow certain analytical practices. Writers interpreting scientific studies carefully describe how the experiment was conducted, listing the number of participants, the activities of the participants, the categories in which they were placed, and the terminology they used. From this description, the writers can then draw conclusions from the studies.

Review paragraph 9 to see how the 1989 study of the Cooper Institute for Aerobics Research was analyzed. Rosellini first looked at the number of people studied (13,000), mentioned the number of fitness categories (five), listed the activity (treadmill performance), and noted the length of time that these participants were studied (eight years). Then she presented the conclusions of the experiment: "moderate physical activity lowered death rates."

Following this presentation of the experiment, Rosellini critiqued the conclusions, noting that the definition of fitness was incomplete. Fitness is more than physical exercise because there is also a genetic component to being fit. Because critics saw this definition as incomplete, they could call the experiments' conclusions into question. The key question that the experimenters did not consider was: Doesn't genetic makeup also affect death rates?

Here are some of the questions you need to ask as you read scientific studies and their analyses:

1. How many participants were in the study? The larger the number of participants, the greater the validity of the conclusions.

2. How long was the study carried out? Studies that are monitored over time are known as longitudinal studies. You need to determine the value of studying a particular question over a period. For example, what is the importance of tracking the 13,000 participants of the Cooper Institute over an eight-year span?

3. What terms were used? Are these terms defined in an acceptable way? Does the definition of a particular term alter the results of the experiment? You saw in the previous experimental analysis that the particular definition of fitness that the researchers gave affected their conclusions.

4. What conclusions were drawn? You should ask if any other conclusions could be drawn from the same information.

5. How can these conclusions be applied to lifestyle changes? You must be sure that a change of lifestyle is warranted by the experimental results. Sometimes experimental results are misinterpreted, and changes in behavior are inappropriate. For example, it may not be the case that the government's recommendations for light, intermittent exercises, as opposed to moderate exercise, positively affects health.

As you read and write about experimental studies, be sure you study and critique the information carefully. As you have seen in the Rosellini selection, conclusions drawn from experimental studies are difficult to prove.

BEFORE YOU WRITE

Before selecting a writing topic, you may want to study the uses of the noun clause and complete Practice A15 (pages 224–225); then study the active and passive constructions and complete Practice B15 (pages 253–254) of the handbook.

WRITING TOPICS

Choose an essay topic from the following questions. Follow the steps of the writing process summarized on the inside front cover as you complete your drafts.

Writing about the Reading

1. In an organized essay, explain the dispute between those who favor "short, intermittent exercise" with "a solid half-hour workout" as they relate to health. Carefully present and analyze the experimental studies that Rosellini discusses to explain both positions. Having analyzed the evidence in this selection, which side of the argument are you on? Why?

Writing from Experience

2. Describe several fitness or exercise programs that you have tried in your life. Which were the most successful, and which were least successful? Why?

3. Describe your current exercise program and be as detailed as you can. What are the benefits that you have seen?

RESPONDING TO STUDENT WRITING

Use some or all of these questions to respond to your draft or to that of your classmate. Read carefully for meaning and make your comments specific.

1. Does the draft begin clearly? What part of the introduction is still unclear to you? What types of revision do you suggest?

2. How is the experimental evidence or the details from personal exercise experiences presented? Are they clear? Are they accurate? How could they be revised?

3. Which paragraph seems the most successful to you? Why?

4. Which paragraph seems the least successful to you? Why?

5. Edit for obvious errors in spelling and punctuation. Edit for the correct use of semicolons, colons, and dashes. If you are unsure about how a particular punctuation should be used, ask your instructor for help.

SELECTION 16: "BURNING CALORIES MAY BE EASIER THAN YOU THINK" BY PATRICIA ANDERSEN-PARRADO

This article concerns how exercise relates to weight loss. As in the previous selection, Patricia Andersen-Parrado debates whether mild or moderate exercise is preferred.

Like Selection 15, "Burning Calories" carefully analyzes experimental studies related to exercise. It is also as technical as Selection 15.

READING/WRITING PREP

Before reading this selection, answer the following questions in a free-writing journal or in group discussion:

1. Do you consider yourself active or inactive?
2. What are some of the physical activities that you do each day?

PREVIEWING

Preview the following selection, in which three important experiments are analyzed carefully. Move through this selection quickly and locate these three experiments.

Before you read critically, see if you can name these three research studies.

Names of the three experiments:

_____

_____

_____

_____

_____

READING CRITICALLY

Now critically read the selection, and complete the following outline as you read or after you finish. You may want to make this outline into a visual cluster of the important information.

Patricia Andersen-Parrado

Burning Calories May Be Easier Than You Think

1 While some people "just can't stay still" and find sports and fitness-related activities to be quite exhilarating, others are content curling up with a good book or movie, and not moving a muscle for hours at a time.

2   While maintaining a healthy weight is probably easier for the former, rather than the latter, group, it's a goal which may be achievable for both types, if you're willing to put at least some action into your day, according to some recent studies.

Fidgeting your way to weight loss

3   At one time or another, we've all read weight-loss articles advising us that "simple things," such as—taking the stairs instead of the elevator, getting up off the couch to change the channel instead of using the remote control, or hopping off the bus a couple of blocks before our destination—are simple ways to burn more calories. Reluctant to heed such advice? Think again.

4   In a recent issue of the journal *Science,* researchers from the Mayo Clinic and Mayo Foundation in Rochester, Minn., set out to learn why some people are more likely to gain weight than others in response to overeating.

5   The researchers studied 16 nonobese adults (12 males and 4 females between 25 and 36 years of age) who underwent measures of both body composition and energy expenditure before and after 8 weeks of supervised overfeeding by 1,000 calories/day.

6   In their calculations to determine daily calorie expenditure, one form of such expenditure looked at was NEAT, which stands for "nonexercise activity thermogenesis." NEAT is defined as " . . . the thermogenesis [burning of calories] that accompanies physical activities other than [sports and fitness-related activities], such as the activities of daily living, fidgeting, spontaneous muscle contraction, and maintaining posture when not [lying down]."

7   While basal metabolism (the minimum amount of energy expended by the body to maintain vital processes, such as respiration, circulation, and digestion), energy expenditure associated with food processing, and "intentional" exercise varied little among the study participants, and had little effect on variations in weight gain. The authors note, however, that "NEAT proved to be the principal **mediator** of resistance to fat gain with overfeeding."

8   While it may be premature to advise everyone to go around "fidgeting," it seems sensible, and certainly not harmful, to encourage such steps as favoring the stairs over the elevator, and sneaking in any other non-strenuous calorie-burners you can think of, into your day, in your efforts toward achieving a healthy weight.

An incentive to do your chores

9   Putting off pulling the weeds or mopping the floors? If you thought it would help you to lose a few pounds, you might be more inspired. Recent studies published in *The Journal of the American Medical Association (JAMA)* also found that improved fitness can be found in both lifestyle physical activities and structured exercise.

10   One of the studies, conducted by Andre L. Dunn, Ph.D., and colleagues at The Cooper Institute for Aerobics Research, Dallas, Texas,

compared the 24-month effects of a lifestyle physical activity program with traditional structured exercise on improving physical activity, **cardiorespiratory** fitness, and **cardiovascular** disease risk factors on 235 sedentary adults (116 men and 119 women). The authors found that both groups experienced significant and comparable improvements in physical activity, cardiorespiratory fitness, and blood pressure. While neither group experienced significant weight loss, both groups did lose a significant percentage of body fat.

11 The second study in this issue of *JAMA*–supporting this hypothesis that significant improvements in health can be made by incorporating less intense physical activity into one's daily routine can result in significant health benefits–looks at the effects of lifestyle activity vs. structured **aerobic** exercise in combination with dietary changes among 40 obese women with an average age of 42.9 over a 16-week period, plus one 1-year follow-up period.

12 The diet plus structured aerobic exercise group participated in three step-aerobics classes held in a dance studio three times a week, whereas the diet and lifestyle group was advised to increase levels of moderate-intensity physical activity–short bouts of physical activity–by 30 minutes daily on most days of the week. After 16 weeks, there was no significant difference in weight loss among the two groups, with the aerobic exercise group losing an average of 8.3 pounds and the lifestyle group losing an average of 7.9 pounds.

13 After the initial 16-week period those who continued to be physically active were most likely to maintain their weight loss. The authors conclude that the "principal finding of this study" is that a program which includes a healthy diet, as well as lifestyle activity, may be just as beneficial and a "suitable alternative" to a healthy diet plus a vigorous aerobic exercise program for women who are overweight.

Lastly . . .

14 The research discussed here in no way suggests that regular vigorous physical activity is not an important part of maintaining a healthy weight–it simply supplies people with options. Given the fact that more than one-third of the U.S. population is obese and that fewer than one fifth of American adults participate in regular, sustained, vigorous exercise we need to do whatever we can to help people slim down sensibly, safely, and for the long-run.

References

Andersen, Ors E., Ph.D., et al. "Effects of lifestyle activity vs. structured aerobic exercise in obese women," *JAMA* 281(4):335–340, Jan. 27, 1999.

Dunn, Andrea, L., Ph.D., et al. "Comparison of lifestyle and structured interventions to increase physical activity and cardiorespiratory fitness," *JAMA* 281(4):327–334, Jan. 27, 1999.

Levine, James A., et al. "Role of nonexercise activity thermogenesis in resistance to fat gain in humans," *Science* 283:212–214, Jan. 8, 1999.

SOURCE: *Better Nutrition* 61, no. 4 (April 1999), p. 34.

OUTLINING/CLUSTERING

I. Argument of the selection

_____

II. Key procedures and conclusions of the Mayo Clinic Study

A. _____

B. _____

III. Key procedures and conclusions of the Cooper Institute Study

A. _____

B. _____

IV. Key procedures and conclusions of the *JAMA* Study

A. _____

B. _____

C. _____

V. Conclusions made in the selection

_____

A SECOND READING

Reread the Andersen-Parrado selection and answer the following questions as you read. Before answering these questions, you may want to write in your reading journal about any questions or comments that you have about the selection.

1. Reread paragraphs 1 and 2. What is the purpose of these two paragraphs?
2. Reread the definition of NEAT in paragraph 6. Put this definition in your own words.

_____

mediator: that which allows for bringing together; **cardiorespiratory:** involving the heart and breathing; **cardiovascular:** involving the heart and blood vessels; **aerobic:** describing sustained exercises like running and swimming

3. In paragraph 10, two groups are compared. Identify these two groups.

4. How is the *JAMA* Study discussed in paragraph 11 different from that discussed in paragraph 10?

5. Reread paragraph 13. What is the one factor that seems required to keep weight off?

READING/WRITING FEATURE: THE LOGIC OF SCIENTIFIC WRITING

Underlying most scientific research, as well as all of the studies that you have read about in these last four selections, is a consistent logic. This is a logic based on the scientific method, or the way by which scientists construct experiments and analyze their results.

The first question in the scientific method is:

1. What questions should one ask?

Research cannot begin unless the scientist has formulated a well-thought-out question. The researchers in the Andersen-Parrado article, for example, are all asking the same thought-provoking question: How much exercise is necessary to maintain or lose weight?

Scientists tend to answer their question by gathering information—what the sciences called *data.*

The second key question these scientists ask is:

2. How should one collect the data?

In answering this question, the scientific researchers do their most important experimental work: they devise the procedures for their experiments. In the experiments analyzed in Selection 16, you note a set number of experimental participants (16 nonobese adults in paragraph 5, 116 men and 119 women in paragraph 10), a set time for the experiment to take place (8 weeks in paragraph 5, 24 months in paragraph 10), and specific activities required of the participants ("supervised overfeeding by 1,000 calories/day" in paragraph 5 or "lifestyle physical activity program" and "traditional structured exercise" in paragraph 10). Respected researchers in the sciences are always clear in their studies about the numbers of participants, the time the experiment will take, and the participants' activities.

The third question of the scientific method that researchers ask is:

3. What generalization is derived from the data?

This is where the researchers interpret their results. Generalizations that come from the research analyzed in this selection could be that light exercise and moderate exercise are equal in maintaining one's weight or that moderate exercise is more effective than light exercise in maintaining one's weight.

The fourth and fifth questions interpret the generalization derived from the experiment:

4. What hypothesis explains the data?

5. What further experiments will test the hypothesis for it to become a theory?

Two important scientific terms are used here: hypothesis and theory. A *hypothesis* is a general scientific idea derived from an experiment or experiments, such as: Mild and moderate exercise burn an equal number of calories. A *scientific theory* is a general principle by which the scientists work. A theory can explain several hypotheses. Theories in the field of weight loss, for example, would have to do with the chemistry and physics of the burning of calories into energy.

The relevance of question 4 to the experiments presented in these last four selections is that scientists who find the results of these weight experiments thought-provoking will devise others to see if the results can be *replicated,* or confirmed once again.

As you continue to read and write about scientific experiments, you should have these five questions of the scientific method in the back of your mind. If the experiments adhere to these questions, then you can be assured that the researchers are relying on accepted scientific practices.*

---

*Adapted from G. Tyler Miller, Jr.: *Chemistry: A Basic Introduction*, 2nd ed, Belmont, CA: Wadsworth, 1981, pp. 3-4.

BEFORE YOU WRITE

Before you select a writing topic, you may want to study the use of "there is" and "there are" and complete Practice A16 (pages 225–226); then study sentence length and complete Practice B16 (pages 255–257) of the handbook.

WRITING TOPICS

Choose an essay topic from the following questions. Follow the steps of the writing process summarized on the inside front cover.

Writing about the Reading

1. In an organized essay, analyze the three experiments presented in the article "Burning Calories May Be Easier Than You Think." What do they suggest about weight loss and exercise? Do you agree with the conclusions that these experiments draw?

2. Reread Selection 15 ("How Far Should You Go to Stay Fit?") and Selection 16 ("Burning Calories May Be Easier Than You Think"). In

an organized essay, compare the experimental results presented in these two selections. Where do the results agree? Where do they disagree? Finally, which results do you agree with more? You may want to refer to pages 35–40 on the compare-contrast organizational pattern as you compose your draft.

Writing from Experience

3. In an organized essay, discuss the various diets you have tried. Which ones were successful? Which were unsuccessful? Provide as much detail as you can.

4. In an organized essay, describe the diet you are presently following. Discuss what you eat, what you don't eat, and how you feel physically and emotionally on the diet. Finally, discuss the diet's strengths and weaknesses.

RESPONDING TO STUDENT WRITING

Use some or all of these questions to respond to your draft or to that of your classmate. Read carefully for meaning and make your comments specific.

1. Read over the introduction. Does it provide a clear direction for the rest of the draft? If not, how could the introduction be revised?

2. For questions 1 and 2, select one or more experiments that need to be explained more fully. Suggest what should be included or revised in the discussion of these experiments.

3. For questions 3 and 4, determine if sufficient details are given to describe the various diets. If not, suggest other information that could be included.

4. Read the conclusion. Does it adequately summarize or synthesize the information in the draft? If not, how can the conclusion be revised?

5. Edit carefully for obvious errors in spelling and punctuation. Edit for errors in pronoun reference agreement and subject-verb agreement, especially with "there . . ." constructions. If you are unsure about a particular punctuation or agreement error, ask your instructor for help.

FOLLOW-UP

Now that you have read several selection on how to exercise to be fit, answer the following questions in a free-writing journal or in group discussion.

1. Describe an exercise program that you would now follow to help stay trim and healthy.

2. Which of the four selections seemed most interesting to you? Explain why. What topics in exercise and fitness do you now want to study further?

ISSUES IN LEARNING:
SELECTIONS 17–20

■━━━■

In the following four reading selections, you will consider the various ways people learn, particularly how they learn in school. You will be exploring how people learn differently because of their varied kinds of intelligences, how children learn in diverse cultures, how talented teachers improve student learning, and how culture and language affect the way a child learns in school. By the end of these selections, you should have a richer sense for how you and others learn.

The four selections are titled:

**Selection 17: "Teaching That Goes Beyond IQ"
    by Elaine Woo
Selection 18: "Japan Firsthand" by Marilyn Sue Chapman
    and Martha Hoppe
Selection 19: From *Possible Lives* by Mike Rose
Selection 20: From *Ordinary Resurrections*
    by Jonathan Kozol**

As you read these selections, you will also learn about the following aspects of reading and writing:

READING/WRITING FEATURES	GRAMMAR/USAGE	WRITING CONVENTIONS
Selection 17 Arguing Your Point	Use of Pronouns	Brackets within a Quote
Selection 18 Journalistic Writing	Use of Who/Whom	A Quote within a Quote
Selection 19 Narratives	Parallelism	Citing Long Quotes
Selection 20 Identifying Mood and Tone	Participial Phrases	Placing Page Numbers After Quotes

READING/WRITING PREP

You may want to answer the following questions in a free-writing journal or in group discussion before you begin reading these four selections. Answering these questions should help you determine how much you know and don't know about ways to learn:

1. How would you define intelligence?
2. What are the qualities of an effective teacher?
3. What does a student learn from peers?
4. What role should parents play in their children's education?

SELECTION 17: "TEACHING THAT GOES BEYOND IQ" BY ELAINE WOO

This article focuses on the ways in which people learn and our incomplete understanding of intelligence. Elaine Woo analyzes the ideas of Howard Gardner, a Harvard psychologist researching intelligence and learning. Early on, she presents Gardner's ideas; then she shows how these theories are applied to classroom teaching, particularly at the elementary school level.

This selection is long but straightforward, using the thesis-support pattern throughout.

READING/WRITING PREP

Before reading this selection, answer the following questions in a free-writing journal or in group discussion:

1. How do you define intelligence?
2. Do you think intelligence can be accurately measured through an intelligence test?

PREVIEWING

Preview the following selection. Read through quickly the first eight paragraphs and then determine the argument that Gardner is making about human intelligence.

Gardner's understanding of intelligence:

_____

_____

_____

_____

_____

READING CRITICALLY

Now critically read the selection and complete the following outline as you read or after you finish. You may want to make this outline into a visual cluster of the information.

Elaine Woo

Teaching That Goes Beyond IQ

1   The assignment–read a chapter in a history book about the Erie Canal and the westward movement–meant trouble for 13-year-old Garrett Santos. A bright child who has trouble reading, the Modesto eighth-grader told his teacher he just wasn't getting it.

2   Her response?

3   Singing. "We studied some old folk songs–'15 Miles on the Erie Canal,' 'I've Been Working on the Railroad,'" Garrett said. During the chapter test, he ran the lyrics through his head to help him recall important facts. "Every time I got to a question I couldn't remember, I thought about the songs."

4   The result? "I got an A on the test. I probably would have bombed it," he said, if his teacher had not tried a less conventional approach.

5   What his instructor did was simple. She found another way to reach Garrett's mind, realizing that for him music opened a door the written word could not.

6   Such new ways to teach rely on a complex and provocative theory called multiple intelligences.

7   It is controversial because it attacks the classical notion of what constitutes intelligence. Yet a growing number of educators say MI (as it's called by adherents) offers tremendous promise for unlocking children's minds.

8   Originated by Harvard psychologist Howard Gardner 12 years ago, the theory rejects the mainstream view that people have a single core mental ability that is measurable in an IQ test.

9   Gardner believes that intelligence entails a set of mental skills that enable us to recognize and resolve problems. He has identified seven types of intelligence that he says we each possess to some degree.

10   The first two are widely accepted: mathematical-logical (as seen in scientists and tax assessors) and linguistic (politicians, lawyers).

11   The others are less conventional: spatial (engineers, inventors); bodily kinesthetic (dancers, surgeons); musical (composers, critics); interpersonal (understanding what makes people tick, as in psychologists) and intrapersonal (being able to understand and learn from one's own's feelings, as in poets).

12   Gardner correlates each type of intelligence to a region of the brain; based on research with brain-damaged people, he suggests that the seven intellectual domains operate **autonomously.**

13   "All of us in my generation were raised on something called IQ," said Brown University professor Ted Sizer, who founded the Coalition of Essential Schools, a highly regarded national school reform network.

14   "What Howard has done is blown that up. If not an IQ as a nice little fraction, what is there? Is there something called innate intelligence? [Gardner] pushes those basic questions if not all the way back to square one, then close to square one."

15   Although gaining acceptance, the theory still inspires criticism, even from experts who like much of what it says.

16   "I don't agree with Gardner's use of the word *intelligences,*" said Al Shanker, the progressive head of the American Federation of Teachers. "I think what he calls intelligences is a talent.

17   "I would view intelligence as some sort of broader function of the mind, a managerial function. You can say someone has musical intelligence, but it's better to say musical *talent.*"

18   Nonetheless, Shanker sees educational uses for MI theory: "Howard Gardner recognizes the importance of mathematical and linguistic competence," the two skill areas most valued in and measured by schools. "What he is saying is there are other competencies that are very important in human life, as well."

19   Gardner said he hopes that the theory will help personalize education, which he says is traditionally based on the idea that all children learn the same way.

20   "The principal educational implication of multiple intelligences is to look at kids very, very carefully and see what would interest kids as much as we can," Gardner said. "It is the direct opposite of uniform schooling, where you teach all kids the same and test them the same."

21   In the classroom, however, Gardner warns that his concept can be misinterpreted to justify activities that may be fun for children but have little value.

22   Moreover, because MI-based schooling is so new, there is little empirical proof of its effectiveness. Test scores have risen at some schools that use his theory, but changed little or slumped slightly at others.

23   Yet stories of MI's effectiveness abound many campuses. Teachers say that discipline problems have decreased and that students seem to retain knowledge longer. This may be because they are more engaged in schoolwork and are given a variety of options for learning–instead of just reading a book or writing an essay.

24   A spatially adept student might be better able to show what he knows about "Charlotte's Web" by creating a cardboard diorama instead of by writing a report. A linguistically talented youth might be more interested in reciting verses about volcanoes than by building a model of one.

25   "Seven kinds of intelligence," Gardner wrote in "Frames of Mind," his 1983 book introducing the theory, "would allow seven ways to teach, rather than one."

26   No one knows how many schools are attempting to apply the theory. But it is safe to say that membership in what has been dubbed "the MI underground" numbers in the hundreds. Project Zero, a Harvard research institute co-directed by Gardner, maintains a list of 55 schools that use it. Another 222 public schools in six states follow an MI-centered instructional program developed by the Los Angeles-based Galef Institute.

27   An MI network, run by a former teacher-turned-consultant in Chicago, has signed up 600 members in three years and offers a newsletter, electronic bulletin board and other resources.

28   Three conferences last year on MI in schools drew 1,600 educators and 500 are expected to attend another conference in Tucson this month. The nation's largest organization of curriculum specialists recently sent its 100,000 members a teacher's guide to MI, written by a Sonoma county consultant who has made a career of spreading MI theory to education's grass roots.

29   Leaders in the education Establishment are receptive to the concept of more than one form of brain power, but worry that oversimplifying MI could result in a lowering of standards by some teachers.

30   "The potential [impact] is very great, provided that school people look at this in a balanced way," Shanker said. "What is likely to happen is some school people will pick this up and turn it into a fad, de-emphasizing substantially all forms of traditional learning and setting up schools where youngsters are doing dance, music and all sorts of other things."

31   In fact, Gardner says he has seen just that sort of misuse of his theory. He recalled visiting a classroom where the teacher had students crawling on the floor, pretending to be wolves. "People think the point is kids crawling on the floor or kids dancing or kids singing. But I say, 'What is that achieving'?

32   "My own interest is in using the idea of multiple intelligences for educational ends. I am very interested in kids understanding more, in kids mastering disciplines, finding something that interests them and getting deeply into it."

33   Gardner was an obscure psychology professor when "Frames of Mind: The Theory of Multiple Intelligences" was published. It has sold steadily—recently, about 20,000 copies a year—and the 10th anniversary edition has been translated into five languages.

34   Gardner deliberately exerts no quality control over schools attempting to make the leap from MI theory to practice. In fact, the past recipient of a MacArthur Foundation genius award confesses he is totally bored by MI.

35   Thus, no two schools seem to do MI exactly the same. Schools that infuse their teaching with MI-inspired practices typically tie in other innovations, so disentangling its purported benefits from other approaches is difficult.

36   The theory's rising popularity coincides with a growing reform movement that includes an emphasis on personalizing education—allowing children to learn at their own pace in so-called ungraded primary classes, for instance, or breaking large classes into small clusters to increase participation.

37   It dovetails with the basic tenet of the school reform movement of the past decade—that all children can learn. And it is an assault on the kind of thinking embodied in "The Bell Curve," the recent book that argues that intelligence is **immutable** and genetically based.

38   Gardner's kinder and gentler view of human potential is "really catching on," said Stanford education professor Mike Kirst. "It plays into the idea that most all kids have intelligence."

39   At a growing number of campuses, that has led to a more creative—and labor-intensive—mode of teaching.

40   Maureen Manning, a fourth-grade teacher at Emma Shuey Elementary School in Rosemead, remembers being the "kind of kid who got nailed by test scores." She knew she was smart, but teachers rarely asked her to demonstrate what she knew in the ways that she felt most comfortable.

41   "I know something. I can sing it, I can dance it," she said.

42   So when Manning became a teacher, she slipped music and art into as many lessons as she could.

43   But she felt out of step, even though she knew intuitively that the traditional ways schools transmit and assess knowledge—fill in the blank, read this chapter and answer questions—are not how many children learn best.

44   Now Manning, a 17-year classroom veteran, has been liberated. About two years ago, most of her colleagues at Shuey embraced MI through a program designed by the Galef Institute, a nonprofit education center in West Los Angeles. The teachers try to integrate as many of the intelligences as they can into all lessons.

45   Students love the new approach. One of Manning's students said: "She turns math into art and PE. It's a more fun way to learn."

46   Attendance is up at Shuey, and so is enthusiasm. "I see a real happiness, a relief" in students, Manning said. "[They think] 'Oh, I can *do* this.'"

47   "It takes the blinders off educators," said Patricia Bolanos, principal of the public Key School in Indianapolis, which became the first school in the country to apply MI theory in teaching gifted youngsters in 1984. "It makes it possible for educators to recognize giftedness in other areas."

48   In 1987, the Indianapolis district opened an MI-based magnet elementary school for students of all ability levels. Two years ago, Bolanos added a middle school and has her sights set on a high school.

49   The Key Schools' 300 students are expected to master the basics through three nine-week courses that blend disciplines and are linked to broad schoolwide themes.

50   Several times a week, students visit the "flow" room, a place for serious play, stocked with puzzles, board games and books. Here they are encouraged to enter a state of "flow" where they lose track of time and, in choosing their own activity, discover "intrinsic motivation" to learn. Observers record their choices and include that information in reports to

51   parents.

Letter grades are out and paper-and-pencil tests are de-emphasized in favor of projects or video-taped presentations that students produce to

52   show their knowledge.

The aspect of Key's program that most raises the eyebrows of traditionalists is that it gives equal weight to educating each of the seven intelligences. So learning to read is considered no more important than

53   learning to play the violin—or dodge ball.

The school also caters to students' strongest intelligences. So those with particular **deficits**—in math or reading, for example—are not given

54   additional help but are advised to seek tutoring.

"It's building on strengths rather than [correcting] weaknesses,"

55   Bolanos said.

56   Other schools are less extreme.

At Garrett Santos' school, Hart-Ransom Elementary in Modesto, teachers have embraced MI, but without abandoning the traditional

57   goals of early schooling—such as learning to write a term paper.

"We are not here to make children proficient in all seven intelligences," district Supt. Dennis Boyer said. "It's fine if they become proficient in all seven, but our mission is to produce an educated child who can do the things our community says children should be able to do. Our community is conservative. Our focus is to move children through the

58   traditional education system."

Boyer said his teachers regard MI as a framework for restructuring the traditional curriculum so that students are given at least seven ways

59   to learn it.

In Jerrianna Boer's seventh- and eighth-grade classes, students learn writing by exploring their reactions to a piece of classical music, first by making crayon drawings that fit the mood, then writing a story infused with those

60   emotions.

"It's a more interesting way to teach," Boer said. "It's also more difficult . . . a lot more work for the teacher than just saying read this
61 story and answer these questions."

How well is it working? Because the school began phasing in the MI approach only last year, Boyer said, it is too soon to tell what impact it
62 will have on standardized test scores.

A two-year study of 1,000 students at four Galef Institute campuses showed significant increases in language ability, but multiple intelli-
63 gences is just one of the major components of its program.

At Key School, Bolanos puts little stock in state-mandated exams, which show Key on a slight downward trend in language arts scores over the last four years. Mary Mickelson, director of testing for the Indiana Department of Education, said she is concerned about the slump but that it may reflect the mismatch between the old-style tests and Key's **radi-**
64 **cally** different approach to learning.

She said a more telling sign of MI's impact may be the Key School's 97% attendance rate, which is about four points higher than the state
65 average.

"Something is happening at that school that causes kids to want to come," Mickelson said. "I suspect students are learning very well."

———————

SOURCE: *Los Angeles Times*, Jan. 20, 1995, p. 1.

OUTLINING/CLUSTERING

I. Gardner's understanding of intelligence

_____

II. The seven types of intelligence

_____

III. How Gardner's ideas are generally used in the classroom

A. _____

B. _____

IV. Maureen Manning's learning and teaching experiences

A. _____

B. _____

C. _____

———————

autonomously: in a self-governing manner; **immutable:** unchangeable;
deficits: monetary shortages; **radically:** fundamentally

V. Ways the Key School teaches its students

A. _____

B. _____

C. _____

A SECOND READING

Reread the Woo selection and answer the following questions as or after you read. Before answering these questions, write in your reading journal about any questions or comments you have about the selection.

1. In paragraph 11, Woo describes the difference between interpersonal and intrapersonal intelligence. In your own words, state what this difference is.

2. Paraphrase the following sentence from paragraph 12: ". . . based on research with brain-damaged people, he suggests that the seven intellectual domains operate autonomously."

3. In paragraph 28, Woo states that some educators worry that Gardner's ideas may be oversimplified when applied to classroom teaching. Give some examples of ways in which Gardner's ideas can be misused by teachers.

4. In paragraph 35, Woo talks about how Gardner's teaching ideas allow a more personal learning experience for students. Why is this so?

5. Why does Boer argue that using Gardner's teaching suggestions requires more work for the teacher (paragraph 59)?

READING/WRITING FEATURE: ARGUING YOUR POINT

Effective essays that try to prove a point move logically. You have previously learned about coherence (Selection 6)–how carefully sentences can work together to create an organized paragraph. When effectively arguing your point in an essay, you consider how paragraphs relate to each other and how these paragraphs relate to your thesis. In a sense, you are examining the coherence of the entire essay when carefully arguing your point.

Let's assume that you are assigned to write an essay on Howard Gardner's seven forms of intelligence. As a critical writer on this topic, you begin by shaping a thesis. You should have in mind questions such as: What do I plan to say about Gardner's model of intelligence, and how can I prove it? Let's say that you come up with this working thesis after some thinking: Gardner's seven forms of intelligence can be effectively applied to elementary school teaching, allowing students to learn more easily.

Having set up your argument, you now need to decide how the points you plan to make will support this thesis. You must identify and explain Gardner's seven forms of intelligence early on because if your reader is unclear about these types of intelligence, he or she will not understand the rest of your essay on classroom learning. You also want to consider the order in which you will present the seven forms of intelligence. That is, which forms of intelligence should be grouped together in your discussion?

Next, you should supply evidence from several elementary schools showing how teachers have applied Gardner's theory to their lessons and how successful their application has been to their teaching. If you had read the Woo article, you could use several bits of information: Maureen Manning's insights, the information about Key School, and comments from the Modesto teachers. With each set of evidence, you should ask yourself two essential questions:

1. How does this evidence relate to the thesis? Is it convincing support? Does it help further explain the thesis? Or does the evidence contradict the thesis?

2. How should the evidence be organized? Which bit of evidence should come first, and which should come last? How does one piece of evidence help explain the other?

Note that you may not need to present the evidence in the same order that Woo presented it. Because you are arguing for classroom application of Gardner's ideas, the evidence should be organized around classroom teaching and Gardner's ideas about intelligence.

All too often, students assume that because they have to prove their point from evidence they have read, any form of organizing this reading material will do. Carefully argued essays that use readings, like carefully coherent paragraphs, move logically from one sentence to the next and one paragraph to the other, finding ways to explore the thesis.

In proving your point well in your essay, you need to review your thesis and evidence for a while before you begin drafting. Therefore, it is helpful to study your thesis and evidence either in outline or cluster form. In this schematic or visual stage, examine your thesis to determine if it is workable. Consider whether it can be more effectively worded or if responses to your evidence could possibly disprove it. Remember that the intelligence of your thesis drives the rest of your essay. A weak thesis can create an essay with little direction, whereas an essay that begins with a thought-provoking thesis encourages a careful reader to move through it with interest and with questions.

Then with your outline or visual cluster in front of you, place your evidence together on the page. Examine how the organization of your evidence works together to prove your point. Arrange and rearrange this material so that you can see if one bit of information should come before another, or if bits of information should be put together. All along, you need to keep asking: How is this evidence related to my thesis?

This is the most important work that is involved in writing college essays–the careful thinking through of your argument and of the points that support this argument. As with your outlining, you need to ask this question after you draft each paragraph: How has this paragraph furthered the explanation of my thesis?

If you find that your thesis is not being explained further in a particular paragraph, you should revise the paragraph before you move on to the next part of your essay.

Of course as a reader, you can ask similar critical questions of the writer:

1. Is the writer's thesis convincing? Can I come up with an argument to disprove it?

2. Does the evidence the writer uses carefully support this argument? Is the evidence organized in a convincing and logical way, or does one bit of evidence merely repeat what was said before? Does the evidence, in fact, contradict the thesis?

In this way, you are able to evaluate what you read.

By arguing your point well or by critically reading a selection to determine the author's point, you make college essay writing and reading a challenge, not just an assignment you have to complete.

BEFORE YOU WRITE

Before selecting a writing topic, you may want to study the effective use of pronouns and complete Practice A17 (pages 227–228); then study using brackets within quotes and complete Practice B17 (page 257) of the handbook.

WRITING TOPICS

Choose an essay topic from the following questions. Follow the steps of the writing process summarized on the inside front cover as you complete your drafts.

Writing about the Reading

1. Explain carefully Howard Gardner's seven types of intelligence and show how they are applied to the classrooms described in "Teaching That Goes Beyond IQ." Do you believe that these types of classroom learning are effective, or do they shortchange students? Be specific in your response.

Writing from Experience

2. Explain Howard Gardner's seven types of intelligence. Then describe the sort of learner you are in as much detail as you can. Which of the seven types of learning best describe you? Explain why.

3. Think back on your classroom educational experiences. Choose one or more of these experiences and apply Gardner's seven intelligence

types to your recollections. Which type or types of intelligence best describe the ways you learned in school?

RESPONDING TO STUDENT WRITING

Use some or all of these questions to respond to your draft or to that of your classmate.

1. Is the thesis clear? If not, how can it be improved?

2. Choose a paragraph in the body that does not effectively explain the thesis. Show how this paragraph can be revised.

3. Choose a paragraph in the body that effectively explains the thesis. State why.

4. (For questions 3 and 4) Are the personal recollections detailed or vague? If they are vague, show how they can be improved.

5. Edit for obvious errors in spelling and punctuation, as well as for fragments, run-ons, and comma-related errors. Determine whether the sentence structure is varied. If it is not, pick one sentence and revise it for variety. If you are unsure about editing for specific errors in punctuation or how to revise for sentence variety, ask your instructor for help.

SELECTION 18: "JAPAN FIRSTHAND" BY MARILYN SUE CHAPMAN AND MARTHA HOPPE

This article describes the experiences of two teachers as they visited schools in Japan. Chapman's and Hoppe's intent is to dispel many of the myths that Americans have about Japanese education.

This selection is clearly written and provides ample detail to describe the Japanese educational system. This information is organized around the five most common myths that Americans have about Japanese public education. By studying this evidence, American readers can compare American public schools with those in Japan.

READING/WRITING PREP

Before reading this selection, answer the following questions in a free-writing journal or in group discussion.

1. Do you believe that Japanese public schools are better than those in America?

2. How do you think Japanese schools differ from American schools?

PREVIEWING

Preview the following selection. Read through the first ten paragraphs quickly to determine who these teachers are and what they wanted to do in Japan.

Description of the two teachers and their purpose for going to Japan:

_____

_____

_____

_____

_____

READING CRITICALLY

Now critically read the selection and complete the following outline as you read or after you finish. You may want to make this outline into a visual cluster of the important information.

Marilyn Sue Chapman and Martha Hoppe

Japan Firsthand

1 We recently experienced the thrill of traveling to Japan for a three-week educational trip. We were able to see firsthand the education system we hear so much about, and are often compared to here in the United States. We did, however, find a few surprises.

2 Our trips were paid for by the Fulbright Memorial Fund, a Japanese scholarship program for American teachers to visit Japan. The program aims to promote greater intellectual understanding between the two countries, improve both educational systems through the exchange of ideas, and enrich international education for American students.

3 Though the Fulbright Memorial Fund is only in its second year of operation, an amazing 2,700 applicants from all 50 states and the District of Columbia applied for the 1998 program.

4 Independent of each other, we had both learned of the program through the union and applied for scholarships. Several months later, we learned we were among the 600 educators and administrators selected to travel to Japan. Three groups of 200 would travel to Japan, one group per month.

5 Martha would travel in October, Marilyn in November. We began preparing for what would be a trip of a lifetime. What follows is a combined synopsis of our experiences.

6   Our first stop was Tokyo, where we attended meetings with top government and Ministry of Education officials, professors, and others.
Then we were divided into groups of 20, and each group traveled to a different prefecture (state) to experience everyday Japan.

7   Martha went to Matsumoto City in the prefecture of Nagano. Marilyn
Sue went to Aizu-Wakamatsu in the Fukushima prefecture.

8   We spent a day and a night with our host families, then we spent
seven days visiting schools, local industries, and attractions, and visiting
with parents, students, and teachers.

9   As a result of these experiences, we discovered an educational system deeply **embedded** in the culture of Japanese society; it is, therefore,
difficult to assess which aspects make the system work or fail.

10   We were able to **scrutinize** the many stories about Japanese education we frequently hear in the United States. In some cases, we learned
they are only myths, and hope to dispel those myths here. In others, we
can only correct common misinformation or add more detail to the picture of K–12 education in Japan.

Myth 1: Japan is pleased with its model system of K-12 education

11   In spite of being very successful on international tests, the Japanese are
not content with their educational system. The Japanese tests indicate
their students show inadequate performance in understanding math
concepts, problem solving, and working together.

12   Major educational reforms are underway, including eliminating
"the test" for entrance into high school, increasing creativity in their students, curbing school violence and bullying, and eliminating Saturday
school.

13   To improve their instruction in mathematics, Japanese officials are
looking to the United States for ideas which concentrate on understanding, solving problems together, and creativity. It seems ironic that, as we
strive to make our educational system more like Japan's, they are striv-
ing to make theirs more like ours.

14   These educational reforms are not without concerns for teachers,
especially since the educational system is so ingrained into society. We
did not uncover a structured plan to provide in-service training about the
reforms to teachers.

15   The teachers are concerned about how to implement the reforms,
especially the reduced classroom hours per month if **bi-weekly** Saturday
school day was eliminated. Though the curriculum has been changed to
accommodate the loss of class time, teacher concern has not lessened.

Myth 2: Japanese students compete intensely in school

16   Japanese education is not all about competition. Still there is enormous
pressure on students, beginning in junior high school, to achieve on their
entrance exams to high school.

17   In Japan, if students score high enough on this test, they can get into good high schools, they can get into good colleges, and if they can get into good colleges, their futures are secure. Beginning in grade school, some students attend weekend or after hours cram schools called "jukus" to help them prepare for these entrance exams.

18   However, from our limited experiences, the Japanese classroom is not a competitive environment. On the contrary, there was a strong sense of classroom and school community, and students and teachers didn't appear to be stressed.

19   For starters, students pitch in to help prepare lunch every day. Up until high school, students and their teachers generally sit down and eat lunch together in the classroom. Then after lunch, cleaning time begins. Every member of the school population takes part in cleaning the school, including classrooms, hallways, and bathrooms.

20   While the Japanese have a longer school year than ours, 227 days as opposed to our 180, many of these days are spent on all-school field trips or festival days. Students might ice skate or go skiing; they might go camping in the woods or visit a local industry or historic site.

21   The length of the Japanese school year will be shrinking with the elimination of Saturday school in the near future. The length of the school day is comparable to ours, but our students spend more of their time in actual instruction.

Myth 3: Japanese students are well-behaved

22 Students were well-behaved and quiet during lecture times. On the other hand, teachers of the primary grades tend to accept as normal a high level of what we might consider "rowdiness" during free times. The authority of both teachers and parents seems to rest in the **intrinsic** motivation of the student to do what is right, good, and expected.

23   It seems as if the Japanese do not reward or punish students as much as American educators. In this way, it is not always the adult's responsibility to make sure that the child behaves, but the child's responsibility. In the classroom, for example, it appeared that the teacher would not insist on the students paying attention. Rather, the students should know to pay attention themselves.

24   The Japanese are also working on reforms to curb increasing school violence and student bullying. They hope to reduce the amount of student to student harassment–another fact about Japanese education we were surprised to learn.

Myth 4: Japanese teachers make good money

25 We've all heard how Japanese society respects and reveres teachers. We have also heard Japanese teachers are paid very well.

26   From conversations we had with Japanese parents and teachers, when it comes to problems of discipline or student performance, "the

teacher is always right." Very rarely do students question the judgment of a teacher, since their parents will always side with the teacher.

27   On the other hand, teachers in Japan work long hard hours. In addition, it is standard for them to put in tons of extra hours on overnight field trips and big projects. Often, the teacher is also the one who is called to deal with a student's behavior problems outside of school.

28   And finally, it seems that Japanese teachers do not earn a whole lot more money for their work than we do. While teacher salaries are higher than ours, the cost of living in Japan is much higher. Teaching is not considered a highly paid job in Japan.

Myth 5: Japanese teachers collaborate to make great lesson plans

29 Much has been written about teacher **collaboration,** lesson faires, crafting research-based lessons, and teacher observations of other teacher's lessons. These have been reported in AFT's *American Educator* (Winter 1998), and the report of the Third International Math and Science Survey (TIMSS).

30   The Japanese teachers we met were extremely busy people, working late hours usually six days a week. Marilyn talked with assistant English language teachers from Australia and the United States who knew nothing about teacher collaboration. The language teachers said the Japanese teachers were too busy during the day to plan together; the Japanese teachers said the same. Both appeared to be unaware of research-based lessons as well. While these teaching techniques must exist in Japan, they appear to have not migrated to the more rural prefectures.

31   When Martha asked teachers about teacher collaboration, they mentioned that they share a teacher workroom in the school where they do their lesson planning. Additionally one teacher can often witness another teacher's lesson through thin walls or across partial walls separating classrooms. In this way, it seemed that "collaboration" meant working alongside one another or knowing what the other teachers were doing.

Sayonara

32 As in America, Japan's greatest resource is its children. Their openness, smiles, and enthusiasm for life will remain with us for a long time to come. We heartily express our thanks to the people and children of Japan for allowing us to explore their culture, schools, and homes, as well as to the Japanese government for providing us the means and opportunity.

33   After the trip to Japan, each participant is expected to prepare a follow-up plan with the aim of sharing what we learned with our colleagues, students, and community members. This article is one part of that task. Beyond the sheer dissemination of information, though, the follow-up plan has encouraged us to constantly reflect on our journey and our experiences.

54   The trip provided us with insight and knowledge that will benefit us, our peers, and our students for years to come. It is in this spirit that we share our impressions and thoughts with you.

SOURCE: *California Teacher*, June 1999, pp. 5+.

OUTLINING/CLUSTERING

I. Teachers' purpose for going to Japan

　　_____

II. Explanation of Myth 1 and evidence to explain it

A. _____

B. _____

C. _____

III. Explanation of Myth 2 and evidence to explain it

A. _____

B. _____

IV. Explanation of Myth 3 and evidence to explain it

A. _____

B. _____

V. Explanation of Myth 4 and evidence to explain it

A. _____

B. _____

VI. Explanation of Myth 5 and evidence to explain it

A. _____

B. _____

---

embedded: fixed firmly; **scrutinize:** investigate, study thoroughly; **bi-weekly:** every two weeks; **intrinsic:** real; **collaboration:** the act of working together

A SECOND READING

Reread the Chapman and Hoppe selection and answer the following questions as you read. Before you answer these questions, write in your reading journal about any questions or comments you have about the selection.

1. What do the Japanese public schools seem to be lacking in regard to mathematics education (paragraph 13)?
2. What do the authors mean when they say that in Japan "the educational system is so ingrained into society" (paragraph 14)?
3. Paragraph 19 talks about who cleans up the schools in Japan. What sort of school atmosphere does this activity help create?
4. Who is responsible for maintaining acceptable behavior in Japanese schools (paragraph 23)? What does this say about the Japanese student and the attitude the Japanese have toward children?
5. Reread Myth 5. Why is it difficult for Japanese teachers to work together?

READING/WRITING FEATURE: JOURNALISTIC WRITING

Some of what you read in college and much of what you read outside of college comes from newspapers and magazines. Features in popular newspapers and magazines are called *journalistic pieces*. Journalistic material is characterized by the following features:

1. Short, clear sentences
2. Short paragraphs
3. Many facts
4. A structure that is easy to determine
5. A lead-in that may delay the thesis
6. An abbreviated conclusion or no conclusion

Journalistic material thus differs from the requirements of college essays, which ask for a clear thesis early on, analysis of the evidence to support this thesis, and a recognizable conclusion.

"Japan Firsthand" is a fitting example of journalistic writing. The thesis comes in paragraph 10 after the lead-in, each myth is clearly named in a subhead, facts are presented to support each myth, little evaluation is given of these facts, and a very short conclusion does not attempt to tie in all of evidence presented.

As a reader, you will find journalistic writing easy to skim and easy to read quickly because the format almost never changes and many clear clues are given about how the piece is structured. You will find this type of journalistic writing as front page and feature material in newspapers and as feature material in magazines—the education section, the foreign affairs column, and so on.

Commentary features in newspapers and magazines, which usually appear in the opinion and editorial sections, are more carefully written—more like the essays that you are being taught to write. In commentary, the facts are analyzed, and a particular thesis is explored. Here, you will have a harder time reading the material quickly and easily determining its structure.

Journalistic writing often provides a starting point for your research. As with "Japan Firsthand," you are given an introduction to the key points about Japanese education. If you are interested in the topic of education in other countries, this piece can encourage you to do further research through articles on Japanese education, through journals related to education, and through full-length education studies.

BEFORE YOU WRITE

Before selecting a writing topic, you may want to study the correct use of *who* and *whom* and complete Practice A18 (pages 228–229) and study the use of quotes within quotes and complete Practice B18 (page 258) of the handbook.

WRITING TOPICS

Choose an essay topic from the following questions. Follow the steps of the writing process summarized on the inside front cover as you complete your drafts.

Writing about the Reading

1. Reread carefully "Japan Firsthand" to determine the most important features of a Japanese education. Explain each of these features, summarizing clearly the details presented in the selection. How do these features in Japanese schools differ from the American public school education with which you are familiar? You may want to review the compare-contrast organizational pattern on pages 38–40 as you draft your essay.

Writing from Experience

2. Assume you are writing a journalistic piece for Japanese readers describing the five key features of the American public schools. Focus on American attitudes toward three or more of the following: the importance American schools place on testing students, the emphasis on competition among students, student behavior in the classroom, and the respect that American students and parents give to teachers in the public schools. Rely on your own educational experiences in American schools as your evidence.

RESPONDING TO STUDENT WRITING

Use some or all of these questions to respond to your draft or to that of your classmate. Read carefully for meaning and make your comments specific.

1. Read through the first part of the draft. Can you locate the thesis? Is it clear? If unclear, how can it be revised?

2. Read through the middle of the draft. Is the evidence used to support the thesis generally clear and accurate? If details from the Chapman and Hoppe selection are mentioned, are they accurately summarized?

3. Which paragraph seems to be best organized and most carefully detailed? Explain why.

4. Which paragraph seems to be less organized with the least amount of detail? How can this paragraph be improved?

5. Edit for obvious errors in spelling and sentence fragments. Edit for punctuation errors and for correct use of pronouns–both *who* and *whom* and vague pronoun references. If unsure, ask your instructor for help with any punctuation or pronoun errors.

SELECTION 19: FROM *POSSIBLE LIVES* BY MIKE ROSE

This selection is from a book-length study of excellent teaching and teachers. In this excerpt, Mike Rose examines why a high school economics teacher is so successful. As a narrative, this selection is a nice balance between description and narration.

This excerpt effectively uses the organizational pattern of description. By the end of the reading, you will have a clear understanding of this very special teacher–both who he is and how he teaches.

READING/WRITING PREP

Before reading this selection, answer the following questions in a free-writing journal or in group discussion:

1. What are the qualities of a successful teacher?
2. What are the qualities of a successful school?

PREVIEWING

Preview the following selection. Read through the first four paragraphs to get a sense for the high school and the teacher that Rose examines. Next, write out what seem to be the major qualities of Rick Takagaki.

Major qualities of Rick Takagaki:

_____

_____

_____

_____

_____

READING CRITICALLY

Now critically read the selection and complete the following outline as you read or after you finish. You may want to make this outline a visual cluster of the important information.

Mike Rose

From *Possible Lives*

1 Driving the residential streets south out of Santa Monica, you see the scenes spliced into so many movies and television shows: stucco, palm trees, agave, bougainvillaea, lawn sprinklers, joggers. I took a left turn at Wilshire Boulevard, passing Princeton, Harvard, Yale, and Berkeley avenues, past a small sign that announced CITY OF LOS ANGELES, east in the thick traffic along a mix of buildings from the 1940s and fifties and sleek new high-rises and minimalls, passing men's shops and video stores, sushi bars and software outlets. Viva la Pasta, Cellular Palace, El Capote Mexican Restaurant. Then a right turn on Barrington Avenue, past the Barrington Plaza, and up alongside University High School. Uni High is close to the Federal Building, the Veterans Administration, UCLA, the Westside financial hub at Westwood and Wilshire (the busiest inter-section in Los Angeles)—all told, some of the most expensive land in the Basin.

2 It is the oldest high school in West Los Angeles. Built in 1924, origi-nally Warren G. Harding High School, Uni changed its name to **forgo** association with the corruption then being revealed about President Harding's administration and to underscore its key role as a feeder school to the University of California, to nearby UCLA in particular. For some time, the school has had a distinguished academic reputation; as an enticement, some real estate ads mention that property is in the Uni High district. It is a beautiful campus, twenty-five acres, terraced and rich with shrubbery and flowers: rose beds, birds of paradise, carob trees, Canary Island pine. Two natural springs run through it. The

administration building—the site of the original cornerstone—is red brick with large windows, cream-colored wood frames. A jacaranda in full bloom is right outside the entrance, thousands of light purple buds spread in a loose circle on the lawn at the base of the tree.

3   There was the smell of honeysuckle in the dim **vestibule** outside the principal's office; lettered neatly on the door's frosted glass, a sign:

PRINCIPAL
MR. MOSCOWITZ

Inside, the sun streamed through open windows across a wide desk and a vintage Columbia Dictaphone. There were old **pennants** and photographs on the wall: the severe Angus Cavanaugh, an early principal; a student named Tom Dixon, big smile, "Winner of Popularity Contest, 1933"; a nameless yell leader, a megaphone with the letters *WGHHS* lying across his bent knee. Warren G. Harding High School.

4   "I brought Rick Takagaki here," Jack Moscowitz explained, "to shake things up. He's a stimulant, a **catalyst,** an irritant. He'll say outlandish things if he has to—and that will get students to question him . . . and argue back." He suggested that I talk to other teachers about Takagaki, and I did. Bonnie Williams, whose room was across the hall from Rick's, started to call him a maverick but caught herself. "No, that's too mild a word. He's irreverent, even **sacrilegious.** Whatever it takes to get kids to think."

5   Rick Takagaki was about five-seven, thin, wiry, in his late forties, and as he taught, he moved quickly from a stool behind his desk to a chair in front of it to an open semicircle surrounded by students. He moved in spurts and stutter-steps, and when he paused to write on the chalkboard, he kept his left leg extended behind him, his right knee bent inward, ready to pivot back around his desk to the center of the class, challenging the students, tweaking them, assuming a range of voices, saying whatever it took. He began his first economics class on the day of my visit by adopting the persona of Adam Smith and arguing for pure ***laissez-faire* capitalism.** "There should be minimal regulation of factories," he stormed. "On his own, the owner will make factories safe. Why? Because it will make workers happy, and that's conducive to high productivity." He stopped, raising a finger, fixing the class with a stare. "That's enlightened self-interest." "How about moral obligation?" a student asked skeptically. "Mr. Chin," Takagaki-Smith shot back, "morality is not the issue. Let the marketplace resolve it."

6   Economics is a high school requirement in the Los Angeles Unified School District, so, in any class you'd observe, no matter how well conceived, you'd find some students who were sullen, or whispering, or daydreaming—a million miles away. "It's always a challenge," Rick explained to me. "To the degree a course is required across the board, like

economics or U.S. government, you'll get students who would rather not be there. But I continually try to bring them into the discussion, take a gamble—and I know when to back off." Most courses were structured around a textbook and taught basic concepts: capital formation, supply and demand, elasticity, inflation, and so on. Rick covered these terms, but did so in a course that was a hybrid of comparative economics and economic philosophy, using handouts, articles, and newspaper clippings to lead his students to analyze the century's major systems: capitalism, scientific socialism, and the various **Hegelian syntheses** that have developed in our time. Some students who were concerned about grades wanted a more traditional course, a straightforward **microeconomics** syllabus. But Rick worried that such a course would lack a critical edge.

7   Takagaki was now **fulminating** against the U.S. Postal Service. "Inefficient! Always in the red!" And he began arguing for privatization. "Hold on," said Scott from the side of the room. (Scott looked like the actor Giancarlo Esposito and had just been accepted to West Point.) "All people couldn't afford that. Thirty-two cents gets your mail out. If it takes longer than Federal Express, well, then that's an efficiency problem—and you can figure out how to remedy that." Rick rocked on the balls of his feet. "There's only one way to solve inefficiency, my man, and that's through competition." Anna, dressed gangbanger-chic, in baggy pants, oversized X-LARGE pullover shirt, sunglasses, sized Rick up and, head back, said, "Yeah, but, like, what happens if the business collapses? And businesses *do* collapse, Tak. Look at LA, huh? Who's going to provide the service then?" "Good thinking, Girl Wonder," Rick conceded, and turned on his heel to begin another disquisition, this one on the evils of **subsidization.**

8   "One of the most important things about Rick Takagaki," Principal Moscowitz had said, "is that he holds students accountable for their opinions. He challenges them, prods them, but out of respect for what they're capable of doing." He told me a story. It seemed that several years ago, some students in an advanced placement government class challenged a penalty Rick gave for a late assignment. OK, he said, fair enough. Since this is a class in government, let's put the issue to the courts. He asked them to set up a trial. He would be the defendant. There would be three judges (two picked by the students, one by Rick), prosecuting and defense attorneys, witnesses. The students had to learn court procedure and rules of evidence, set up the date and time of the trial, subpoena witnesses. Mr. Moscowitz himself was called to testify. After extensive argument, the judges decided that, while Mr. Takagaki had the right to grade as he saw fit and to deduct points for late assignments, in the case under consideration there were **mitigating** circumstances. The students were not guilty. Rick rescinded the penalty.

9   Rick had abandoned the voice of Adam Smith and was now pacing the room as John Maynard Keynes, talking in somber tones about factors of production. "What," he asked, "are the secondary effects of failed

industry? What happens when a factory closes down?" "There are a lot of 'em," Amanda ventured, her legs stretched out in front of her, her heels tapping the floor. "Say it's automotive. It closes. It affects the rubber plant, steel, glass, uh, the people who make covering for the seats." "All right. OK," Rick said, leaning back against the chair in front of his desk. "And what else happens?" José, who, during preclass **banter** about prom tuxedos, identified himself as "the Kmart Poster Boy" noted that when a factory closes, the surrounding economy suffers, too. "Workers can't buy groceries; they don't go out to lunch; they don't buy a new TV . . ." Rick got **pensive,** rubbed his chin, and wondered out loud about converting such industries, retooling. "What about our local defense plants?" he asked. "Couldn't we save them by turning them to commercial production?" "I don't know about that," Amaury said, pulling himself up quickly from a slump. "I was reading that orders are down for commercial aircraft, too. Retool? Retool for what?" He leaned across his desk toward Rick, worked-up, the words coming quickly. "I've been thinking about this, Tak. We haven't been able to see how basically weak our economy is, because . . . well, we've been in a state of war, sort of. The cold war has created a kind of wartime economy, so to speak. We've been artificially geared toward defense. People don't know otherwise. They don't know how to think about the economy in different ways." "Jeez . . . all *right,*" Rick said, shifting to a voice that sounded like Cheech Marin's. "Stu-pen-dous," and he held out his hand, palm open, as if presenting Amaury to the class.

----

10   Rick typically spent his lunch break in his room, leaving the door open for anyone who wanted to talk, hang out, or just have a place to eat alone. During my visit, several groups came together and dispersed, following an easy rhythm of food and talk. Over by the filing cabinets, a group of Asian students–Chinese, Japanese, Korean, Filipino–ate lunch from plastic containers and gossiped and laughed. "Hey, Mr. Takagaki," one girl asked Rick as he walked by, "did you know that when Chinese people go on a diet, they eat with one chopstick?" Next to them, four boys– one African American, three White (two with long 1960s hair)–reviewed the Lakers' game ("Did you see that airball?") the movie *Sliver* ("William Baldwin is *so* lame"), and Uni's chocolate fundraising drive (lame as well)–and then made plans for a basketball game later that day. A group from Rick's AP government class (students accepted at places like Yale and Brown) sat and stood around him by his desk, discussing the legality of a district proposal to conduct random weapons searches; reading and ridiculing a flier advertising Mace: "Stops drunks and psychotics . . ."; challenging Rick on books he'd recommended ("You know, Tak," said a boy in a Thelonius Monk T-shirt, "*Demian* was impossible"); and teasing one another about the prom: dates, clothes, hair, ride. Some of this was addressed to Rick, some to each other, Rick moving in and out, listening,

laughing, throwing it back, pushing on them about probable cause, reading lists, and the amount of money they were going to spend on the prom. Toward the end of the break, a girl came in and motioned Rick to the door. She looked upset and asked to talk to him about something another teacher had said to her. He pulled two chairs into a corner, out of earshot, and listened, nodding.

11   I took the opportunity to talk with Ayal Goury, one of the guys who had been dissecting *Sliver.* Brown hair, thin, cut-offs, Keds, he was planning to go to Hebrew University in Jerusalem to study social science. "Tak doesn't realize the influence he has on people," Ayal said. "I had been thinking of gong to NYU and majoring in business, but Tak's classes made me realize I needed to go experience things. Learn more about human behavior. I guess he got me to look at life in a different way. To take a step back, you know, and think and do the right thing. I mean, it's gotta be about more than getting a great stock deal and buying a car— that's ridiculous."

12   What was it that made Rick Takagaki a teacher of such influence? There were, of course, the qualities that Jack Moscowitz and Bonnie Williams described: he's stimulating, **cynically irreverent,** and has a quick, sparring style. From what I could tell, the role playing was effective, too. In addition to assuming roles himself, Rick encouraged his students to do the same: "Imagine you're the CEO of a large corporation." "Imagine you're the owner of a home in East LA, and you're losing it to a redevelopment project." All this opened up the discursive possibilities in the room. Some of the students seemed to have a lot of fun with it.

13   The many voices Rick assumed contributed to his appeal. In addition to the stern diction of Adam Smith and John Maynard Keynes (or, at other times in the semester, Marx and Lenin and Castro), he spoke in a number of styles, some from popular culture, some from the neighborhoods he had come to know. Rick grew up with second-generation *Nisei* parents in the racially mixed Crenshaw District, went to predominantly African-American elementary and junior high schools, and attended the very diverse LA High. He was at home across a range of cultures, and that familiarity revealed itself in his phonology and gesture. A hip-hop Socrates. What gets lost in most discussions of multiculturalism and education—from the right and the left—is the potential for joy in diversity: cultural gestures and practices **counterpointing** each other, mixing, sliding about in a vibrant social space. For its first several decades, University High School was almost exclusively White and Protestant. But as Japanese settled on nearby Sawtelle Boulevard in the mid-1930s— many opening nurseries on the then-spacious land—and as Jews migrated west from earlier settlements around downtown LA and then the Wilshire-Fairfax district, the ethnic composition of the high school began to change. It changed again in the mid-1970s as **mandated** integration brought students in from other sections of the city, parents as far

away as Huntington Park and South Gate (in the old industrial corridor, near Watts and Bell) having learned about the school's reputation. The mix, of course, has led to problems, given the broader ethnic conflicts in Los Angeles, but Uni remains a civil place, and Rick in his classroom tried to create a comfortable, at times comic, environment, where ethnic differences not only were respected but played out and played with.

14   But the heart of Rick's influence, I think, was his belief in each student's moral agency. For all the linguistic jabbing and hip cynicism, he conveyed admiration for his students' ability to make decisions, to come to reasoned judgment, to take a stand. Among the posters around the room, on prominent display was the photograph of the lone Chinese student stopping a row of tanks on Tiananmen Square.

15   "I was trained to believe," Rick told me as we drove down Sawtelle Boulevard, headed for home, "that you need to reach every student, every minute. Yet what you come to realize is that in the broad sweep of their lives, you're little more than a speck of sand . . ." he was tired; the classroom persona fading. He was more the Rick Takagaki his friends knew outside school, contemplative, soft-spoken. "If you can keep both of these things in your mind at the same time," he continued, "then . . . then you'll be a good teacher."

SOURCE: Mike Rose, *Possible Lives* (Boston: Houghton-Mifflin, 1995), pp. 46–51.

OUTLINING/CLUSTERING

I. Some words the principal (Jack Moskowitz) uses to describe Takagaki

A. _____

B. _____

C. _____

---

forgo: do without; **vestibule:** small entrance hall; **pennants:** long flags; **catalyst:** driving force; **sacrilegious:** disrespectful to sacred things; *laissez-faire* **capitalism:** not interfering in people's economic matters; **Hegelian syntheses:** philosophical concept in which opposing ideas join to form a new idea; **microeconomics:** study of individual elements in an economy; **fulminating:** shouting; **subsidization:** a form of economic assistance to citizens by the government; **mitigating:** alleviating; **banter:** playful talk; **pensive:** thinking deeply; **cynically:** in a manner questioning one's sincerity; **irreverent:** showing disrespect; **counterpointing:** presenting an opposite point; **mandated:** commanding

II. Some interesting ways Takagaki teaches

    A. _____

    B. _____

    C. _____

III. How Takagaki uses a mock trial to solve a classroom dispute

    A. _____

    B. _____

    C. _____

IV. Why Takagaki has a positive influence on his students

    A. _____

    B. _____

    C. _____

A SECOND READING

Reread the Rose selection and answer the following questions as you read. Before answering these questions, write in your reading journal about any questions or comments you have about this selection.

1. In paragraph 5, Takagaki takes on the persona of the economist Adam Smith. What is his purpose for teaching this way?

2. The principal says of Rick Takagaki that "he holds students accountable for their opinions." What does he mean here?

3. What was the educational purpose of having a jury decide on a classroom dispute (paragraph 8)?

4. Why do you think Takagaki stays in with his students at lunch (paragraph 10)?

5. Reread paragraph 15. Here Rick talks about what it takes to be a good teacher. Discuss what he is suggesting.

READING/WRITING FEATURE: NARRATIVES

A *narrative* is a work of fiction or nonfiction that recreates an experience through description and dialogue. Successful narratives make the experience real, even if it is made up. The Rose selection is a fitting example of a successful narration. By the time you finish reading about Rick

Takagaki, you have a rich understanding of the high school, the students, and, most importantly, Rick and the sort of teacher he is.

Successful narratives include detailed descriptions of people and places. Look at paragraph 1 of the Rose selection. See how careful Rose is in describing the area surrounding the high school in paragraph 1 and the high school campus itself in paragraph 2. Before we even are introduced to the economics teacher, we know where he teaches, down to the shrubbery on the campus: "rose beds, birds of paradise, carob trees" (paragraph 2).

Rose succeeds in describing Takagaki mainly through *dialogue*–the words used in conversation. Note how Rose has taken down the words of the principal, Takagaki's own words, students' commentary about him, and teachers' statements about Takagaki's teaching. All paint a clear picture of the kind of successful teacher Rick is. Note also that Rose knows what sort of dialogue to choose–thought-provoking commentary that leaves much to the reader's imagination. For example, just what does the principal mean when he says of Takagaki: "He's a stimulus, a catalyst, and irritant" (paragraph 4)? What does Takagaki mean when he talks about his role of a teacher as being "little more than a speck of sand . . ." (paragraph 15)?

Furthermore, successful narratives are a careful blending of description and dialogue. In the Rose selection, for example, note how the writer moves gracefully from what people say about Rick to Rose's description of him and his school.

Finally, narratives that work do not try to do too much. They have one purpose in mind, in this case to describe this very accomplished teacher, and do not diffuse this purpose with other narratives.

As a careful reader and writer of narratives, ask yourself the following questions:

1. Can I visualize what is being described? What is left unclear?

2. Does the dialogue provide information that I need to understand the purpose of the narrative? Does the dialogue reveal important information about the speaker or what the speaker is describing? Is there too much or too little dialogue?

3. Is there a purpose to the narrative that I can infer, or does the narrative seem to try to say too much and have several purposes?

4. Do the description and dialogue work together to create a believable world and a purpose?

Narrative writing differs from the essays you will often write in college. In your essays, you are more commonly asked to state your purpose early on and prove it with convincing evidence. In effective narratives, like Rose's, there is a purpose, but it is up to you to infer what it is. No well-crafted narrative will begin by stating: "In this narrative, I plan to . . ." What the writer plans to do and how effective he or she is in doing it is up to you, the reader, to determine.

A narrative is creative rather than expository writing. As you continue to read and write in college, you may discover that you are more talented in writing the narrative rather than in composing the successful academic essay.

BEFORE YOU WRITE

Before selecting a writing topic, you may want to study parallelism and complete Practice A19 (pages 229–230); then study the use of long quotes and complete Practice B19 (pages 259–260) of the handbook.

WRITING TOPICS

Choose either topic from the following questions. Follow the steps of the writing process on the inside front cover as you complete your drafts.

Writing about the Reading

1. Having read about Rick Takagaki, the economics teacher, determine why you think he is so successful. Carefully examine Takagaki the person, examples of his teaching, and what students and colleagues say about him. Be sure to bring out what the description and dialogue are inferring about Takagaki's teaching. Are there any other qualities of a successful teacher that are not shown in Takagaki?

Writing from Experience

2. Write a narrative in which you describe the *best* or the *worst* teacher you ever had. Use detailed description and dialogue to bring this teacher to life. If you can't remember the dialogue that took place with your teacher, re-create it the best you can from memory.

RESPONDING TO STUDENT WRITING

Use some or all of these questions to respond to your draft or to that of your classmate. Read carefully for meaning and make your comments specific.

1. (For question 1) Early on in the draft, is there a clear, general statement made about why Takagaki is such a successful teacher? If there is not, how can this statement be improved?

2. Is the detail presented to describe Takagaki or the teacher of your choice clear? Are there any other details you would like to add here?

3. Is dialogue included in the middle of the draft? In essay 1, is the dialogue analyzed for what is inferred about Takagaki? If it is not, what else should be commented on? In essay 2, is the dialogue appropriate,

that is, does it reveal important characteristics about the teacher that is described? If not, how can the dialogue be improved?

4. Select a paragraph that is most detailed and well organized. Explain why you believe this is the most successful paragraph.

5. Edit for obvious errors in spelling and sentence fragments, pronoun errors, and incorrect use of parallelism. If you are unsure about a particular error, ask your instructor for help before making the correction.

SELECTION 20: FROM *ORDINARY RESURRECTIONS* BY JONATHAN KOZOL

This selection by Jonathan Kozol, titled *Ordinary Resurrections,* is an excerpt from a series of recollections on effective teachers. For many years, Kozol has been writing about the negative effects that urban schools have on minority children. Here, Kozol changes his theme somewhat and describes some gifted teachers that have improved the lives of young people in the South Bronx of New York City.

This excerpt powerfully describes several of these teachers, one teacher in particular. Relying on the organizational pattern of description, Kozol relates incidents in the classrooms he observes that show how these teachers improve the lives of these children of poverty.

This selection will hold your interest because the narratives concerning these teachers are so well crafted.

READING/WRITING PREP

Before reading this selection, answer the following questions in a free-writing journal or in group discussion:

1. What conditions can make teaching in poor urban schools challenging?

2. Do you remember a teacher who was able to win over a class of difficult students? In what specific ways was this teacher successful?

PREVIEWING

Preview the following selection. Read through the first two paragraphs and then move through the excerpt quickly to get a sense for the teachers that Kozol will describe. Before you read critically, write a sentence describing the problems that urban New York City school teachers face when teaching arts and music.

The teaching of arts and music in New York City's urban schools:

_____

_____

_____

_____

_____

READING CRITICALLY

Now critically read the selection and complete the following outline as you read or after you finish. You may want to make this outline into a visual cluster of the important information.

Jonathan Kozol

From *Ordinary Resurrections*

1 New York City once had comprehensive art and music programs for the children in the elementary schools. Most of this was terminated years ago as a cost-saving measure at a time of what was called "the fiscal crisis" in New York, around the same time that the city also took school doctors from the elementary schools and more or less **dismantled** what had once been very good school libraries in order to save money on librarians and books. Since that time there have been several long-extended periods of great prosperity in New York City, and the city's revenues, of course, have soared in recent years during the escalations of stock values, which have brought unprecedented profits to the banking and investment principalities of Wall Street; but the savage cutbacks in the personnel and services available to children in the city's public schools, who now are overwhelmingly black and Hispanic, have not been restored.

2 So third-grade kids at P.S. 28 learn to make do, and make music, with imaginary flutes; and the children here at P.S. 30 get a couple of hours of good choral practice once or twice a week with a retired black instructor who received his love of music from a mother born to segregation in the South and does his best to pass these treasures on to children born into another kind of segregation, nearly as absolute but possibly a good deal less **genteel** and less protective than the somewhat milder kind of rural isolation that his mother knew some sixty years before.

3 The detail that stuck with me was the way he reached his hand out to the child who was lying on her stomach next to him and lightly

touched her on her hair. I've seen Mr. Bedrock do exactly the same thing: reaching out one of his hands to graze one of the children on the shoulder, or an elbow, or her hair, not even looking up but knowing somehow that the child's there. The children in his class like to pretend that they're eavesdropping on his conversations, peering up at him obliquely like small **espionage** agents, with stage smiles. He'll just reach out while he and I are talking and locate the child's hand or arm and maybe draw the child in to him and hold her head beneath his arm like a good-natured soccer ball, and then look down and act surprised, as if to say, "What have we here?"

4   Mr. Bedrock used to teach at Temple University. He was a war resister in the 1960s and served time in prison. He's a deeply serious man, and he's politically tough-minded. His observations about life among the children, his belief in their intelligence and moral goodness, and his recognition of the obstacles that many face, as well as his intense, unsparing condemnation of New York for its apparently eternal acquiescence in the racial isolation of these children, had a powerful effect in focusing my own perceptions of the neighborhood and reinforcing my beliefs about the structural **inequities** that narrowed opportunity for many of these girls and boys.

5   Political loyalties, however, as some of us learn belatedly, do not automatically equate to qualities that make a teacher likable, exciting, or successful in the classroom. I think that Mr. Bedrock's **pedagogic** victories have less to do with his political beliefs than with his willingness to let the children know him as the somewhat undefended, open-hearted, earnestly affectionate good person that he really is.

6   "She misbehaved" he told me once about a child who was making faces at him while we spoke, "because she knows I love her."

7   Sometimes his students do get out of hand. When they do, he seems to know the way to get them back under control. Mrs. Gamble has imaginary music for this purpose. Mr. Bedrock has his own approaches, which do not exclude raising his voice from time to time, although his far more usual approach to moments of disorder is to show a truly pained expression on his face and to convey his disappointment in a voice of mournful sorrow. "I don't understand why there is *any* need for table six to talk about the definition of a simile," he said one day this fall when I was in his class. "I admit it isn't a terrific lesson but you're *not* making things easier by talking." When the children saw him smiling after those distressing words, they looked relieved and actually did quiet down to keep their teacher happy.

8   Both Mr. Bedrock and Mrs. Gamble are politically sophisticated people. Yet both respect, and keep alive, another part of the imagination that does not belong especially to politics or even, really, **intellection;** they both retain their playfulness and, even more than that, they *learn* some of that playfulness from being in the company of children.

9   I was with Mr. Bedrock once in April when he took a group of older boys for mathematics. The subject of the lesson was "improper fractions." Isaiah was in the class that day and the idea of "proper" or "improper" fractions struck him as amusing. Mr. Bedrock asked him what he found so funny and Isaiah simply said the words with an exaggerated English accent, in the phrasing you might hear in films about the British upper class. Mr. Bedrock picked up on Isaiah's humor and continued with the lesson on improper fractions in a very funny, very "proper-sounding" imitation of an English gentleman. It was only a brief moment in a long day of instruction, but it helped to lighten up the lesson and perhaps to animate a subject that the students here apparently had had a hard time learning.

10   In the cafeteria one day, a child in his fourth-grade class came up to him with several very tiny cakes with decorations in the frosting, which she'd brought from home. She held them on her hand and told him, "Look!" and asked him if he wanted one for his dessert. They were the size of postage stamps. There was something so mysterious about the way she seemed to speculate upon those little cakes!

11   "I don't know . . . ," he said, "They look too good to eat."

12   He peered into the child's hand as if the cakes were tiny works of medieval sculpture. "Did your mother make them?"

13   "No," the child said, "they're from the store."

14   "I don't know . . . ," he said again, making it seem a difficult decision. Then he chose one of the cakes and popped it in his mouth and ate it in one swallow.

15   "Is it good?"

16   "I'm full!" he said.

17   The child laughed and went back to her table.

18   Why does this remind me of the moment in the garden of the church when Mother Martha and Katrice were watching Otto and the other children playing in the sprinkler? It is, perhaps, only the pleasing insignificance of a spontaneous connection between adult **sensibilities** and juvenile amusement. Elio's pants are falling off. The priest, who went to court this afternoon to get a teenage boy released from the Manhattan lockup called "The Tombs" and who returned with the frustration that she almost always feels when coping with the overloaded courts, is suddenly relaxed and carefree, and gets soaked!

19   Grown-ups need these moments just as much as children do. The water refreshes the bodies of the children and renews the **torpid** air of afternoon. The laughter of the children is refreshing too. Carried away by unimportant **bellicose** preoccupations, some of them call out from time to time to make sure that the grown-ups are not missing anything that's going on.

20   "Look, Katrice!"

21   "What is it, child?"

22   "Look, Katrice!"

23   "I'm looking!" says Katrice.

24   "Look! Look, Katrice!" another child cries.

25   "Lord's sake, child!" says Katrice. "What more do you want of me? I'm *looking!*"

26   She sounds slightly put upon. It's part of her manner, though. Her Caribbean lilt, as always, is quite beautiful and full of tenderness. I am reminded of imaginary music.

SOURCE: Jonathan Kozol, *Ordinary Resurrections* (New York: Crown, 2000), pp. 280–284.

OUTLINING/CLUSTERING

I. Why teaching arts and music in New York City's urban schools is a problem

_____

II. Mr. Bedrock's style of teaching

A. _____

B. _____

C. _____

III. How Mr. Bedrock maintains classroom harmony

A. _____

B. _____

C. _____

IV. How Mr. Bedrock teaches mathematics creatively

A. _____

B. _____

V. What children can teach their teachers

A. _____

B. _____

---

dismantled: taken apart; **genteel:** well bred; **espionage:** spying;
inequities: unfairnesses; **pedagogic:** pertaining to teaching;
intellection: thinking; **sensibilities:** feelings; **torpid:** sluggish;
bellicose: warlike

A SECOND READING

Reread the Kozol selection and answer the following questions as you read. Before answering these questions, write in your reading journal about any questions or comments you have about the selection.

1. What is unfair for Kozol about the prosperity in New York City and its neglect of the arts and music in the public schools (paragraph 1)?

2. Why is touch so important for Mr. Bedrock's relationship with his students (paragraph 3)?

3. Paraphrase the following sentence: "I think that Mr. Bedrock's pedagogic victories have less to do with his political beliefs than with his willingness to let the children know him as the somewhat undefended, open-hearted, earnestly good person that he really is" (paragraph 5).

4. What is the important point that Kozol makes about playfulness and teaching (paragraph 8)?

5. What is Kozol suggesting about the way Katrice scolds her students (paragraph 26)?

READING/WRITING FEATURE:
IDENTIFYING MOOD AND TONE

Reading fictional and nonfictional literature involves understanding your responses to the world the writer creates. This response emerges from the inferences you make from the language the writer chooses, the style he or she selects, and the kind of narrative being told. You have previously been introduced to ways to make inferences, to diction, and to style in Selections 2, 7, and 11.

Your response to a narrative is its *mood*–that is, the feeling you derive from the work. The mood of the work, as the mood in life, spans a wide spectrum of emotions from extreme joy to debilitating sadness. In the Kozol selection, a mood most readers would describe is a comforting, caring feeling that the teachers have for their students and a feeling of despair for the insensitivity that the school system has regarding its children's education.

Putting into words the mood you sense for a narrative is a helpful practice to develop because you must then consider the important tools the writer uses: the connotations of words, his or her style, the nature of the narrative, and the kinds of characters developed. In the *Ordinary Resurrections* excerpt, for example, Kozol uses gentle words like "lightly touched" and "draw the child in to him" (paragraph 3) to create a sense of comfort that Mr. Bedrock orchestrates in his classroom. Throughout this paragraph and others describing Mr. Bedrock's teaching, the language

Kozol selects has nonthreatening connotations. Similarly, Kozol describes peaceful, playful actions to explain Mr. Bedrock's teaching: a child lying on her stomach or Mr. Bedrock lightly touching a child's hair (paragraph 3).

Here are some tips to use when identifying the mood of a narrative:

1. Right after reading, write down those words that come to your mind about the feelings you have. They do not necessarily have to complement each other at this time.

2. What characters seem the most striking or peculiar? What feelings do they evoke in you?

3. Is the style simple or complicated? How does the style help you express your feelings for the work?

4. Do the descriptive words (for example, *peace, disorder, fear, love,* and so on) seem to fit into any pattern?

5. Now look back at the list of words you initially wrote down. Are there any that seem to work together? Are there any more you want to add or any you want to delete?

6. Finally, write a sentence or two that best describes your feeling, or mood, regarding the work you read.

Identifying tone involves similar practices. The *tone* of a work or fiction or nonfiction is the writer's unstated attitude toward his or her subject. Determining tone is a more difficult task because you must infer the writer's, not your, feelings toward the subject. Often the author expresses a sympathetic or unsympathetic tone toward his or her subject.

The tone in this excerpt of *Ordinary Resurrections* seems to focus on the caring teachers Kozol has found in the New York City School system. Kozol has tremendous respect for those loving teachers who consistently see the world through their students' eyes. You can infer this respect for sensitive teachers from the positive connotations of the language he uses to describe them. You can also infer a strong dislike for large, bureaucratic school systems that ignore what is best for all children. For example, note how Kozol describes the school system's economic decisions as "savage cutbacks in the personnel and services available to students" (paragraph 1). "Savage" has strong negative connotations of cruelty and brutality, in contrast to the positive connotations of the words that Kozol selects to describe the kind teachers. You can thus conclude that there is a striking difference in Kozol's mind between teachers and the system for which they work. You can, in fact, say that the tone of Kozol's excerpt is dual: on the one hand, sympathy for the teachers and, on the other, a strong dislike for the system that makes decisions about the teachers and the students.

To correctly identify the author's tone, you must consider the following suggestions:

1. See which character earns your greatest respect. This is often the character the author respects as well.

2. Put into words the issues that the narrative examines: prejudice, political beliefs, religious beliefs, patriotism, and so on.

3. From the events in the narrative, put into words what you think the author's attitude is toward these issues and give a few reasons why. For example, you can conclude that Kozol is unsympathetic toward educational bureaucrats making decisions in offices away from children but is very sympathetic to teachers who find ways to understand children and who ignore many of the demands of their school system.

Determining mood and tone as you analyze works of fiction and non-fiction will make your reading more focused. Similarly, when you write narratives, consider what mood you want to evoke in your reader and the tone that your narrative suggests. Revise your drafts with these considerations in mind.

BEFORE YOU WRITE

Before selecting a writing topic, you may want to study the participial phrase and complete Practice A20 (pages 230–231); then study where to place page numbers after a quote and complete Practice B20 (pages 260–261) of the handbook.

WRITING TOPICS

Choose an essay topic from the following questions. Follow the steps of the writing process summarized on the inside front cover.

Writing about the Reading

1. In this excerpt from *Ordinary Resurrections,* Jonathan Kozol describes the teaching strengths of Mr. Bedrock. Select relevant details from this excerpt that demonstrate the kind of teacher Mr. Bedrock is. Analyze each detail carefully and determine what you can infer from each detail or anecdote. Finally, explain why you believe Mr. Bedrock is such a successful teacher.

2. In the last two selections, you have read about two very talented teachers: Rick Takagaki and Mr. Bedrock. Compare the teaching abilities of these two gifted men, showing how their teaching styles are similar and how they differ. Be specific in your discussion of these similarities and differences, providing revealing details from each of their teaching experiences. You may want to refer to the discussion of the compare-and-contrast organizational pattern in Chapter 3 as you draft your essay.

Writing from Experience

3. Describe a teacher that you have had who was as compassionate as Mr. Bedrock. This teacher could have come from any level of your education—elementary, secondary, or college. Where possible, describe narrative moments that show the ways in which this teacher was effective. Be as detailed as you can. Write so that your reader can determine a definite mood from your narrative. Some of the moods your narrative can create include pleasure, peace, comfort, or belonging.

4. Write a narrative in which you describe how you were mistreated by a particular teacher, at any level of your education. State clearly what your teacher did to make you feel uncomfortable and describe your response to this negative treatment. Again, strive for a narrative that creates a definite mood and tone.

RESPONDING TO STUDENT WRITING

Use some or all of these questions to respond to your draft or to that of your classmate. Read carefully for meaning and make your comments specific.

1. Does the draft have a clear direction, that is, do you know what the writer plans to do? If not, provide ways to make the beginning clearer.

2. (For questions 1 and 2) Does the writer provide accurate and important detail from the excerpt to support the points made? If not, which details should be included or deleted, or which are inaccurate?

3. (For questions 3 and 4) Does the writer provide sufficient detail in the narrative? What sections of the narrative are unclear and need further detail?

4. Of all the paragraphs in the draft, which is the most successful? Explain why.

5. Edit for obvious errors in spelling and punctuation. Also edit for grammatical errors and incorrect punctuation of quoted material. If you are unsure about a particular punctuation in the draft, ask your instructor for assistance.

FOLLOW-UP

Now that you have read several selections on how young people learn, answer the following questions in a free-writing journal or in group discussion.

1. List several characteristics that describe an effective school.

2. Of the four writers on learning that you have read, which do you agree with most? Which do you agree with least? State why. Which areas of learning do you think these writers have not covered, and which areas would you like to learn more about?

PART III

A Writer's Handbook

■━━━━━■

A HANDBOOK OF GRAMMAR, USAGE, AND WRITING CONVENTIONS

This handbook addresses the most important topics in grammar, usage, and writing convention that you need to know to edit your writing. A short topic is introduced, and a practice follows. With each practice, you will be editing for that specific topic on a sample student writing.

This handbook is divided into two sections: A. Grammar and Usage, which deals with sentence-level issues of grammar and punctuation, and B. Writing Conventions, which addresses ways to effectively present material and correctly cite your evidence in these paragraphs. In the Writing Conventions section, you will also complete five review practices to test your understanding of all that you have learned up to that point.

A.

GRAMMAR AND USAGE: EXPLANATIONS AND PRACTICES

The topics covered in this part of the handbook are the following:

 1. **Editing for sentence fragments without subjects**
 2. **Editing for sentence fragments with adjective clauses**
 3. **Editing for sentence fragments with adverbial clauses**
 4. **Editing for run-on sentences as comma splices**
 5. **Editing for run-ons as fused sentences**
 6. **Subject-verb agreement**
 7. **Punctuating the compound sentence**
 8. **Punctuating the adverbial clause**
 9. **Using the adjective clause**
10. **The compound-complex sentence**
11. **Using the semicolon**
12. **Using the colon**
13. **Using appositives**
14. **Using the dash**
15. **Using the noun clause**
16. **The use of "There is . . . " and "There are . . . "**
17. **Effective use of pronouns**
18. **Use of "who" and "whom"**
19. **Parallelism**
20. **Using participial phrases**

1. EDITING FOR SENTENCE FRAGMENTS WITHOUT SUBJECTS

A common error found in college student writing is the sentence fragment. A *sentence fragment* is often defined as an incomplete thought. However, many people disagree with each other over what is a complete or incomplete thought. As you continue to write, you will find that certain rules in grammar and punctuation will help you determine what constitutes a complete thought in writing.

An important term that you need to understand to begin identifying sentence fragments is a clause. A *clause* is a group of words containing a subject and a verb.

A *verb* is a word stating an action (I *run*), a condition (I *require*), or an assertion (I *want*). It must agree with the subject in number; that is, it is either singular (one) or plural (more than one):

She *reads.* (singular verb)
They *read.* (plural verb)

A verb must also agree with a subject in person. Person includes first (I, we), second (you), and third (he, she, it, they).

A *subject* is the second necessary part of a sentence. It must agree with the verb in number and person:

I read. (first person)
You read. (second person)
He reads. (third person)

Sometimes students write a group of words that they think is a sentence but is lacking a subject. Without a subject, this group of words then becomes a sentence fragment. Study the following example:

Robert couldn't read to his children. And couldn't help them with their homework.

Do you see how the first sentence is complete because it has a subject and a verb ("Robert" and "could not read"), whereas the second is a fragment because there is no subject, only a verb ("could not help")?

As you write, look over your sentences to see if you can identify a subject and verb in each sentence.

PRACTICE A1: EDITING FOR SENTENCE FRAGMENTS WITHOUT SUBJECTS

The following is a section of a reading journal on the Merina selection. It contains four sentence fragments that do not have subjects. Correct each one by supplying a subject, identify each error by sentence number, and then make the correction in the space provided.

(1) Robert Mendez is an amazing man. (2) At age 35 he could not read. (3) Now has published articles and poetry. (4) He speaks about literacy throughout the country. (5) Even spoke at the United Nations. (6) And has time to help his son.

(7) To me, Robert Mendez showed how important reading is. (8) And showed us all that it's never too late to learn.

1. _____

_____

2. _____

_____

3. _____

_____

4. _____

_____

---

2. EDITING FOR SENTENCE FRAGMENTS WITH ADJECTIVE CLAUSES

Students often write sentence fragments, or incomplete thoughts, in the form of dependent clauses. Remember that a clause is a group of words with a subject and a verb. A *dependent clause* is a group of words that must be attached to a complete sentence.

One type of dependent clause is the *adjective clause,* which is a dependent clause modifying a noun. Adjective clauses are always introduced with one of the following words, called *relative pronouns:* who, that, which whom, whose.

Look at the following sentence fragments using adjective clauses:

Who published her first article twenty years ago.
Which was titled <u>Sugar</u>.

Sentence fragments with adjective clauses are easily corrected by attaching them to the sentence that comes before, as in the following two examples:

Melannie Svoboda was the writer *who published her first article twenty years ago.*
In third grade, Svoboda wrote her first book, *which was titled <u>Sugar</u>.*

Sentence fragments with adjective clauses can also be corrected by making the adjective clause into a sentence of its own. This is accomplished by replacing the relative pronoun with another word that becomes the subject of the sentence:

She published her first article twenty years ago.
Her first book was titled <u>Sugar</u>.

PRACTICE A2: EDITING FOR SENTENCE FRAGMENTS WITH ADJECTIVE CLAUSES

Read the following paragraph from an essay on a student's learning experience. It includes three sentence fragments with adjective clauses. Identify each sentence by number, and then rewrite each one in the space provided. You can correct these fragments in more than one way.

(1) My senior high writing teacher was terrific because she helped me understand my writing strengths. (2) That were often hard for me to identify. (3) She was the kind of teacher who spoke to each of her students individually. (4) And who never made us nervous when she called us up to her desk. (5) Mrs. Frank always had something nice to say about my writing. (6) Which became clearer and stronger as the semester went on.

1. _____

_____

2. _____

_____

3. _____

_____

---

3. EDITING FOR SENTENCE FRAGMENTS WITH ADVERBIAL CLAUSES

Another common way to write sentence fragments is to mistakenly use an adverbial clause for a complete sentence. As with fragments with adjective clauses, you can easily correct this adverbial clause fragment by attaching it to the previous sentence.

Like an adjective clause, an adverbial clause is a dependent clause. An *adverbial clause* is a group of words with a subject and a verb that together modifies a verb, adjective, or adverb. Adverbial clauses begin with *subordinating conjunctions.* These conjunctions signal the following relationships: time, purpose, comparison, contrast, and condition. They present the same kinds of relationships as some of the organizational patterns you have studied in Chapter 3.

Here is a list of the most common subordinating conjunctions. They will help you identify adverbial clauses and sentence fragments with adverbial clauses:

time: *after, before, until, when, whenever, while, as*
purpose or reason: *because, since*
comparison: *just as*
contrast: *although, though*
condition: *if, as if, unless, in order that, so that, whether*

Look at the following two clauses. See if you can determine which one is the complete sentence and which is the sentence fragment with an adverbial clause.

Computers help many young adults learn to read. Although they do not solve all of their reading problems.

Do you see that the second clause is the sentence fragment? Your clue is that it begins with the subordinating conjunction "although." Look how this fragment can be easily corrected:

Computers help many young adults learn to read although they do not solve all of their reading problems.

It is helpful to memorize these subordinating conjunctions so that you can more easily spot adverbial clauses in your writing and correct possible sentence fragments.

PRACTICE A3: EDITING FOR SENTENCE FRAGMENTS WITH ADVERBIAL CLAUSES

Read the following paragraph from the middle of an essay on a student's reading experiences in elementary school. It contains three sentence fragments with adverbial clauses. Identify each error by sentence number and then make the correction in the space provided.

(1) I remember the first book I read in first grade. (2) As if it were yesterday. (3) It was a small reading book about trains. (4) I was six, and I loved learning as much as I could about trains. (5) Because I had taken a train ride as a very young child. (6) When my mother had to visit her parents in the neighboring state of Oregon.

1. _____

_____

2. _____

_____

3. _____

_____

4. EDITING FOR RUN-ON SENTENCES AS COMMA SPLICES

Writing run-on sentences is a common writing error. A *run-on* sentence is the opposite of a sentence fragment. In a run-on, two sentences are incorrectly joined, either with or without a comma. If the sentences are incorrectly joined with a comma, the error is called a *comma splice*.

Look at the following example of a comma splice:

Malcolm X desperately wants to learn to read, he begins by studying the dictionary.

You can correct a comma splice either by placing a period between the independent clauses, making two separate sentences, or by placing a semicolon (;) between them, joining the two sentences into one correctly punctuated sentence. Semicolons are often used to join two clauses that are closely related in meaning.

Look at how this comma splice can be corrected in two different ways: the first with a period and the second with a semicolon:

1. Malcolm X desperately wants to learn to read. He begins by studying the dictionary.
2. Malcolm X desperately wants to learn to read; he begins by studying the dictionary.

You can also use coordinating conjunctions to correct comma splices. *Coordinating conjunctions* are connecting words, for example: *and, but, so, or, for, yet.* When coordinating conjunctions join two independent clauses, a comma comes before the conjunction. Be sure the conjunction you use shows a correct relationship between the two independent clauses, for example:

Malcolm X desperately wants to learn to read, *so* he begins by studying the dictionary.

The coordinating conjunction "so" correctly relates these two independent clauses because it shows the reason why Malcolm X studies the dictionary.

PRACTICE A4: EDITING FOR RUN-ON SENTENCES AS COMMA SPLICES

Read the following paragraph from the body of an essay describing an ideal elementary school. It contains three comma splices. Identify each by sentence number and then rewrite each one correctly in the space provided. You can correct these three comma splices in several ways.

(1) Reading would be an important part of each school day, it would take place in the morning and in the afternoon. (2) In the morning, students would learn some phonics rules. (3) The teacher would present the lesson, the students would do an exercise showing that they understood the lesson. (4) The afternoon would be different. (5) Students would choose any book they wanted to read, they would be given an hour of silent reading with no interruptions.

1. _____

_____

2. _____

_____

3. _____

_____

5. EDITING FOR RUN-ONS AS FUSED SENTENCES

A second type of run-on sentence is called a fused sentence. A *fused sentence* incorrectly joins two sentences together without any punctuation between them. Look at the following example of a fused sentence:

Luis wants to help his son Ramiro he has gotten himself involved with gang members in Chicago.

You can correct this fused sentence by placing a period between the two sentences, making two separate sentences, or by placing a semicolon between them, thus making one correctly punctuated sentence. Look at how the previous sentence is corrected in two ways:

1. Luis wants to help his son Ramiro. He has gotten himself involved with gang members in Chicago.
2. Luis want to help his son Ramiro; he has gotten himself involved with gang members in Chicago.

As with comma splices, you can also use coordinating conjunctions to correct a fused sentence. Remember that coordinating conjunctions are the connecting words, which include:

and, but, so, for, or, yet

Be sure that the conjunction you choose shows a correct relationship between the sentences, for example:

Luis wants to help his son Ramiro, for he has gotten himself involved with gang members in Chicago.

Luis wants to help Ramiro because his son has gotten involved with gangs. "For" is therefore an appropriate conjunction.

PRACTICE A5: EDITING FOR RUN-ONS AS FUSED SENTENCES

Read the following paragraph from the body of an essay on "La Vida Loca." It contains three fused sentences. Identify each by sentence number and then rewrite each one correctly in the space provided. You can correct these fused sentences in several ways.

(1) Luis lived a rough childhood he broke the law many times. (2) He once beat up a policeman. (3) Luis was involved in several robberies he also used drugs at an early age. (4) One of the drugs was heroin. (5) At his worst, Luis sniffed spray he had a near death experience.

1. _____

_____

2. _____

_____

3. _____

_____

---

6. SUBJECT-VERB AGREEMENT

Students sometimes make errors in subject-verb agreement, especially when the subject is separated from the verb. A *subject-verb agreement* error occurs when the subject does not agree in number with the verb. Usually an "s" is added to a present-tense verb to make it singular, as in the following example:

Ressler *believes* that a violent childhood can lead to a violent adult life.

The "s" is commonly removed when the subject is plural, as in this sentence:

Ressler and his research team *believe* that emotional violence is as dangerous as physical violence.

When a prepositional phrase separates the subject from the verb, writers often mistake the object of the preposition for the subject of the sentence. They then wrongly make the object of the *preposition* agree with the verb. The following examples are incorrect:

Every one of Ressler's killers *show* some sort of violent childhood.
Ressler's emphasis on environmental factors *are* helpful to study the behavior of serial killers.

In the first sentence, the subject is "one," not "killers," so the verb should read "shows" and not "show." In the second sentence, "emphasis" is the subject and not "factors," so the verb that it agrees with should be "is," not "are." In both cases, the prepositional phrase separates the subject of the sentence from the verb with which it must agree.

When you are editing your writing for grammar and usage errors, be careful to identify the subject correctly in sentences that have interrupting modifiers such as prepositional phrases.

PRACTICE A6: EDITING FOR SUBJECT-VERB AGREEMENT

Read the paragraph from the middle of an essay on serial killers. It contains two errors in subject-verb agreement. Identify each error by sentence number and then make the correction in the space provided.

(1) Monte Ralph Rissel has a seriously disturbed childhood. (2) One of his major problems were that he came from a divorced family. (3) Monte was forced to stay with his mother, but he wanted to be with his father. (4) A big part of Monte's childhood years were spent with siblings who took drugs. (5) His mother spent her time away from Monte with her new husband. (6) She seemed unconcerned about her son's whereabouts.

1. _____

_____

2. _____

_____

---

7. PUNCTUATING THE COMPOUND SENTENCE

A *compound sentence* is defined as two or more independent clauses joined together. These two independent clauses can be joined by coordinating conjunctions, which include *and, but, so, or, for, yet,* and *nor.*

These words were introduced earlier in the discussion on run-ons. When you write sentences of comparison and contrast, you often use coordinating conjunctions.

Independent clauses can also be joined by semicolons. You also learned about semicolons when you studied ways to correct run-ons.

When you use coordinating conjunctions, you must place a *comma* before the conjunction to show where one independent clause ends and another begins. Look at how the coordinating conjunction "and" joins these two independent clauses:

Some individuals are very upset with our government, *and* they may resort to violence to show their anger.

Often writers use these same conjunctions to join words or phrases. In these cases, you should not use a comma. See how the coordinating conjunction "and" joins two noun phrases and two verb phrases without a comma:

Federal law enforcement and state agencies were involved in tracking down Ted Kaczynski. (noun phrases joined by "and")
Thomas Powers *creates a profile of Ted Kaczynski and analyzes his behavior.* (verb phrases joined by "and")

In writing compound sentences, you can combine information that seems related. Furthermore, you can begin to vary your sentence structure so that you are not just writing simple sentences.

PRACTICE A7: CORRECTLY PUNCTUATING COMPOUND SENTENCES

The following paragraph on terrorism has two errors in punctuating a compound sentence. Identify each error by sentence number and then make the correction in the space provided.

(1) Some groups in America believe that they are losing their freedom and they blame the federal government. (2) These groups see the federal government as passing unnecessary laws. (3) Many of these laws either prevent them from owning and using firearms or they do not allow them to live in certain areas. (4) Some of these more militant groups feel they need to protect themselves and have banded together. (5) Such militant groups are made up of both young and old Americans.

1. _____

_____

2. _____

_____

8. PUNCTUATING THE ADVERBIAL CLAUSE

You have already learned something about adverbial clauses in editing for sentence fragments with adverbial clauses. Remember that an adverbial clause contains a subject and verb and that it modifies a verb, adjective, or adverb. Also remember that adverbial clauses always begin with *subordinating conjunctions* showing time, purpose or reason, comparison and contrast, and condition. You can review this list under Editing for Sentence Fragments with Adverbial Clauses discussed earlier in this handbook.

The punctuation rule to remember is: If you place an adverbial clause at the beginning or middle of the sentence, it must be set off with commas.

Study how these two sentences are punctuated:

When high school boys are lonely, they sometimes act out violently to get attention.
High school boys, when they are lonely, sometimes act out violently to get attention.

If you place an adverbial clause at the end of a sentence, it is not set off with commas:

High school boys sometimes act out violently to get attention when they are lonely.

Using adverbial clauses will add exactness to your sentences. You will be showing your reader your train of thought, demonstrating how one of your thoughts relates to another in terms of time, purpose, condition, or comparison.

PRACTICE A8: USING ADVERBIAL CLAUSES

The following paragraph on boys' aggression contains two errors in punctuating adverbial clauses. Identify each error by sentence number and then make the correction in the space provided.

(1) When boys are young and in school teachers often want them to sit quietly. (2) These boys are often considered emotionally disturbed when they do not listen to their teachers. (3) Some boys when they are asked to cooperate in small classroom groups feel uncomfortable. (4) These boys would rather work alone. (5) They have not learned the social skills that girls their age have mastered.

1. _____

_____

2. _____

_____

9. USING THE ADJECTIVE CLAUSE

The adjective clause is a dependent clause that modifies a noun. You were introduced to the adjective clause in the earlier section, Editing for Sentence Fragments with Adjective Clauses. The adjective clause has several interesting uses for a writer. Unlike the adverbial clause, the adjective clause must come after the noun that it modifies. You cannot place it anywhere you like in the sentence. Adverbial clauses are introduced by subordinating conjunctions, whereas adjective clauses commonly are introduced by words called *relative pronouns:* who, that which, whom, and whose.

Writers using the descriptive organizational pattern often rely on adjective clauses because they qualify and explain a particular noun. Consider the following example:

According to the author, television is a medium that has lost its popularity.

Do you see how "that has lost its popularity" describes television? Without this adjective clause, the sentence would be meaningless: "According to the author, television is a medium."

An *essential adjective clause* is one whose information is necessary to the meaning of the sentence, as in the example above. It is *never* set off with a comma.

A *nonessential adjective clause* is one that adds information to the independent clause but that is not essential to the meaning of the kernel sentence. It is *always* set off with a comma. Study the following example:

Television, which has been around for over fifty years, is now having to compete with other forms of entertainment technology.

The fact that television is over fifty years old is not essential for your knowing that television is in competition with other forms of technology.

As you read adjective clauses, you naturally pause before nonessential clauses, but you tend to move more quickly over an essential clause. Reread the two preceding examples. Do you hear a pause with your reading of the second sentence and no pause with your first?

PRACTICE A9: USING THE ADJECTIVE CLAUSE

The following paragraph on "Taking the Fun Out of Watching Television" contains two errors in punctuating an adjective clause. Identify each error by sentence number and then make the correction in the space provided.

(1) Television which I don't personally watch very often is in a state of change. (2) It is not the only form of home viewing that people can turn to. (3) The VCR is one of the inventions, which has given the viewer more choices. (4) Instead of watching a situation comedy, the viewer can

watch a movie she has rented from Blockbuster. (5) The VCR also allows the viewer tape a show and view it at a later date.

1. _____

_____

2. _____

_____

10. THE COMPOUND-COMPLEX SENTENCE

The compound-complex sentence is the most intricate sentence that you will write. It contains elements of both the complex sentence and the compound sentence, which you may have already studied. A compound sentence contains at least two independent clauses, while a complex sentence includes one independent and at least one dependent clause. A *compound-complex sentence* contains at least two independent clauses and at least one dependent clause. You need to follow all the punctuation rules that you learned for adverbial and adjective clauses, as well as those for the compound sentence. Figure H.1 shows how simple, compound, and compound-complex sentences are related.

FIGURE H.1
SIMPLE, COMPOUND, AND COMPLEX SENTENCES

Simple Sentence

    independent clause
Television commercials are not informative.

Compound Sentence

    independent clause   **conjunction   independent clause**
Television commercials are not informative,   but   people still watch them.

Compound-Complex Sentence

    dependent clause   **independent clause**
Although much money is spent on them, television commercials are not informative,
conjunction   independent clause
    but   people still watch them.

Study the following two sentences:

Although commercials are hugely profitable, they do not necessarily sell products.
Yet commercials are still being made.

Now see how they are combined into a compound-complex sentence:

Although commercials are hugely profitable, they do not necessarily sell products, yet commercials are still being made.

When you punctuate a compound-complex sentence, you should keep two basic punctuation rules in mind:

1. Dependent clauses at the beginning of a sentence are set off with a comma.
2. Two independent clauses joined by a conjunction are set off with a comma.

Did you notice that these two rules were used in our compound-complex sentence about commercials?

You can write compound-complex sentences that have several independent and dependent clauses, but they tend to become overwhelming. Like overly long paragraphs dealing with several ideas, long compound-complex sentences tend to lose their focus. In contrast, compound-complex sentences that are not overly long add sophistication to your writing. They show your reader that you have control of several punctuation rules and can correctly relate several bits of information in one sentence.

PRACTICE A10: THE COMPOUND-COMPLEX SENTENCE

Read the following paragraph on commercials. It contains three errors in punctuating compound-complex sentences, and two errors are in one sentence Identify the errors by sentence number and then make the corrections in the space provided.

(1) Although we may not pay attention to the television commercials which we watch every day they have become more sophisticated and they are now part of the programming itself. (2) Jingles no longer are effective ways to sell a product on television. (3) Many commercials now have long narratives that in some ways are similar to the narrative in the programs they sponsor. (4) One can say that commercials and programs are part of the same sales package so the viewer moves effortlessly from program to commercial. (5) These commercials are far different from those shown on television in the fifties and sixties.

1. _____

_____

2. _____

_____

_____

11. USING THE SEMICOLON

Student writers often have questions about how to use the semicolon correctly. There are three basic uses of the *semicolon.*

1. Semicolons can be used to join two independent clauses without a coordinating conjunction. These two sentences are often closely connected in meaning:

Rap music is a very popular musical form; it speaks of life in America's cities.

Note how the second independent clause is a further explanation for the first.

2. Semicolons are also used to join two independent clauses connected by the following conjunctions, called *conjunctive adverbs.* These conjunctive adverbs serve as transitions:

accordingly, moreover, nevertheless, furthermore, thus, therefore, however, consequently

Study the following sentence using a conjunctive adverb to join two independent clauses:

Rap music has become a popular black music form; however, gangsta rap seems to have offended many listeners of rap.

Note how "however" shows a contrast in meaning between the two independent clauses.

Do not use a semicolon when these adverbs are used within an independent clause, as in the following sentence:

Rap, however, is still a popular form of black music.

In this case, "however" does not join two independent clauses.

Note that in the first sentence, a semicolon comes before the conjunctive adverb and a comma comes after, so that the sentence pattern is:

independent clause + semicolon + conjunctive adverb + comma + independent clause

In the second sentence, "however" is used within the independent clause and is set off with a comma before and after it, so that the pattern is:

comma + however + comma

Like coordinating and subordinating conjunctions, conjunctive adverbs show your reader how the two clauses relate. In fact, conjunctive adverbs can be classified according to three of the organizational patterns that you have studied:

Cause-Effect	**Comparison**	**Contrast**
accordingly	moreover	nevertheless
thus	furthermore	however
therefore		
consequently		

Begin to use these conjunctive adverbs when your writing involves these organizational patterns.

If you choose, you can replace a semicolon with a period when you are joining two independent clauses:

Rap music has been a popular black music form. However, gangsta rap seems to have offended many listeners of rap.

3. A semicolon can be used to separate two independent clauses when you have already used commas in one or both of the clauses. In this case, a semicolon replaces a comma:

Rap music speaks of many urban concerns like gang life, poverty, and drug use; and rappers continue to reinterpret these topics.

Note how the commas in the first independent clause list nouns in a series, while the semicolon separates the two independent clauses. You would not be incorrect, though, if you replaced the semicolon with a comma as in the following:

Rap music speaks of many urban concerns like gang life, poverty, and drug use, and rappers continue to reinterpret these topics.

The following figure shows the three ways in which you can use semicolons and provides a clear summary for the sometimes baffling uses of the semicolon.

PRACTICE A11: USING THE SEMICOLON

The following paragraph on rap music has two sentence errors requiring the use of a semicolon. Identify each error by sentence number and then make the correction in the space provided.

(1) Rap music has captured the attention of American popular music lovers however its source is still the black urban culture. (2) The topics rap explores are those that speak most strongly to the black urban youth. (3) This is not to say that rap is only heard by African Americans. (4) Many young people from all races can relate to rap's topics. (5) Rap is a

FIGURE H.2

USES OF THE SEMICOLON

To join two independent clauses without a coordinating conjunction

  independent clause   **independent clause**
Rap music has gained in popularity; it is likely going to last a long time

To join two independent clauses with a conjunctive adverb

  independent clause **conjunctive adverb** **independent clause**
Rap music has gained in popularity; therefore, it is likely going to last a long time.

To separate two independent clauses when you have already used commas in either clause

    independent clause using commas
Rap music has gained in popularity among high school listeners, college listeners,
    independent clause
and many adults; and it is likely going to last a long time.

---

black art form, furthermore it is a music that is being produced and distributed largely by African Americans.

1. _____

_____

2. _____

_____

---

12. USING THE COLON

The *colon* has two important uses that you may want to apply to your writing:

 1. Colons are used to introduce an itemized list of words or phrases:

Country-and-western music lyrics often discuss the following social topics: failed relationships, crime, and employment problems.

 Note in this sentence that the colon comes after an independent clause, or complete statement, and is often placed after phrases like "in this manner," "in this way," or "in the following."

 2. Colons can also introduce a sentence if the sentence is especially important:

Rap music has one overriding intent: It wants to bring to light the real issues of urban life.

Colons add a degree of sophistication to your writing, showing your reader that you can effectively use more than just a period and a comma.

PRACTICE A12: USING THE COLON

The following paragraph on rap and country-and-western music contains two errors requiring the use of a colon. Identify each error by sentence number and then make the correction in the space provided.

(1) Rap and country-and-western music do not seem to have much in common. (2) Yet if you study these forms of music, you can look at how they explore the following topics, men's attitudes toward women, drug use, and making money. (3) They may not often agree on these issues, but they open these topics up to their listeners. (4) Listeners of rap and C&W may come from different ethnic and social groups. (5) Yet they both listen to these musical forms to answer the same question, How does this music help me understand my life?

1. _____

_____

2. _____

_____

---

13. USING APPOSITIVES

An *appositive* is a noun or pronoun that can replace another noun or pronoun that comes before or after it. If an appositive has a *modifier* attached to it, this group of words is called an *appositive phrase.* Here are examples of an appositive and an appositive phrase:

1. The author Hoeger has a clear understanding of terms related to fitness. (appositive)
2. Hoeger and Hoeger, the authors of this textbook, have a clear understanding of terms related to fitness. (appositive phrase)

In the first example, the appositive "Hoeger" and the subject "author" are synonyms. One can replace the other. In the second example, the appositive "authors" has a modifier attached to it "of this textbook," words that make it an appositive phrase. Note that the appositive phrase is set off by commas. Appositives are usually set off by commas. The only exception is when the appositive is a single word name. That is why the last name "Hoeger" in the first sentence is not set off by commas.

To add sentence variety to your style, you can place an appositive phrase at the beginning of a sentence. Again, you would set the appositive phrase off with a comma:

The authors of the textbook, Hoeger and Hoeger have a clear understanding of terms related to fitness.

Appositives and appositive phrases are effective tools that can be used to add sophistication to your writing style.

PRACTICE A13: USING APPOSITIVES

The following paragraph on fitness and health has two errors in punctuating appositives. Identify each error by sentence number and then make the correction in the space provided.

(1) Jim Fixx seemed to be the picture of health. (2) When Fixx was fifty pounds overweight, he began to jog. (3) The jogger, Fixx, reached the level of running 60 to 80 miles a week. (4) Fixx a fifty-two year old died suddenly of a heart attack. (5) He ignored the fact that his family had a long history of heart disease.

1. _____

_____

2. _____

_____

---

14. USING THE DASH

A dash, like the semicolon and colon, has specific punctuation uses. If you type or use the word processor, the dash is made by two unspaced hyphens. If you are writing by hand, it is simply two short, consecutive lines.

A *dash* is used to set off words, phrases, and sentences that the writer wants to emphasize. Often this material is listed in a series (three or more bits of information). Look at how the dashes are used in the following sentences on fitness and weight:

1. To be thin, to be fit, to be healthy--these are the goals of so many people today.
2. Some researchers--experts in their field, be it noted--are now suggesting that overweight people can be fit.

Note that in both sentences, the material set off by dashes is important to the meaning of the sentence. In the first sentence using a series, the three goals of people today are the sentence's focus. In the second sentence, the writer uses dashes to show that these researchers are experts in their field.

Dashes must not be consistently used in place of periods, commas, or colons. They should be called upon sparingly when you want to emphasize a particular part of your sentence.

PRACTICE A14: USING THE DASH

The following paragraph on weight and fitness contains two sentences that need to be punctuated with a dash. Identify each error by sentence number and then make the correction in the space provided.

(1) You are tired, you are sick, you are weak; these are some of the misconceptions we have about overweight people. (2) Some studies are now showing that being overweight is not necessarily a reason to be unhealthy. (3) These studies show that overweight but fit people are actually healthier than thin but unfit people. (4) The Cooper Institute in Dallas, a respected organization on fitness and health, I might add, showed that death rates among overweight but fit men was markedly less than those of thin but unfit men. (5) This research is interesting and needs to be made public to those who still believe that thin is always healthy.

1. _____

_____

2. _____

_____

---

15. USING THE NOUN CLAUSE

Like the adjective and adverbial clauses, the noun clause cannot stand alone. A *noun clause* is a dependent clause that replaces a noun. It is usually found in the object and subject complement position but can also be found as the subject of a sentence.

Words that introduce a noun clause include *that, what, whoever, whomever, whichever, whatever, how, why, when, whether,* and *where.*

Look at how noun clauses are used in the following sentences as objects and subject complements:

1. I know *that moderate exercise promotes health.* (noun clause as object of the sentence)

2. Exercise is *what keeps most people fit.* (noun clause as subject complement)

Noun clauses are less often used as subjects; but when they are in the subject position, they add emphasis to the information in the noun clause. Look at the following sentence using a noun clause as a subject:

3. *That exercise is a necessary part of fitness and health* is a common idea among doctors today. (noun clause used as subject)

Do you see how the focus of this sentence is on exercise and its importance in fitness and health?

Using noun clauses as subjects allows you another option to vary your sentence structure and to provide emphasis for information that you find important.

PRACTICE A15: USING THE NOUN CLAUSE

The following paragraph on exercise contains two sentences with noun clauses used as subject complements. To emphasize these noun clauses and for sentence variety, move these noun clauses to the subject position. Identify these sentences by number and then rewrite them in the spaces provided.

(1) It is amazing that exercise has changed our ways of thinking about health. (2) In the fifties, there were very few who exercised regularly. (3) Few then connected a healthy diet with regular workouts. (4) Today most all doctors recommend walking, jogging, or some form of aerobic exercise to stay healthy. (5) Researchers are now studying the amount of exercise people need. (6) It still remains a mystery whether moderate or more intense exercise is better for our health.

1. _____

_____

2. _____

_____

---

16. THE USE OF "THERE IS . . ." AND "THERE ARE . . ."

Often you will write sentences relying on the "There is . . ." and "There are . . ." constructions. Here are two examples:

1. There is one experiment on weight loss that I find particularly interesting.
2. There are several experiments on weight loss that I find interesting.

In writing and revising these sentences, be sure that your verb correctly agrees with its subject. "There" is never a subject, but it always points to the subject that comes after the linking verb "is" or "are." In sentence 1, the subject is "experiment," so the linking verb must be singular (is); whereas in sentence 2, the subject is "experiments," so the verb must be plural (are).

Because the subject comes after "there," writers often assume "there" is the subject and incorrectly match a plural subject with a singular verb, as in the following:

3. There is several experiments on weight loss that I find interesting. (subject-verb agreement error)

In sentence 3, because "experiments" is the subject, the verb that agrees with it must be "are," not "is."

As you edit for subject-verb agreement errors in your drafts, keep these rules regarding "There is . . ." and "There are . . ." in mind.

PRACTICE A16: THE USE OF "THERE IS . . ." AND "THERE ARE . . ."

The following paragraph on exercise and weight loss contains two errors incorrectly using "There is . . ." and "There are . . ." Identify the error by sentence number and then make the correction in the space provided.

(1) There is several studies that have come out recently on how much exercise one needs to maintain or lose weight. (2) The results are fairly consistent in showing that exercise is an important factor in weight control or loss. (3) There is a few questions that still remain. (4) How much exercise is needed to keep weight off or lose weight? (5) And what constitutes light exercise as opposed to moderate exercise?

1. _____

_____

2. _____

_____

17. EFFECTIVE USE OF PRONOUNS

A common error that teacher's find in student essays is misuse of pronouns. A *pronoun* is a word that replaces a noun. ("he" for Howard Gardner; "it" for a type of intelligence). If you place a pronoun too far from the noun that it replaces, you may confuse the reader because the precise noun you are referring to may be unclear. This mistake is often called an error in *pronoun reference*. Here is an example of such an error:

The Gardner group is interested in several types of intelligence, while my professor's committee is focusing on one intelligence test. It will serve to help change the way we teach.

Does the pronoun "it" refer to the "Gardner group" or to the "professor's committee"? This sentence could be corrected by replacing the "it" with the noun itself:

The Gardner group is interested in several types of intelligence, while my professor's committee is focusing on one intelligence test. The Gardner group will serve to help change the way we teach.

Whenever a pronoun can replace more than one noun that comes before it, you would be wise to repeat the noun to which it refers.

Note how the pronoun reference in the following sentence is clear:

Gardner notes that children are not taught effectively if we only study one type of intelligence. They need to be given several ways to learn a particular skill.

"They" refers only to the children, not to "Gardner" or "we."

Use pronouns whenever you can and when they clearly replace a noun. Pronouns tie sentences together and are an important tool for coherence. Pronouns also help to avoid repeating the same noun over and over. Look at the following two sets of sentences:

Gardner is concerned that psychologists simplify the way people learn. Gardner thinks that this simplification prevents some people from learning as much as they can. (original sentence)

Gardner is concerned that psychologists simplify the way people learn. *He* thinks that this simplification prevents some people from learning as much as they can. (revised sentence using pronoun)

In the revised sentence, "he" replaces "Gardner" without creating any confusion, and the writer avoids repeating Gardner's name.

PRACTICE A17: EFFECTIVE USE OF PRONOUNS

The following paragraph on Howard Gardner contains two errors in pronoun reference. Identify each error by sentence number and then make the correction in the space provided. In each case, rewrite the sentence and replace the vague pronoun with the appropriate noun.

(1) Howard Gardner believes that each student and each adult learns in different ways. (2) He should therefore be taught in ways that are personalized. (3) Some learners are visual; others are comfortable with language.

(4) A visual learner should not just be given books to read and lectures to listen to. (5) They often provide very little visual information that this learner can utilize.

1. _____

_____

2. _____

_____

18. THE USE OF "WHO" AND "WHOM"

You learned about relative pronouns when you were introduced to adjective clauses and completed Practice A9. "Who" and "whom" are particularly confusing pronouns, and students tend to mix them up in their writing.

There are two basic rules for the use of "who" and "whom" when you write:

1. "Who" serves as the subject of an independent or dependent clause.

Who visited the Japanese schools?
It was the Americans *who* visited the Japanese schools.

A way to check that "who" is the correct pronoun is to replace it with the pronouns: *he, she,* or *they.* Then see if the sentence sounds grammatically correct. In the preceding sentences, you can correctly say: *They* visited the Japanese schools (not *Them* visited . . .).

2. "Whom" serves as the object of an independent or dependent clause.

To *whom* were the teachers speaking?
It was the Japanese students to whom the teachers were speaking.

A way to check that "whom" is used correctly is to replace it with *him, her,* or *them.* In the preceding sentences, you can correctly say: The teachers were speaking to *them* (not . . . to *they*).

Although "who" and "whom" are often interchanged in speaking ("Who did she talk to?" instead of the grammatically correct "Whom did she talk to?"), it is still not acceptable in your writing. Use the test for replacing "who" and "whom" with the appropriate pronoun in your editing when you are unsure about which pronoun to use.

PRACTICE A18: THE USE OF "WHO" AND "WHOM"

In the following paragraph describing the Japanese school system, there are two errors in the use of "who" and "whom." Identify each error by sentence number and then make the correction in the space provided.

(1) The two teachers found that the Japanese were students who wanted to help in their schools. (2) They noted that it was the students who the teachers asked to help clean up their school. (3) By working with their teachers in keeping the school clean, the Japanese students were not as likely to litter their campus. (4) The students were a school group who felt responsible for the cleanliness of their school. (5) In American schools, is it the students who we can turn to in order to keep our schools clean?

1. _____

_____

2. _____

_____

---

19. PARALLELISM

When you list items (nouns, verbs, adjectives, adverbs), you need to be sure that they are in the same grammatical form. If you begin a list with an adjective, for example, you should continue to use adjectives. By being consistent in this way, you are following the rules of *parallelism.*

Study the following examples:

Mike Rose describes a teacher who is intelligent, dynamic, and he is also creative.
(not parallel)
Mike Rose describes a teacher who is intelligent, dynamic, and creative.
(parallel)

Note how in the revised sentence, the writer lists three adjectives.

Look at this second example:

Rick Takagaki involves his students in role playing, group discussion, and they participate in mock trials.
(not parallel)
Rick Takagaki involves his students in role playing, discussion, and mock trials.
(parallel)

In the revised sentence, the writer lists three noun phrases.

Note that in the preceding examples, commas are used up to the conjunction "and." A series is defined as three or more words or phrases. When you write a parallel series of words or phrases, separate each word or phrase with a comma, up to the conjunction that you choose.

PRACTICE A19: PARALLELISM

In the following paragraph on the Rose selection, there are two errors in parallelism. Identify each error by sentence number and then make the correction in the space provided.

(1) Mike Rose is interested in studying outstanding teachers. (2) For Rose, these outstanding teachers are innovative, personable, and they are sincerely devoted to their students. (3) In Rick Takagaki, Rose finds just such a teacher. (4) Takagaki takes on the voices of various economists, brings in outside newspaper material on economics, and he even spends his lunch time in his classroom with any students who want to come in. (5) For Rose, Takagaki is a teacher whom other teachers can learn from.

1. _____

_____

2. _____

_____

---

20. USING PARTICIPIAL PHRASES

A *participial phrase* is a verb form that functions as an adjective. A participial phrase is made up of a verb ending in "ed," "ing," or "en" plus words that modify it. By using participial phrases, you add variety to your writing. Participial phrases can be found anywhere in a sentence, and they are often set off with a comma. When participial phrases begin a sentence, they are always set off with a comma, as in the following example:

Respecting his students' thinking, Mr. Bedrock had tremendous influence in the classroom.

If you place this participial phrase in the middle of the sentence, you would also need to use commas:

Mr. Bedrock, respecting his students' thinking, had tremendous influence in the classroom.

Try to place participial phrases as closely as possible to the nouns they modify. Note that in the preceding examples, the participial phrases come before or after the word that they modify ("Mr. Bedrock").

Like adjective clauses, participial phrases can be essential or nonessential. A *nonessential participial phrase* can be seen as additional information in a sentence, and it is set off by commas. The previous examples use nonessential participial phrases. The essential meaning of these sentences is that Mr. Bedrock had tremendous influence in the classroom.

In contrast, an *essential participial phrase* is central to the meaning of the sentence, and it is not set off with commas. Note how the following participial phrase is essential to the meaning of the sentence:

Only those students respecting Mr. Bedrock did well in his class.

In this sentence, it is essential for the reader to know that those students "respecting Mr. Bedrock" did well in his class.

If you reread all three of these sentences, you will find that you naturally pause when you come to a nonessential participial phrase and do not pause when you come upon an essential participial phrase.

PRACTICE A20: USING PARTICIPIAL PHRASES

The following paragraph is from an essay written on Ordinary Resurrections. *There are two errors in punctuating a participial phrase. Identify each error by sentence number and then make the correction in the space provided.*

(1) Mr. Bedrock is a truly gifted teacher. (2) Wanting his students to be comfortable he tries to be playful in the class. (3) Yet Mr. Bedrock's playfulness does not mean that his students do not learn. (4) Mr. Bedrock assuming that frightened students tend to block what they hear makes playfulness as important as the content he is teaching. (5) His students respond well to this mixture of work and play.

1. _____

_____

2. _____

_____

B.

WRITING CONVENTIONS: EXPLANATIONS AND PRACTICES

The topics covered in this part of the handbook are the following:

1. **Mentioning the author and work**
2. **Using quotes**
3. **Writing clear introductions**
4. **The topic sentence**
5. **Writing effective topic sentences**
6. **Commenting on quotations**
7. **Evidence that is too general**
8. **Organizing the body of your writing**
9. **Using transitions**
10. **Avoiding redundancies**
11. **Vague phrasing**
12. **Editing for colloquialisms**
13. **Sentence variety**
14. **Paraphrases that sound too much like the original**
15. **Use of the active and the passive construction**
16. **Editing for sentence length**
17. **Using brackets within a quote**
18. **Using a quote within a quote**
19. **Citing long quotations**
20. **Citing page numbers after a quote**

1. MENTIONING THE AUTHOR AND WORK

In your reading journals and in other writing assignments in college, you may need to mention the author and title of the work you are studying.

The four straightforward rules to follow when you introduce an author or a title are as follows:

1. You underline the title of a book, such as an autobiography or novel, or in word processing, you can italicize the title: <u>The Autobiography of Malcolm X</u>, <u>Uncle Tom's Cabin</u>. You also underline a magazine or newspaper title: <u>The New York Times</u>, <u>Time Magazine</u>. You capitalize all words in the title except for little words like "the "of," or "a." You capitalize these small words only when they begin the title, as in <u>The Autobiography of Malcolm X</u>.

2. The title of articles or the titles of chapters in a book are set off with quotation marks, as in the article title to Selection 1: "Literacy: A Family Affair." Note that the quotation marks enclose the entire article title. As with book titles, little words are not capitalized, unless they start a title or come after a punctuation mark like a colon (:).

3. If a title is particularly long, you may abbreviate it after you have introduced it completely the first time. You can refer to <u>The Autobiography of Malcolm X</u> as <u>Malcolm X</u> or <u>Autobiography</u> the next time you mention it in your writing, or you may refer to the "Literacy: A Family Affair" article simply as "Literacy" or "Family Affair" the next several times that you mention this article.

4. When you refer to the author for the first time, you should mention the complete name: first name, last name, and middle name or initial, if it is included. For example, you would first introduce the author as Anita Merina, then Merina. Never use an author's first name in your writing: never, for example, Anita.

PRACTICE B1: MENTIONING THE AUTHOR AND WORK

The following is the first part of a reading journal entry on "Literacy: A Family Affair." There are four errors in the correct use of author and title. Identify each error by sentence number and then make the correction in the space provided.

(1) I liked this reading selection, "Literacy: A family Affair." (2) <u>Literacy</u> gave me a lot to think about. (3) I especially liked the way "literacy" described Robert Mendez. (4) Anita shows how Robert could not read for 35 years, yet became a very successful citizen.

1. _____

2. _____

_____

3. _____

_____

4. _____

_____

---

2. USING QUOTES

In writing about your reading, you may want to quote part of the selection directly. Sometimes a direct quote is more effective than a paraphrase.

Here are the rules you need to follow when quoting material:

1. Introduce the quote by mentioning the author, as in the following:

Svoboda says, "To write a book is a serious undertaking."

Remember that the comma comes after says, and the period stays within the quotation marks. Commas and periods always stay inside quotation marks.

2. Verbs other than "says" that you can use to introduce a quote are *notes, discusses, states, remarks, declares,* and *affirms.* Synonyms for the word "suggests" are *implies* and *intimates.*

3. When you quote a phrase rather than a sentence, you do not introduce the phrase with a comma, as in the following:

Svoboda notes that book writing is "a serious undertaking."

Remember that the period still stays within the quotation marks.

4. Sometimes your sentence using quoted material is a question. In this case, the question mark stays outside the quotation marks, as in the following:

What does Svoboda mean by "a serious undertaking"?

The question mark stays *inside* the quotation marks only when the quote itself is in the form of a question, as in the following:

Svoboda asks, "What do you think of me now?"

5. If you want to cut out a part of the quote, use *ellipsis points* (. . .). These three dots show that a word or phrase has been taken out of the quoted sentence. Just be sure that what you take out does not change the meaning of the complete quote, as in the following:

Svoboda notes, "To write a book is a serious undertaking. . . . "

Note that what was taken out, "a major commitment," does not markedly change the meaning of this quote.

6. Never copy a phrase or sentence from a selection unless you quote it. Copying is called *plagiarism,* and it is considered stealing someone else's words or ideas, as in the following:

Svoboda notes that writing is such a perilous business, much like living.

This sentence is copying a large chunk of Svoboda's sentence, so it is plagiarized. You need to identify with quotation marks those words that are not your own. See how this plagiarized phrase is corrected:

Svoboda notes that "writing is such a perilous business," much like living.

PRACTICE B2: USING QUOTES

Read the following paragraph from a student essay on "The Eight Beatitudes of Writing." There are two errors in punctuating a quote. Identify each error by sentence number and then make the correction in the space provided.

(1) Melannie Svoboda claims that writing can humble you because it is such a complex activity. (2) She states "Writing would be less humbling if at the start I knew what I thought. . . ." (3) She notes that even what she has published is not the final word on a subject. (4) Svoboda concludes that she finally must, "write provisionally, for the time being."

1. _____

_____

2. _____

_____

---

3. WRITING CLEAR INTRODUCTIONS

In Chapter 2, you learned that introductions begin essays that explain or persuade. Introductions are important because they introduce the topic that the writer explores and place it in an interesting framework. Effective introductions also include the point or thesis that the writer is making and generally list the pieces of evidence that the writer uses in the body to further explain and support this thesis.

Look at how an essay on phonics versus whole language begins:

Phonics and whole language ways of teaching reading have lately become issues in the news because some states are changing their reading method from whole language to phonics. Phonics teaching and whole language teaching are very different ways of teaching reading. In fact, they are so different that I cannot think of any teaching topic they agree on. For one, phonics begins with sound, whole language with meaning. Second, whole language teachers say students do not have to sound out every part of a word to know what it means, while phonics teachers insist that readers sound out every syllable. Finally, phonics teachers only give students books with words their students can sound out, but whole language teachers encourage students to read what they are interested in, even if the words are too hard.

Note how the topic is interestingly presented in the first sentence and that the thesis is laid out in the second sentence: phonics and whole language are very different teaching methods. Also see how the evidence is clearly presented: sound versus meaning, how to sound out words, and books to read. You can assume that these three topics will be carefully explained in the essay's body.

Try to write introductions in expository and persuasive essays that clearly introduce your topic and argument and present the major points you intend to cover in the body of your essay.

PRACTICE B3: WRITING CLEAR INTRODUCTIONS

The following is an introduction from an expository essay on a student's most memorable experiences in elementary school. Read this introduction carefully and then answer the four questions that follow.

I have heard that people change lives. I think this statement accurately describes my early years. The people I met in my elementary school years made a lasting impression on me and changed me in very important ways. When I first started school, I was very shy. My kindergarten teacher showed me how to make friends and how to carry on conversations with my classmates. In third grade, I had difficulty reading. A parent aide in this class spent the entire year tutoring me on all of the reading work I could not understand. And finally, in fifth grade before I started middle school, I met a friend in my class who showed me how wonderful a sport baseball was both to play and to watch. These are the three childhood experiences I want to explore to show how each experience changed my life for the better.

1. How does this writer introduce the topic of his essay? _____

_____

2. What is the writer's argument? _____

_____

3. List the evidence the writer will likely develop in his body to support

this argument. _____

_____

4. Do you think this is a successful introduction? Why? _____

_____

4. THE TOPIC SENTENCE

Although some paragraphs do not need a topic sentence, others do. You should write a topic sentence for your paragraph when you present many details but your reader cannot determine how they are related.

Remember that a *topic sentence* is the general sentence in the paragraph that serves to organize the rest of the sentences. Study the following paragraph on the Malcolm X selection and see how the first sentence–the topic sentence–is more general than the detail sentences that follow it and how it adds focus to these details:

> *Malcolm X has a powerful desire to learn to read.* He studies the dictionary and copies each word out. When it is time to sleep in prison and the lights are out, he reads by the light in the corridor. He would also read into the morning hours, so that he rarely got more than four hours of sleep a night.

Do you see how all three sentences after the first provide evidence for Malcolm X's passion for learning to read? He copies words out of the dictionary, reads by the hallway light, and reads into the morning hours. All three of these details make better sense because the topic sentence organizes them under Malcolm X's insatiable desire to read.

Topic sentences are commonly placed at the beginning of a paragraph, but they can also be found at the end.

PRACTICE B4: THE TOPIC SENTENCE

Read the following two paragraphs from the middle of an essay describing a four-year-old, Karen. Each of these paragraphs needs a topic sentence, either at the beginning or the end. Read these two paragraphs and write an appropriate topic sentence that would tie the evidence together.

(1) Karen kept on opening her book. (2) She carefully turned the pages. (3) She smiled at several of the pictures she saw. (4) She even wanted to show me some of these pictures and talk about them to me.

Topic sentence: _____

_____

(1) Karen started watching a news program and made a sad face. (2) She watched a baseball game for a few minutes but kept on looking away. (3) She watched a commercial on beer and began playing with her doll. (4) When she changed the channel to a situation comedy, Karen walked out of the room.

Topic sentence: _____

_____

---

5. WRITING EFFECTIVE TOPIC SENTENCES

Effective topic sentences direct the reader to the major point you are trying to make in your paragraph. Sometimes topic sentences are too *general* or do not give your paragraph enough direction. Your goal as a writer is to be sure that the topic sentence in your paragraph ties the details of that paragraph together or gives a purpose for the details.

Look at the following two topic sentences on the causes of gang activity. See how the first is too general or vague and the second, more purposeful or directed:

1. There is one main reason for gang activity. (vague)
2. The main reason for gang activity is that gang members do not have a positive male model to look up to. (directed)

In the first sentence, the main reason for gang activity is not given. All you know is that there is one main reason. In the second sentence, in contrast, the writer directs you to the key difference: no positive male role models. Using the second topic sentence, the writer can more easily organize the details of this paragraph around what a positive male role model should be.

When your teacher or classmate determines that your draft lacks organization or direction, many of your paragraphs probably do not have a focused topic sentence. In this case, it is helpful for you to read over the sentences in the paragraphs making up your body to look for overarching ideas that organize the details you present. If you find that they do not, in your second draft you may want to write focused topic sentences that bring out the purpose of your details more clearly.

PRACTICE B5: WRITING EFFECTIVE TOPIC SENTENCES

In the following two paragraphs on the reasons for gang activity, you will find two weak topic sentences. Read both paragraphs and study the details. Then in the space provided, identify the number of the weak topic sentence and revise each one.

(1) Gang members have problems at home. (2) Mothers are often not interested in raising their sons. (3) Fathers are often absent. (4) When the parents are involved, they tend to punish by hitting their sons. (5) The parents often create a disorganized home life for their sons.

(6) The gang provides a lot for each member. (7) There is usually a father figure that the young members can go to for help. (8) The members of the gang protect each other from violence, as if they were brothers.

(9) Also, the gang members often have a loyalty for each other that they may not have at home.

1. _____

_____

2. _____

_____

REVIEW 1: PRACTICES 1–5

The following are the last two paragraphs from a draft that discusses the "La Vida Loca" selection. There are six errors: an error introducing a quote, an error introducing the selection, two sentence fragments, one comma splice, and one fused sentence. Identify each error by sentence number and then make the correction in the space provided. There are several ways to correct some of these errors.

(1) Rodriguez presents some important reasons for gang activity. (2) He shows how a dangerous neighborhood encourages dangerous behavior, young people get physically hurt in these neighborhoods. (3) And exposed to all sorts of drugs. (4) Which often make these people addicts at an early age. (5) These young drug addicts must find ways to pay for their drugs they often rob to get quick money.

(6) "La Vida Loca" is an honest account of how poor boys get involved in violence and drugs. (7) It is hard to believe that young people go through so much pain at such an early age. (8) This pain is the, "small but intense fire" that Rodriguez believes is burning in each of these young people.

1. _____

_____

2. _____

_____

3. _____

_____

4. _____

_____

5. _____

_____

6. _____

_____

6. COMMENTING ON QUOTATIONS

When you write about the reading, it is important to use quotations to support your arguments. Sometimes quotes express a point better than you can.

When you quote from a reading, it is often wise to comment on this quoted material. By doing so, you are showing your reader how the quote fits into your argument. Do not assume that your reader will automatically know why you included a particular quote.

Look at how the comments on the quote in the following paragraph provide further explanation and make the paragraph more coherent:

> This young man seems to be very disturbed. When he entered puberty, he often expressed his anger, especially toward his mother. Ressler comments that "he would become violent because he wanted two hot dogs instead of one, or because he was unable to have chocolate syrup on his ice cream." *The reasons for his anger are so unimportant. It almost seems that he is looking for reasons to get violent with his mother.*

The commentary here is essential to the writer's argument. The quote suggests that this young man is disturbed, but the writer's commentary on the nature and reason for his anger shows the reader how destructive this young man's relationship is with his mother.

As you write about various readings, remember to carefully choose your quotes, selecting those that best express your argument. Comment on these quotes when you want to draw out certain points that are not immediately clear in the quotes themselves.

PRACTICE B6: COMMENTING ON QUOTATIONS

The following two paragraphs come from an essay on "Childhoods of Violence." Each paragraph ends with a quote, but the writer has not commented on either quote. Read each paragraph and, in the space provided, include a sentence or two of comment to further explain the quote.

(1) What is interesting about the killers Ressler and his group studied is that they tended to share certain childhood experiences. (2) There is evidence that many of these killers came from families with mental illness and criminal histories. (3) Also, Ressler notes, "All the murderers– every single one–were subjected to serious emotional abuse during their childhoods."

Comment on quote in sentence 3: _____

_____

(4) Ressler believes that the mothers of these killers played an important role because they were often absent. (5) He notes that these killers had mothers who did not seem to care about them and who often neglected them entirely. (6) Ressler emphasizes that "these children were deprived of something more important than money—love."

Comment on quote in sentence 6: _____

_____

_____

7. EVIDENCE THAT IS TOO GENERAL

Sometimes paragraphs in your writing use evidence that is too general; so the support you give sounds as general as your topic sentence. When the evidence in your paragraph is too general, your paragraph tends to lose its *focus*.

Let's say you write a paragraph on the loneliness of the Unabomber. You start with a topic sentence that says:

The Unabomber shows a disturbingly lonely character.

You would assume that this paragraph would provide examples for how the Unabomber is lonely.

Look at how this first paragraph on the alleged Unabomber is too general, whereas the paragraph that follows is nicely detailed:

The Unabomber shows a disturbingly lonely character. He lives in a lonely cabin. He was mean to a woman he liked. Finally, he wasn't very close to his father. *(evidence is too general)*

The Unabomber shows a disturbingly lonely character. He lives in a Montana cabin without windows. This man began harassing a woman at work because she refused to date him. Finally, the Unabomber was so separated emotionally from his father that he refused to attend his funeral. *(evidence is nicely detailed)*

Do you see how the second paragraph describes the cabin as not having windows and how the Unabomber harassed the woman he liked and was so distant from his father that he didn't even attend his funeral? These details make the Unabomber's loneliness much more real. Simply saying that his cabin was lonely, he was mean to a woman, and he was distant from his father are details that do not convince the reader that the Unabomber is lonely.

Remember that convincing paragraphs that set a nice balance between general and specific statements inform and reinforce the main idea of the paragraph. However, general statements used as support simply weaken your argument.

PRACTICE B7: EVIDENCE THAT IS TOO GENERAL

In the following paragraph on terrorism, two sentences of support are too general. Identify each sentence by number in the space provided. Then suggest what information is needed to make each sentence more detailed.

(1) Terrorism has become a disturbing problem in America. (2) The 1995 bombing of the Oklahoma City federal building is the most appalling example of terrorism. (3) There were several people involved. (4) New York also had its Federal Trade Center bombed in 1993. (5) This was also a painful incident.

1. _____

_____

2. _____

_____

---

8. ORGANIZING THE BODY OF YOUR WRITING

Often in their writing, students know what they want to say, but they have not thought out the order in which they want to say it. Readers of this writing often find two, sometimes three, important points mentioned in the same paragraph of their body. Usually these paragraphs of support begin coherently, but they move into a topic that needs to be developed separately.

Look at how the following paragraph on boys' aggression begins well, but it moves into a new topic toward the end:

> Some biologists believe that the aggression one sees in boys is biological. The hormone that causes these differences is called testosterone. These biologists say that testosterone is responsible for certain structures in the male brain that are different from those in the female brain. *Attention deficit disorder (ADD) is what many aggressive boys have been diagnosed as having. In school, those boys with ADD talk too much and fight with their classmates.*

Note how the first three sentence discuss aggression and biology, but the italicized sentences introduce a new topic on attention deficit disorder. This material is best discussed in a separate paragraph.

As you revise the body of your writing, look to see how a paragraph or group of paragraphs develops a specific supporting point. When a paragraph introduces a new supporting point, consider making it into a new paragraph.

PRACTICE B8: ORGANIZING THE BODY OF YOUR WRITING

In the following paragraph from the body of an essay on male aggression, there are two sentences that belong in a separate paragraph. Identify these two sentences by number in the space provided and explain what new topic they introduce.

(1) John is a ten-year-old who is picking fights at school and in his neighborhood. (2) The teachers have complained that he is usually unruly on the playground. (3) And his mother says that many parents in her neighborhood do not want John to play with their children because he is too rough. (4) I believe that a major cause of his violent behavior is that John's father has recently separated from his wife. (5) Strong male role models are an important way that young boys learn how to deal with their anger constructively. (6) John's father was just such a strong male figure.

Sentences introducing a new paragraph and the topic they introduce:

1. _____

_____

2. _____

_____

---

9. USING TRANSITIONS

Effective writers often show their readers how they think. They signal clearly when they want to show cause, effect, an example, a contrast, a similarity, and so on. *Transitions* are words and phrases that show these turns of thought in your writing.

The following are lists of some of the most common transitions categorized by organizational patterns:

support	effect	sequence	contrast	comparison
for example	therefore	first, second, and so on	however	similarly
for instance	consequently	later, then next, finally	nevertheless on the other hand	

When using a transition, be sure *to set if off with a comma.* If the transition comes at the beginning of the sentence, set it off with *one* comma. If a transition comes in the middle of a sentence, set it off with *two* commas. Look at the effective use of the transition "nevertheless" in the following sentences:

1. Nevertheless, television still seems to be a big part of many people's lives.
2. Television, nevertheless, still seems to be a big part of many people's lives.

Sentence 1 uses one comma; sentence 2 uses two commas.

Using transitions appropriately helps give your writing style more authority. In using transitions, your audience sees how you are organizing your thinking because you are providing them with the appropriate signals.

PRACTICE B9: CORRECTLY PUNCTUATING TRANSITIONS

The following paragraph on television viewing contains two sentences that incorrectly punctuate transitions. Identify these errors by sentence number and then correct the error in the space provided.

(1) Television was very popular in the fifties. (2) There were certain shows that almost every television viewer watched. (3) For example "I Love Lucy" seemed to have everyone talking about the episode viewed the night before. (4) One of the reasons for the popularity of such shows was that if you could not watch it that night, you would probably never see it again. (5) Television therefore had a more immediate appeal then. (6) VCRs and the Internet have changed all that today.

1. _____

_____

2. _____

_____

---

10. AVOIDING REDUNDANCIES

Sometimes writers, students and professionals, repeat themselves. Unnecessary repetition is called *redundancy*. The opposite of a redundant style is a *concise style*. In speaking, repeating yourself is acceptable; in fact, it is a natural way of continuing your train of thought and keeping your listeners interested. Speaking happens in time, but writing happens in space. The printed words remain on the page, and you can reread whatever you want. However, spoken words are lost once they are uttered, so repetition may be necessary. Because writing can be studied, excessive redundancy is unnecessary.

Generally, if you write something effectively once, you need not repeat it. However, in conclusions of summary, you may repeat your major points.

Redundancies can take the form or phrases or sentences, for example:

1. Today's television commercials are well conceived, *effectively planned* narratives. (phrase redundancy)
2. Some television commercials involve carefully scripted story lines. *These commercials involve narratives that are thoughtfully plotted.* (sentence redundancy)

In example 1, "well conceived" and "effectively planned" are phrases that are synonyms, so you do not need to use both descriptions of television commercials. You can avoid redundancy here by deleting "effectively planned" and simply saying that "today's television commercials are well conceived narratives." In example 2, the second sentence does not further the argument of the first sentence. "Carefully scripted story lines" are the same as "narratives that are carefully thought out." In revising these sentences, you should delete one of them.

Here are some redundant phrases that you will come across. Be sure to edit them as you revise your drafts:

full and complete, totally complete, totally true, totally false, completely different, basic and fundamental, true facts, important essentials, future plans, end result, final outcome, personal beliefs, past memories (Part of this list was taken from Joseph M. Williams, *Style*, 2nd ed., Glenview, IL: Scott, Foresman, 1985, p. 69).

Certain adjectives like *full, true, complete*, and *different* do not require additional description. If something is full, it cannot be fuller; and if something is true, it cannot be truer. In the case of *full and complete* or *basic and fundamental*, the writer is repeating the adjective with its synonym. Full means complete, and basic means fundamental.

In all of these cases, the rule remains the same in writing: One word is more effective than two.

PRACTICE B10: AVOIDING REDUNDANCIES

The following paragraph has two redundancy errors. Identify each error by sentence number and then make the correction in the space provided. There are several ways to correct the two redundancy errors.

(1) To look at commercials as part of the program itself is a thoughtful, intelligent concept. (2) One often sees commercials as separate parts of television. (3) They are usually considered distinct elements in programming. (4) If a commercial is part of the program, then the viewer will likely not want to channel surf. (5) I have even heard viewers say that the commercial is a more interesting narrative than the program itself. (6) This movement to join commercials with the program itself is a new advertising strategy.

1. _____

_____

2. _____

_____

REVIEW 2: PRACTICES 1–10

*The following two paragraphs are from an essay on the commercials selection
"Where's the Pitch?" There are six errors: four grammatical errors and two essay
convention errors. Edit for the article being introduced incorrectly, a sentence
fragment, an error in punctuating an adjective clause, and an error in
punctuating a compound sentence. There is also a sentence that should begin
a new paragraph. Identify each error by sentence number and then make the
correction in the space provided. For the sentence that should begin a new
paragraph, merely identify the sentence number.*

(1) "Where's the Pitch?" is a thought-provoking article. (2) It is hard to
believe that commercials are so closely related to the shows they sponsor. (3) When you considered commercials in the past you often looked
at what product was being sold. (4) Never thinking that the commercial
was a short program in its own right. (5) We now look at commercials as
a part of the program and we sometimes are even more impressed with
the commercial than with the show itself.

(6) The Super Bowl which is the most often watched sports event of
the season is often sponsored by Nike. (7) Now it makes sense to me that
Nike's commercials are part of the football game itself. (8) What is sold
in the commercial is also sold by the football players. (9) Both are selling
the desire to be physically fit and to win. (10) There is another commercial that interests me–the most recent Pepsi commercial I saw.

1. _____

_____

2. _____

_____

3. _____

_____

4. _____

_____

5. _____

_____

6. _____

_____

---

11. VAGUE PHRASING

Sometimes writers select a word or phrase that does not accurately describe the idea or experience they are writing about. This tendency is called *vague phrasing.* The noun "thing" is often used when a writer could have used a more exact word:

The journalist describes the violence in gangsta rap music, a *thing* that concerns many Black politicians and artists.

Do you see how "thing" can be replaced with a more precise word like "topic" or "issue"? Look at how the sentence gains focus with its revision:

The journalist describes violence in gangsta rap music, an issue that concerns many Black politicians and artists.

Adjectives, too, can be inexact. The adjective "good" and "bad" tend to be overused. Usually, a more specific adjective would be more effective:

According to this same journalist, rap music can provide African-American musicians with many *good* social questions to consider. (vague)
According to this same journalist, rap music can provide African-American musicians with many *thoughtful* social questions to consider. (revised)

Do you see how "thoughtful" adds focus and detail to the sentence, whereas "good" adds little information to the kind of questions rap music provides? "Good" merely suggests that something positive is happening to the rap music lyrics.

Editing for vague phrasing is often one of the last revisions that you will make to your draft; however, it is often an important activity. By choosing detailed vocabulary, you let your reader know that you have thought out your topic carefully and are moving it away from a more general discussion.

PRACTICE B11: VAGUE PHRASING

In the following paragraph on rap music, there are two italicized words in need of revision because they are vague. Study these words in the context of the paragraph and then replace them with more detailed words of your own choosing. Rewrite both sentences in the spaces provided.

(1) What makes rap music so unique? (2) It's music with a strong political view. (3) Many of the scary *things* in our society can be put into its
lyrics. (4) Rap talks about *bad* experiences with the police and troubles
in relationships. (5) Rap can also speak about urban poverty and violent
youth. (6) Somehow all of this pain is made less hurtful by the poetry that
structures these political statements.

1. _____

_____

2. _____

_____

12. EDITING FOR COLLOQUIALISMS

A *colloquialism* is an informal word or phrase that is more often used in
speech than in writing. Colloquialisms vary with ethnic, racial, and
age groups. What is colloquial to a teenager may not be for the parent.
When a colloquial word or phrase is extremely casual, it is called *slang*.
Informal writing can be found in letters to friends, e-mails, journal
entries, and even some narratives when you are writing dialogue to
realistically present a character. In formal writing, such as essays written in college, colloquialisms are usually not the most acceptable language to use.

Below is a short list of colloquial words and phrases used in today's
speech and their more formal synonyms:

Colloquialism	Formal Synonym	Colloquialism	Formal Synonym
kid	student	folks	relatives
kind of or sort of	somewhat	gotta	must
brainy	intelligent	dumb	slow
hang out	spend time	chill	relax
buff	in shape	old man	father (boyfriend)
old lady	mother (girlfriend)	choked	did poorly
bail	quit	pig	terrible person
cool	fine	crash	sleep
psycho	disturbed person	freak out	get very upset
freaky	strange	bummed	upset

continued

cuz	because	funky	out of the ordinary
guy	person	cop	police
beat it	leave	piece	gun
weirdo	strange person	crazy	insane
junkie	drug addict	bombed	drunk
jock	athlete	nerd	bookish, unathletic person
dope	drugs	booze	liquor
folks	parents		

As you edit your essays, ask yourself if a particular word or phrase is more often used in conversation with your friends. If so, it may be a colloquialism that could be replaced by a more formal word or phrase.

PRACTICE B12: EDITING FOR COLLOQUIALISMS

In the following paragraph from a formal essay on rap music, there are two colloquialisms that should be edited. Identify the colloquialism by sentence number and then replace the colloquialism with a more formal word or expression in the space provided.

(1) Rap music is far out! (2) Why do I say this? (3) I say this because rap talks about issues that I rarely read about in school. (4) Rap is the music of urban street life in all of its reality. (5) Furthermore, many of the lyrics are quite thoughtful and sometimes kinda poetic.

1. _____

_____

2. _____

_____

_____

13. SENTENCE VARIETY

Effective and interesting writing uses various sentence structures. The use of several sentence patterns in your writing is called *sentence variety.* The most common sentence pattern in English is subject + verb + direct object or complement.

Look at the following sentence using this common English sentence pattern:

Physical activity concerns bodily movement.
    Subject   +   Verb   +   Direct Object

Sentences in essays become monotonous when this same pattern (S + V + DO) is used in several consecutive sentences, as in the following four sentences:

Exercise concerns structured bodily activity. Walking requires bodily activity. Jogging leads to bodily exercise. Stretching also allows for structured bodily activity.

Do you see how these four sentences each follow the same pattern (S + V + DO) and become monotonous by this repetition in structure?

You can achieve sentence variety in your essays in several ways. The three most common structures include the following:

1. Beginning a sentence with a prepositional phrase:

   In a recent report, it was found that moderate physical exercise provides measurable health improvement.

2. Beginning or ending a sentence with an adverbial clause:

   Because exercise reduces the risk of heart disease, diabetes, and certain forms of cancer, doctors are frequently recommending exercise to their patients.

3. Using transitions or conjunctive adverbs to join two sentences:

   Exercise also improves the health of the skeletal and muscular system; *moreover,* it also helps reduce symptoms of depression.

Revise for sentence variety at the end of the writing process, after you have revised for content and organization. As you read your draft, listen for the monotony caused by repeating one sentence pattern several times. Start using the preceding three structures to achieve sentence variety.

PRACTICE B13: SENTENCE VARIETY

In the following paragraph on physical activity, two sentences need to be revised for sentence variety. Read over this paragraph and then revise these two sentences using the directions that come after the paragraph.

(1) Exercise is a very important factor in maintaining health. (2) Exercise can reduce risks of heart disease and diabetes. (3) Exercise is now encouraged by doctors. (4) Over 60 percent of Americans do not exercise enough. (5) The Surgeon General has determined that the lack of exercise is a serious American health concern.

1. Combine sentences 2 and 3 by making sentence 2 into an adverbial clause using "because."

_____

_____

2. Combine sentences 4 and 5 by using the conjunctive adverb "therefore" before sentence 5.

_____

_____

_____

14. PARAPHRASES THAT SOUND TOO MUCH LIKE THE ORIGINAL

You may remember from Chapter 2 that paraphrasing is an essential skill used by readers to make sense of difficult sentences. In writing, it is always acceptable to include paraphrases in your essays.

Sometimes, however, the paraphrase sounds too much like the original, and it almost becomes plagiarism. Remember that plagiarism is copying someone else's words without using quotation marks to credit the original writer. When you paraphrase, it is best to put the sentence in your own writing style. Your reader will then hear a consistent voice—not one that abruptly changes from your writing style to that of the author you are paraphrasing.

Look at the following paragraph analyzing the article "Can You Be Fit and Fat?" Note how sentence 5 sounds too much like the original sentence and does not fit into the style of the earlier sentences. Here is the sentence from the selection that is paraphrased too closely in sentence 5: "However, even the much-touted BMI is not a perfect measure of fatness." (paragraph 10, page 145).

> (1) The BMI is a new way of measuring weight. (2) The number you derive from these calculations can show you if you are dangerously overweight. (3) Two numbers are important. (4) The number 25 suggests that you are overweight, the number 30 that you are obese. (5) Yet even the much acclaimed BMI is not an infallible measure of overweight.

Do you see how sentence 5 is too close to the original sentence? Sentence 5 uses a more sophisticated vocabulary than the previous sentences and thus sounds out of place.

There are two ways of correcting this problem:

1. The writer could quote the sentence directly:

   Sheehan notes, though, that "even the much-touted BMI is not a perfect measure of fatness."

2. The writer could make the sentence sound more like his or her own style. To make a paraphrase conform to your own style, avoid having the original sentence directly in front of you as you write

your own sentence, referring to the original sentence only when you want to verify a fact or figure. The previous paraphrase could be more correctly written in this way:

Yet even the BMI has its problems when calculating overweight.

PRACTICE B14: PARAPHRASES THAT SOUND TOO MUCH LIKE THE ORIGINAL

In the following paragraph on overweight and fitness, sentence 6 sounds too much like the original from "Can You Be Fit and Fat?" In the space provided write a sentence that is more in keeping with the style of the paragraph.

Here is the original sentence: "A tantalizing study from the Stanford University School of Medicine found that thigh flab can reduce the risk of cardiovascular disease."

(1) Body types can affect your health. (2) People who are heavy in the hips, thighs, and buttocks tend to be healthier than those who carry their weight around their middle. (3) This is probably because the weight around the middle tends to constrict vital organs. (4) Also additional fat in the middle can negatively affect one's cholesterol, blood pressure, and blood sugar. (5) Studies have also shown that heavy thighs can also be a health plus. (6) A tempting bit of research from Stanford University Medical School determined that thigh fat can decrease the possibility of cardiovascular disease.

1. _____

_____

_____

15. USE OF THE ACTIVE AND THE PASSIVE CONSTRUCTION

Active and passive constructions are sentence structures that affect your writing. The *active construction* follows the traditional pattern of subject + verb + direct object (Exercise reduces the risk of colon cancer). The *passive construction* uses the following pattern that makes the direct object the subject of the sentence and the original subject a prepositional phrase:

subject (original object) + (are/were) + verb (ed) + by + original subject (The risk of colon cancer is reduced by exercise.)

The active construction offers a more direct, understandable style to your writing, whereas the passive voice creates a more indirect, less understandable voice. In most cases, select the active construction over the passive construction in your writing.

In some cases, the passive construction is preferred, particularly under the following conditions:

1. When you want to emphasize the object of the sentence:

    The exercise research was conducted by the government. (Here it is the exercise research that you want to focus on and not the government.)

2. When you do not know who the subject or agent is:

    An agreement has been reached about the value of exercise. (You do not know who reached an agreement.)

PRACTICE B15: USE OF THE ACTIVE AND THE PASSIVE CONSTRUCTION

In the following paragraph on the value of exercise, two sentences are in the passive construction. Change these two sentences to the active voice. Identify the sentence by number and rewrite it in the space provided.

(1) The value of exercise is being studied by many scientists. (2) They are currently examining whether strenuous exercise is more valuable than moderate activity. (3) Moderate exercise is being recommended by recent government research. (4) Some scientists contend that this research favoring moderate exercise does not provide convincing scientific evidence. (5) The jury is still out whether moderate or strenuous exercise is more beneficial to your health.

1. _____

_____

2. _____

_____

REVIEW 3: PRACTICES 1–15

The following two paragraphs come from an essay on fitness and exercise. These paragraphs have six errors: two in essay conventions (redundancy and a vague topic sentence) and four in grammar (comma splice, verb agreement, sentence fragment, and the incorrect use of a semicolon). The grammatical and vague topic sentence errors can be corrected in several ways. Identify each error by sentence number and make the correction in the space provided.

(1) Just how much exercise is necessary to stay trim and fit? (2) Fast running or walking? (3) These are the questions that are being asked today; and there are several studies being conducted. (4) These studies are generally well thought out, well considered.

(5) The conclusions to these experiments say a lot. (6) One of these experiments show that walking regularly and jogging can have the same positive results. (7) In other words, you can lose weight if you jog, you can lose weight if you walk fast. (8) This conclusion is going to be discussed and analyzed in the months and years to come.

1. _____

_____

2. _____

_____

3. _____

_____

4. _____

_____

5. _____

_____

6. _____

_____

16. EDITING FOR SENTENCE LENGTH

In several practices in the handbook, you have studied various types of sentences: simple, compound, complex, and compound-complex. Here is an example of each type of sentence for you to review:

1. Simple sentence: I enjoy exercise.
2. Compound sentence: I enjoy exercise, but I dislike dieting.
3. Complex sentence: Though I enjoy exercise, I dislike dieting.
4. Compound-complex sentence: Though I enjoy exercise, I dislike dieting, but I diet anyway.

The compound-complex sentence is the longest sentence that writers use. When sentences exceed this length, they are too cumbersome and tend to lose their focus. As you edit your drafts, you should shorten these overly long sentences.

Look at the following overly long sentences:

1. I don't enjoy dieting, but I do enjoy exercising, so I exercise, but I force myself to diet.

2. When I diet, I try to find foods that I enjoy eating, so I won't get bored with the food, and so I won't soon quit my diet.

In sentence 1, you note a string of four simple sentences joined by coordinating conjunctions. This sentence is really an overly long compound sentence. Generally avoid stringing more than two simple sentences together with coordinating conjunctions. Study the following revision of this first sentence:

1. (revised) I don't enjoy dieting, but I do enjoy exercising. Thus I exercise, but I force myself to diet.

Note how this long, cumbersome sentence has been edited into two manageable compound sentences with the addition of the transition "thus."

In sentence 2, notice how this compound-complex sentence has an additional simple sentence tacked onto it, which makes the sentence unwieldy. This sentence can be revised as follows:

2. (revised) When I diet, I try to find foods that I enjoy eating, so I won't get bored with the food. In this way, I won't soon quit my diet.

The revision keeps the compound-complex sentence but makes the last simple sentence a separate sentence in its own right. This allows the information in the original sentence to be more manageable.

Your goal as a writer is to compose sentences that present enough information, but not too much. Overly long sentences become unfocused. Refer to the rules for constructing simple, compound, complex, and compound-complex sentences when you find that a sentence is simply too long. Break up these longer sentences into shorter ones.

PRACTICE B16: EDITING FOR SENTENCE LENGTH

The following paragraph on dieting has two sentences that are too long. Identify each by sentence number and then make the revisions in the space provided. You may revise these long sentences in several ways.

(1) I have always had a weight problem, so I have resorted to several diets in my lifetime, but none of them seem to work over the long haul, and I end up gaining more weight than when I started the diet. (2) I have come to the conclusion that no diet is foolproof. (3) What I have learned is that I must eat sensibly and never overeat. (4) When I overeat, I increase my appetite, and so I want to continue to eat, and then I don't know when to stop, so I start gaining weight again. (5) To maintain your weight or to lose weight, you must change your attitude toward food and eating.

1. _____

_____

2. _____

_____

_____

17. USING BRACKETS WITHIN A QUOTE

Often you may want to add a comment within your quote, either to emphasize a point or to make a reference clearer. Whatever you insert within a quote should be placed in *brackets* ([ ]), not parentheses.

Look at how brackets are used in the following quotes:

The excerpt states that "he [Howard Gardner] has identified seven types of intelligence."
The excerpt states that Gardner "correlates each type of intelligence to a *region of the brain* [my italics]."

In the first example, the information within the brackets explains whom the "he" refers to. Sometimes a quote contains a confusing noun or pronoun that you may want to identify in brackets this way. In the second example, a writer wants to emphasize a particular fact within the quote, so the writer has italicized this information. To let the reader know that "region of the brain" is not italicized in the original quote, the writer inserts "my italics" in the brackets.

Using brackets appropriately adds sophistication to your quoting style.

PRACTICE B17: USING BRACKETS WITHIN A QUOTE

The following paragraph is on multiple intelligences. There are two errors in the correct use of brackets within a quote. Identify each error by sentence number and then make the correction in the space provided.

(1) Howard Gardner does not believe that intelligence is a simple aptitude to measure. (2) Gardner contends that "intelligence entails a set of mental skills that enable us *to recognize and resolve problems* (my italics)." (3) This understanding of intelligence focuses on problem solving rather than simply manipulating words and numbers. (4) Gardner has thus "identified seven types of intelligence (which includes verbal and mathematical) that he says we each possess to some degree." (5) Gardner's findings have important implications for classroom teaching.

1. _____

_____

2. _____

_____

18. USING A QUOTE WITHIN A QUOTE

What happens when you have a quote within the original quotation? You use single quotation marks (' ') to identify the quote within your quote and double quotation marks (" ") around the section that you choose to quote. Look at how the following quote from "Japan Firsthand" is handled. In the original sentence, "the test" was in quotes:

Chapman and Hoppe note that Japan's schools are changing: "Major educational reforms are underway, including eliminating 'the test' for entrance into high school."

The single quotation marks around this phrase is the writer's signal that these words were placed in quotes by the authors of the article.

PRACTICE B18: A QUOTE WITHIN A QUOTE

The following paragraph is on Japanese education. You will find two errors in using a quote within a quote. Identify each error by sentence number and then make the correction in the space provided.

(1) Japanese education has many points that differ from that in America. (2) In regard to Japanese primary schools, the authors note, "Teachers of the primary grades tend to accept as normal a high level of what we might consider "rowdiness" during free times." (3) Clearly, the Japanese educators believe that playfulness among children is normal behavior. (4) It is in high school where the pressure seems more than in American high schools. (5) High school students must pass an entrance exam in order to be accepted into Japanese universities, so the authors explain that "some students attend weekend or after hours cram schools called "jukus" to help them prepare for these entrance exams."

1. _____

_____

2. _____

_____

19. CITING LONG QUOTATIONS

Earlier in this section (Practices B2 and B6), you were introduced to some of the basic rules for quoting from reading material. The excerpts you quoted were short, often no more than a sentence. At times you may want to quote long citations, called *block quotes*. A long quote is *more than four lines of your paper* (not of the selection).

Follow these procedures when you use block quotes:

1. If you are typing your essay, indent block quotes *ten spaces* from the left-hand margin. Be sure that every line of your quote is indented. If you are writing your paper, indent these quotes as you would the first sentence of your paragraph.

2. If you are typing, double-space the block quote.

3. Introduce the long quote with a colon (:), not a comma.

4. Do not place quotation marks around the block quote, as you would with shorter quotes that form part of your paragraph.

Here is an example of how a long quote should appear in your essay:

Rose is careful to describe the high school in great detail. Look at how he introduces University High School:

> It is the oldest high school built in West Los Angeles. Built in 1924, originally Warren G. Harding High School, Uni changed its name to forgo association with the corruption then being revealed about President Harding's administration and to underscore its key role as a feeder school to the University of California, to nearby UCLA in particular.

Note that there are no quotation marks around the beginning and ending of the block quote. Also note that the quote is introduced with a colon.

Avoid using too many long quotations in your essay. However, when you do use a block quote, follow these four procedures carefully.

PRACTICE B19: CITING LONG QUOTATIONS

The following is a paragraph on the Rose selection that contains two errors in introducing a block quote. Identify each error by sentence number and then make the correction in the space provided.

(1) Rick Takagaki is a very devoted teacher. (2) He even spends time with his students during lunch hour. (3) Look at how Rose describes the lunch break in Rick's class,

> (4) "Rick typically spent his lunch break in his room, leaving the door open for anyone who wanted to talk, hang out, or just have a place to eat alone. (5) During my visit, several groups came together and dispersed, following an easy rhythm of food and talk. (6) Over by the filing cabinets, a group of Asian students–Chinese, Japanese, Korean, Filipino–ate lunch from plastic containers and gossiped and laughed.

1. _____

_____

2. _____

_____

_____

20. CITING PAGE NUMBERS AFTER A QUOTE

Many instructors will ask that you quote from what you have read. You have already learned some basic rules earlier in this section, and this discussion provides additional information about ways to quote from your reading.

Some instructors may require you to place the page number after a quotation. This is especially helpful to readers who want to know exactly where the quote came from. For research papers in particular, you will be asked to cite page numbers for the quotes that you choose.

The Modern Language Association (MLA) has standards for quoting humanities material–the arts and history. The MLA asks you to follow these procedures when you quote:

1. Place the page number in parentheses:

   Kozol notes, "So the kids at P.S. 28 learn to make do" (280).

   Note that you do not need to place "page" or the abbreviations "p." or "pp." before the page number. Note also that there is no period after the quote, but only one after the page number.

2. If the quote ends with a quotation mark or exclamation point, place the question mark or exclamation point *within the quotation* and a period after the parentheses.

   In regard to the cake this student gave Mr. Bedrock, she asks him, "Is it good?" (56).

   Note that the question mark is within the quotation mark, and a period is added after the page number in parentheses.

By citing page numbers, you make it easier for the reader to locate and study the quotes you have chosen.

PRACTICE B20: CITING PAGE NUMBERS AFTER A QUOTE

The following paragraph on Ordinary Resurrections *has two errors in using page numbers after quoted material. Identify each error by sentence number and then make the correction in the space provided.*

(1) Kozol strongly believes that teachers and children need to work together in the classroom in a respectful and pleasing way. (2) Part of this

cooperation involves teachers being less serious than they often are. (3) Kozol notes, "The laughter of the children is refreshing too." (284). (4) Laughter makes both the teacher and the students more connected to each other. (5) Even in regard to a teacher who is scolding a student, Kozol remarks that her response to the student "is quite beautiful and full of tenderness" (p. 284). (6) Kozol is clear that a disciplined class does not have to be quiet and fearful.

1. _____

_____

2. _____

_____

REVIEW 4: PRACTICES 1–20

In the following two paragraphs written on how people learn, you will find six errors. Two essay convention errors are in placing a page number after a quote and a redundancy. Four grammatical errors are a sentence fragment, a comma splice, a subject-verb agreement error, and an error in punctuating a participial phrase. Identify each error by sentence number and then make the correction in the space provided.

(1) Learning is a most complicated matter. (2) Howard Gardner claims that there are several types of intelligence that, he says, "we each possess to some degree" (page 15). (3) How can the mind contain so many varied, diverse types of thinking? (4) The mind is still a mystery to those studying it.

(5) What we do know is that people learn best in a positive environment, they are uncomfortable learning in an environment that puts people down. (6) This is what Mike Rose shows in his study of talented teachers. (7) Those teachers who believe that everyone of their students has the potential to learn. (8) Sitting in the classrooms of many talented teachers Rose finds that the best teachers relate to students on several levels. (9) The lonely student in a sea of faces in these classrooms are the most in need of these rare teachers who care and find interesting ways to teach.

1. _____

_____

2. _____

_____

3. _____

_____

4. _____

_____

5. _____

_____

6. _____

_____

GLOSSARY OF GRAMMAR
AND USAGE TERMS

The following are some grammar and usage terms used in this text. Each term is defined, and an example is provided.

active construction: sentence structure following the traditional subject + verb + direct object pattern.
I completed my first essay.

adjective: a word describing a noun, expressing some quality of it.
I want to comment on the most *convincing* essays.

adjective clause: a clause that modifies a noun or pronoun, sometimes called a relative clause. Adjective clauses often begin with words called relative pronouns: *who, that, which, whom, whose.*
I chose to discuss the essay *that had the most interesting beginning.*

adverb: a word that modifies a verb, adjective, or other adverb. It can also modify an entire sentence. An adverb answers the question when, where, why, or how.
I *quickly* read through your essays. (modifies verb)
This is the *most* convincing essay that I have ever read. (modifies adjective)
I read your essays *very* slowly. (modifies adverb)
Fortunately for you, I did not lower your grade for an overly short conclusion. (modifies entire sentence)

adverbial clause: a clause usually modifying a verb in another clause. Adverbial clauses begin with subordinating conjunctions, which show time, contrast, condition, or cause. The most common subordinating conjunctions include *after, although, before, because, if, since, when,* and *whether.*
When I receive your essays, I read them quickly.

agreement (pronoun): a matching in number and gender between a pronoun and the noun that it refers to.
Those students who wrote on crime will receive *their* graded essays next meeting. (number)
John Baldwin did not turn in *his* last essay assignment. (gender)

agreement (subject-verb): a match between a subject and a verb; a singular subject agrees with a singular verb, a plural subject with a plural verb. Singular verbs in the present tense usually end in "s"; plural verbs usually do not end in "s."
The essay *assignment seems* difficult. (singular subject and verb)
These essay *assignments seem* difficult. (plural subject and verb).

appositive: a noun that renames another noun.
My brother Ken writes composition textbooks.

263

appositive phrase: a noun plus other words that rename another noun; they are set off with commas.

My friend, a neighbor as well, likes the composition text that we use.

brackets: punctuation marks indicating that you have added a comment to a quote.

In describing my research paper, my professor said, "I am greatly *impressed* [my italics] with the way you comment on your quotes."

clause: a group of words that include a subject and a verb; it can stand alone as a sentence (independent clause), or it can be part of another clause (dependent clause).

When you write an introduction, you should mention the author and title of the work *that you plan to discuss.*

colloquialism: an informal word or phrase more often used in speech than in writing.

My essay has a *funky* sound to it.

colon: a punctuation mark used in three ways:

(1) To introduce a long block quotation.

(2) To introduce an itemized list.

Here is what you will need to write your essay effectively: a word processor, writing software, and a printer.

(3) To introduce a complete sentence that you want to emphasize.

There is one habit that you must follow: You must revise your draft.

comma: a punctuation mark that, among other duties, serves to:

(1) Separate words or phrases in a series.

The humanities includes the arts, history, and literature.

(2) Separate two independent clauses connected by a coordinating conjunction.

Reading literature requires a careful examination of words and phrases, and it also demands rereading.

(3) Introducing an adverbial clause at the beginning of a sentence.

Although reading literature requires a new way of studying, students can learn these new ways of reading.

(4) Introduce nonessential phrases and clauses.

Malcolm X, who wrote his autobiography, was an amazingly intelligent man.

(5) Introduce a quote in sentence form.

My friend asked, "Why do you want to go to college anyway?"

comma splice: the incorrect use of a comma to join two independent clauses.

A topic sentence many begin a sentence, it may also conclude one.

complex sentence: a sentence with one independent clause and at least one dependent clause.

When you finish the first draft of your essay, it is wise to let it "sit" awhile.

compound sentence: a sentence made up of at least two independent clauses joined by a conjunction or semicolon.

An essay needs sound general statements, and it also needs appropriate general details supporting these general statements. (conjunction)

An essay needs sound generalizations; it also needs appropriate general details supporting these statements. (semicolon)

compound-complex sentence: a sentence with at least two independent clauses and at least one dependent clause.

When you finish reading an article, you should try to summarize the most important points, and you should write these points in your own words.

conjunction: a word that connects parts of a sentence together. It can be:

(1) A coordinating conjunction: *and, but, so, or yet, for,* and *nor.* Coordinating conjunctions *and, or,* and *nor* can join words or phrases. All of them can join independent clauses.

You should edit for grammar *and* essay convention errors. (phrase)

You should edit for grammar and usage errors, but you should do this only after you have completed a rough draft. (clause)

(2) A subordinating conjunction: *after, although, as, because, before, since, though, when, whenever,* and *while.* These conjunctions introduce adverbial clauses.

As you write your rough draft, you can change anything you have written.

(3) A conjunctive adverb: *however, indeed, moreover, nevertheless,* and *therefore.* These words can join two independent clauses that require a semicolon or period to separate them.

Evidence is necessary in an essay; *however,* it is not effective without sound general statements. (semicolon)

Evidence is necessary in an essay. *However,* it is not effective without sound general statements. (period)

coordinating conjunction: *See* conjunction.

dash: a punctuation mark used to set off words, phrases, and sentences that you want to emphasize.

The essay--all of it--should move logically from one paragraph to the next.

dependent clause: *See* clause.

ellipsis points: punctuation of three dots showing that you have deleted a part of the quote.

In describing my essay, my professor noted that ". . . it lacked appropriate detail yet provided important general points."

essential clause or phrase: a group of words necessary to the understanding of the sentence. It is not set off with commas.

The thesis support organizational pattern is the major organizational pattern *that composition students must master.* (essential clause)

Students *understanding the thesis support organizational pattern* often write organized essays. (essential phrase)

fragment: *See* sentence fragment.

fused sentence: two sentences incorrectly joined with no punctuation between them.

Preview skimming is an aid to comprehension it saves time for the student in the long run.

independent clause: *See* clause.

modifier: any word or group of words used to describe another word or group of words. Modifiers serve as adjectives or adverbs.

Critical reading is an *important college-level* skill. (adjectives)

In college one must know how to read *critically.* (adverb)

nonessential clause or phrase: a group of words whose information in the sentence is not essential to the sentence's meaning. It is set off with commas.

Preview skimming, which is taught in Chapter 1, is used throughout the textbook. (nonessential clause)

Preview skimming, a topic in Chapter 1, is used throughout the textbook. (nonessential phrase)

noun: any word that can follow the words *a, an,* or *the.* It can be either singular or plural. Plural nouns usually end in "s" or "es."

The reading *selection* in *Chapter 1* deals with *literacy.* (singular nouns)

noun clause: a dependent clause that serves as a noun in another clause or in a phrase. It is introduced by words like *that, what, whoever,* and *whomever.*

Reading narratives requires *that you carefully analyze the words a writer uses.*

noun phrase: a group of words focusing on a noun. The words next to the noun usually modify it.

A necessary feature of most narratives is character.

object: a noun that receives the action of a verb or completes the noun slot of a prepositional phrase.
Narrative writers often use *description*. (verb + direct object)
The writers of *narratives* are sometimes short story writers as well. (preposition + object)

parallelism: using the same grammatical structure in listing a series of items.
You should revise your draft, edit for grammatical errors, and proofread for typos. (repetition of verb phrases)

participial phrase: a verb phrase that serves as an adjective, the verb usually ending in "ing," "ed," and "en." Nonessential participial phrases are set off with commas. Essential participial phrases are not.
Knowing the power of words, writers of narratives choose words carefully. (nonessential participial phrase)
I spoke to the woman *sitting in the chair.* (essential participial phrase)

passive construction: sentence structure making the direct object the subject of the sentence and the original subject a prepositional phrase.
The essay was written by my friend. (My friend wrote the essay. [active voice])

phrase: a group of words working together that do not have both a subject and a verb. Phrases include noun phrases, verb phrases, adjective phrases, and adverb phrases.
Writers in journalism frequently select topics *of human interest.* (noun phrase and adjective phrase)
Many writers continue *to work tirelessly on their writing.* (verb phrase and adverb phrase).

plagiarism: presenting another person's words or ideas as if they were one's own. Plagiarism is not an acceptable writing practice.

preposition: a connecting word that is joined to a noun and that explains a noun or a verb. The preposition plus a noun is called a prepositional phrase.
Writers *for exercise and health* may be published *in medical journals or sports magazines.* (prepositional phrases explaining a noun and prepositional phrase explaining a verb)

pronoun: a word that can replace a noun or noun phrase in either subject or object form. The most common pronouns are *I, you, he, she, it, we, you, they* (subject case); *me, you, him, her, it, us, you, them* (object case)
Narratives are different from expository essays; *they* are both different from lab reports.

pronoun reference: the pronoun that replaces a noun or pronoun previously mentioned. Students sometimes do not clearly refer pronouns to a specific noun or pronoun that has come before. This error is known as a vague pronoun reference.
Critical reading can sometimes be difficult because *it* requires much concentration.

redundancy: a word, phrase, or sentence that is unnecessarily repeated.
You wrote a *convincing* and *cogent* essay. ("Convincing" and "cogent" are synonyms.)

relative pronoun: any pronoun that connects a dependent clause to an independent clause. They include: *that, what, whatever, which, whom, whose, whoever,* and *whomever.*
An essay *that* provides ample and accurate detail more easily supports its argument.

run-on: *See* fused sentence.

semicolon: a punctuation mark often used to join:
(1) Two independent clauses without a conjunction.

The natural sciences often rely on the scientific method to complete their research; this method follows specific steps.

(2) Two independent clauses that use a conjunctive adverb to join them.

Writing in the natural sciences often uses the sequence of events organizational pattern; however, this is not they only pattern you will find in this scientific writing.

(3) Two independent clauses with a coordinating conjunction if there are commas in one or both clauses used for other reasons.

The major organizational patterns I use in my writing are thesis support, cause and effect, and compare and contrast; and each pattern relies on a different set of transitions.

sentence: a group of words made up of at least one independent clause.

The natural sciences include biology, chemistry, and physics.

sentence fragment: a part of a sentence functioning like a whole one, occurring in the form of a clause or a phrase.

When the scientist conducts an experiment. (clause fragment)

The scientist's experimental results. (phrase fragment)

simple sentence: a complete sentence made up of one independent clause, although it may have several phrases.

In narrative writing, a student needs to study descriptions as well. (one prepositional phrase, one independent clause, one noun phrase)

subject: a word or words that the verb agrees with in number and person; a necessary part of any clause.

Short stories and novels both rely on description and narration.

subordinate clause: another name for a dependent clause.

subordinating conjunction: *See* conjunction.

topic sentence: the sentence in a paragraph that states the main point. It is often found at the beginning of a paragraph, but it can be at the end of a paragraph or inferred from the details in a paragraph.

vague phrasing: the inexact use of a word or phrase.

Revising is one of the most effective things you can do to improve your essay. ("Things" is vague; it is better replaced with a phrase like "writing habits.")

verb: an essential part of a clause stating an action, condition, or assertion, and agreeing with its subject in number and person.

Reading and writing *are* often related activities.

INDEX

CREDITS

"Literacy: A Family Affair," Anita Merina. *NEA Today.* April, 1995, 4–5. Used by permission.

Melannie Svoboda. "The Eight Beatitudes of Writing." *America.* Nov. 11, 1995. Vol. 173. No. 15, 23–25. Used by permission.

Sharon Curcio. *Corrections Today.* "Finding Modern Ways to Teach Today's Youth." April 1995. Vol. 57. No. 2, 28–30. Reprinted by permission of the American Correctional Association, Lanham, MD.

From *The Autobiography of Malcolm X* by Malcolm X, with the assistance of Alex Haley. Copyright © 1964 by Malcolm X and Alex Haley. Copyright © 1965 by Alex Haley and Betty Shabazz. Reprinted by permission of Random House, Inc.

"La Vida Loca (The Crazy Life): Two Generations of Gang Members." Copyright, 1992, Los Angeles Times. Reprinted with permission.

Copyright © 1993 by Robert K. Ressler and Tom Shachtman. From *Whoever Fights Monsters* by Robert K. Ressler and Tom Shachtman. Reprinted by permission of St. Martin's Press, LLC.

"Look Back in Anger." Copyright, 1996, Los Angeles Times. Reprinted with permission.

Barbara Dority. "The Columbine Tragedy: Countering the Hysteria." *The Humanist.* July 1999. V 59, 7–11. Reprinted by permission.

"Taking the fun out of watching television," by Charles Gordon. *Maclean's.* June 8, 1998. V. III No 23, 11. Reprinted by permission.

"Where's the Pitch?" Copyright, 1998, Los Angeles Times. Reprinted with permission.

"Salt-N-Pepa Have a New CD and Newfound Faith," Veronica Chambers. From *Newsweek,* 10/27/97 © 1997 Newsweek, Inc. All rights reserved. Reprinted by permission.

Denise Noe. "Parallel Worlds: The Surprising Similarities (and Differences) of Country and Western and Rap." *The Humanist.* August 1995, vol 55. No. 4, 20–3. Reprinted by permission.

Lifetimes Physical Fitness and Wellness: A Personalized Approach 6th Edition by Werner W.K. Hoeger and Sharon A. Hoeger © 2000 Morton Publishing Co. Pages 2–5. Reprinted with permission.

Jay Sheehan. "Can You Be Fit and Fat?" *Fitness Magazine.* July 1999. 100–4. Reprinted by permission.

"How Far Should You Go to Stay Fit?" by Lynn Rosellini. Copyright, November 10, 1997, U.S. News & World Report. Visit us at our Web site at www.usnews.com for additional information.

Patricia Andersen-Parrado. "Burning Calories May Be Easier Than You Think." *Better Nutrition.* April 1999. Vol. 61, 34–5. Reprinted by permission.

"Teaching That Goes Beyond IQ." Copyright, 1995, Los Angeles Times. Reprinted with permission.

Marilyn Sue Chapman & Martha Hoppe. "Japan Firsthand." *California Teacher,* the newspaper of the California Federation of Teachers, AFT, AFL-CIO.

Excerpt from *Possible Lives:* The Promise of Public Education in America. Copyright © 1995 by Mike Rose. Reprinted by permission of Houghton Mifflin Company. All rights reserved.

From *Ordinary Resurrections* by Jonathan Kozol. Copyright © 2000 by Jonathan Kozol. Reprinted by permission of Crown Publishers, a division of Random House, Inc.

SUGGESTIONS FOR COMPLETING YOUR ESSAY

PREWRITING

1. Choose your topic; study all its parts. Know what you need to discuss. Write in your free-writing journal.

2. With your topic in mind, review the reading selection or selections pertaining to your topic. Reread your margin comments, underlinings, and reading journal.

3. Study your Outlining/Clustering activity. Which parts of the outline or cluster can you use to answer your essay question?

4. Review your answers to A Second Reading. Can you include any of this information in your draft?

5. Write a rough outline or complete a clustering diagram, including the most general points you intend to cover.

DRAFTING

1. From your outline or cluster, begin writing. Be sure that your essay has three basic parts: a beginning, a middle, and an end.

2. Aim to present your ideas in an organized way. Do not focus on surface concerns at this time.

3. Do not expect that your first draft will be perfect.

4. Go back to any part of your draft as you are composing, making changes in ideas and organization.

REVISING

1. Let your draft sit awhile, a day or two if possible.

2. Reread and make changes in ideas and organization. Add, take out, or rearrange your material.

3. If you are writing an expository essay, be sure that your introduction tells your reader where your draft is going, and check to see that the middle paragraphs support these general points.

4. Let your peers and instructor read your draft. Listen to the ideas they have to improve your draft. Include those suggestions that you agree with into your next draft.

5. After you have made changes in ideas and organization, edit for grammar and usage and essay convention errors. Review the grammar and usage and essay convention material that you have studied in the selection you are reading, and apply this knowledge to editing your essay. Also apply the grammar and usage and essay convention knowledge that you have learned from the previous selections.

6. Strive for a final draft that is logical, organized, and free of grammar, usage, and essay convention errors.

SUGGESTIONS FOR READING YOUR SELECTION

PREREADING

1. First glance at the title, source, and date to get a sense of how recent the selection is, where it came from, and what the title suggests the selection is about.

2. Read carefully the first and last paragraph to get a sense of the argument of the selection and of its conclusion. What the selection is arguing for is usually in the first paragraph, and what the selection says about this argument is usually in the last paragraph.

3. Skim quickly through the middle of the selection to determine the details that will be used and how the selection is organized. Here you will also get a sense of the kind of evidence the author uses: statistics, anecdotes, interviews, analysis of research, and so on.

4. Before you begin reading critically, see if you can put the argument of the selection in your own words.

CRITICAL READING

1. Read carefully with this argument in mind.

2. As you read, highlight, underline, and make margin comments. Make note of where the argument seems to be, the important points made, and how the selection concludes. In the margins, comment on the kinds of evidence the author uses: examples, steps, characteristics, and so on.

3. In the margins, paraphrase difficult sentences, and ask questions about any part of the article that you do not understand.

4. When you finish your critical reading, see if you can summarize the argument, the key points made, and the conclusion of the selection. If you choose, write an outline of these important points, or write a reading journal entry commenting on the selection.

REREADING

1. Read again to answer those questions that your critical reading brought out.

2. Ask your peers or instructor for help with any sections that you still do not have answers for.

3. Reflect on what you have read: How does this selection relate to other readings on this topic that you have completed? How has it changed your position on this topic?

4. Evaluate what you have read. How effective or ineffective was this reading selection? Can you put into words your reasons for liking or disliking the selection?

CPSIA information can be obtained
at www.ICGtesting.com
Printed in the USA
FFOW042015050313
957FF